"This 'how-to' workbook is unique in that it provides seasoned clinici
ing this population a vision about how sex-offender treatment compa..... .. ..
know, while it also provides a user-friendly, detailed guide for the novice wishing to learn this
highly specialized treatment. The case examples presented are excellent teaching tools regarding
how to handle challenging group therapy situations successfully. Differences in treating men and
women and how to appropriately alter modalities for adolescents and children are clearly outlined.
This book will make the sexual recovery therapy model highly accessible to anyone who takes the
time to read it."

Rana Duncan-Daston, EdD, MSW, LCSW
Radford University School of Social Work,
Southwest Virginia Higher Education Center,
Abingdon

"This 'How-To Workbook' contains helpful information and guidance for skilled therapists engaged in the treatment of sex offenders. It outlines unique issues and characteristics for specific groups. The description of sexual recovery therapy provides a framework and tools for establishing an environment of treatment and recovery for the sex offender. A series of questionnaires designed to elicit clarity for both the therapist and the client are helpful adjuncts to the therapeutic
process. Most important, the book offers hope to both those engaged as treatment providers and to
individuals involved in the journey of reclaiming a healthy and productive life."

Alisa H. Moore, MSW
Executive Director,
Mount Rogers Community
Services Board

"A deeply compassionate approach to sexual offenders without condoning what they do. It is
loaded with helpful tools for helping offenders of all ages recover, including the sexual recovery model, and in-depth approach for changing learned behavior. These tools are invaluable for
therapists, patients, and families. I highly recommend this book!"

Marilou Inocalla, MD
Smyth Counseling Center,
Marion, VA

"This compilation/book is a fount of user-friendly, no-nonsense information. What works well
over time is rationally detailed and well-documented. Confidence as a therapist will be
greatly enhanced by this timely publication."

M. Anderson Douglass, MD
Psychiatrist and Medical Director,
Providence Service Corporation

"An important, well-conceived, carefully written, and much-needed addition to the growing literature in the field of sex-offender treatment. It definitely lives up to its billing as a 'how-to'
workbook. The book is well-organized, concise, readable, practical, and above all provides clear
and workable methods of conceptualizing and treating these clients. In addition to providing many
useful treatment strategies, the book will also help clinicians in this field to identify and modify,
where necessary, their own emotional and cognitive responses when working with these clients, a
key but often neglected factor in being an effective therapist in the mental heath field."

John Ludgate, PhD
Licensed Clinical Psychologist;
Author, *Maximizing Therapeutic
Gains and Preventing Relapse
in Emotionally Disordered Clients*

Sex-Offender Therapy
A "How-To" Workbook for Therapists Treating Sexually Aggressive Adults, Adolescents, and Children

THE HAWORTH PRESS
Haworth Series in Clinical Psychotherapy

Terry S. Trepper, PhD
Editor

College Students in Distress: A Resource Guide for Faculty, Staff, and Campus Community
by Bruce S. Sharkin

Cultural Diversity and Suicide: Ethnic, Religious, Gender, and Sexual Orientation Perspectives
by Mark M. Leach

Sex-Offender Therapy: A "How-To" Workbook for Treating Sexually Aggressive Adults, Adolescents, and Children by Rudy Flora, Joseph T. Duehl, Wanda Fisher, Sandra Halsey, Michael Keohane, Barbara L Maberry, Jeffrey A. McCorkindale, and Leroy C. Parson

Sex-Offender Therapy
A "How-To" Workbook for Therapists Treating Sexually Aggressive Adults, Adolescents, and Children

Rudy Flora
Joseph T. Duehl
Wanda Fisher
Sandra Halsey
Michael Keohane
Barbara L. Maberry
Jeffrey A. McCorkindale
Leroy C. Parson

The Haworth Press
Taylor & Francis Group
New York and London

For more information on this book or to order, visit
http://www.haworthpress.com/store/product.asp?sku=5753

or call 1-800-HAWORTH (800-429-6784) in the United States and Canada
or (607) 722-5857 outside the United States and Canada

or contact orders@HaworthPress.com

The Haworth Press, Taylor & Francis Group, 270 Madison Avenue, New York, NY, 10016.

PUBLISHER'S NOTE
The development, preparation, and publication of this work has been undertaken with great care. However, the Publisher, employees, editors, and agents of The Haworth Press are not responsible for any errors contained herein or for consequences that may ensue from use of materials or information contained in this work. The Haworth Press is committed to the dissemination of ideas and information according to the highest standards of intellectual freedom and the free exchange of ideas. Statements made and opinions expressed in this publication do not necessarily reflect the views of the Publisher, Directors, management, or staff of The Haworth Press, Inc., or an endorsement by them.

Identities and circumstances of individuals discussed in this book have been changed to protect confidentiality.

Cover design by Kerry E. Mack.

Library of Congress Cataloging-in-Publication Data

Sex-offender therapy: a "how-to" workbook for therapists treating sexually aggressive adults, adolescents, and children / Rudy Flora . . . [et al.].
     p. cm.
   Includes bibliographical references.
   ISBN-13: 978-0-7890-3123-5 (soft : alk. paper)
   1. Sex offenders—Rehabilitation—Handbooks, manuals, etc. 2. Teenage sex offenders—Rehabilitation—Handbooks, manuals, etc. 3. Child sex offenders—Rehabilitation—Handbooks, manuals, etc. 4. Psychosexual disorders—Treatment—Handbooks, manuals, etc. I. Flora, Rudy.
   [DNLM: 1. Paraphilias—therapy. 2. Psychotherapy—methods. 3. Sex offenses—prevention and control. WM 610 S5145 2007]

RC560.S47S469 2007
616.85'8306—dc22
                                                                                    2007010701

This workbook is dedicated to my late father and mother.

Rudy Flora

I would like to dedicate this book to all the courageous, dedicated men that I have had the privilege to treat over the course of several years. Through their hard work, they have learned how to understand themselves, their victims and offenses and in so doing have inspired me to do my best work.

Joseph T. Duehl

To the love of my life, for his support, and my family and friends.

Wanda Fisher

To Jim, Emily, Olivia, and Seth. May my work help to make a better place for each of you.

Sandra Halsey

Rachel, the best part of my life began with you and continues on. Thank you for making me laugh out loud.

Michael Keohane

I dedicate my portion of this endeavor to Mitchell for the inspiration and to all the victims, survivors, and those in lifelong recovery.

Barbara L. Maberry

To my family, who allows me to work, "Down the Street."

Leroy C. Parson

ABOUT THE AUTHORS

Rudy Flora, LCSW, ACSW, CSOTP, is a clinician in private practice in Virginia who provides individual, family, and group treatment services to sexually aggressive adults, adolescents, and children. A former probation officer and author of *How to Work with Sex Offenders* (Haworth), he also serves as an adjunct faculty member at Radford University's School of Social Work in the Abington Program.

Joseph T. Duehl, MSW, LCSW, CSTOP, is a clinician in an outpatient PTSD unit at the Veterans Administration in Virginia. He also serves as an adjunct faculty member at Radford University's School of Social Work in the Roanoke Program. He is certified to train in psychodrama and works with adult sex offenders in private practice.

Wanda Fisher, LCSW, MS, CSTOP, is a clinician at Smyth County Counseling Center in Virginia. She works with adult sex offenders and sexually aggressive children and adolescents. She has experience in an in-patient psychiatric hospital and as a former Child Protection Worker and currently works in private practice.

Sandra Halsey, MSM, LCSW, CSTOP, is a clinician in private practice in Virginia who provides individual, family, and group treatment services to sexually aggressive adults, adolescents, and children. She has former experience in an in-patient psychiatric hospital and an outpatient community mental health clinic.

Michael Keohane, MSW, LCSW, CSTOP, is a supervisor at The Highlands Community Services Board in Virginia. With a history of working with the chronically mentally ill, he is also in private practice as a clinician with adult sex offenders.

Barbara L. Maberry, MSW, CSOTP, is a clinician in private practice in Virginia. She works with sexually aggressive adults, adolescents, and children and has a history of working with sexually aggressive children in a residential program.

Jeffrey A. McCorkindale, Licensed Polygraph Examiner, is a former police officer, now in private practice, providing polygraph services for sexually aggressive adults and adolescents.

Leroy C. Parson, MA, LPC, CSTOP, is a school guidance counselor in Virginia. He also works in private practice as an adult sex-offender clinician.

CONTENTS

Preface

This is a workbook that is written for the practicing clinician who works with sexually aggressive adults, adolescents, and children. Beginners or advanced therapists may find the information useful. Also, academia, attorneys, criminal justice personnel, human service caseworkers, judges, law enforcement, legislators, probation officers, prosecutors, students, and other mental health professionals may benefit from the material. In addition, certain sections are written for the lay reader, including patients and their families, who may be seeking help.

To be specific, this book is about patients who are impaired by sexual addiction, sexual disorders, sex offending, and other sexual misconduct behaviors. Both genders, male and female, are represented in this workbook.

The work is designed to be user-friendly, easy to read, and is intended to serve as a helpful resource guide. This workbook is not a cookbook—a mix of quick fix, therapy cure-alls—but rather a step-by-step information guide for therapists who treat sexually aggressive patients. A number of case summaries, work exercises, and clinical suggestions are included. The reader is walked through a sexual disorders program. A number of therapeutic interventions are offered. Information on the polygraph and the FDA approved plethysmograph is provided. All of the sexual disorders are included. In addition, special population patients are reviewed. Clinical techniques and ways to treat patients are provided.

Today, there are many texts on sexual addiction, sex offending, and sexual disorders—but most of the material is about the evaluation process, features of the problem behavior, or "how-to books" for the patient. However, there is little available information on how to actually treat such patients. Also, even more of concern, is that there is little work focused upon sexually aggressive adult females, male and female adolescents, and children—all rising population groups.

Seven therapists and one polygraph examiner participated in the writing of this workbook. Each represents expertise in certain fields of sexual addiction, sexual abuse, child and adolescent psychopathology, clinical psychotherapy, dual diagnoses, sexual offending, polygraph, plethysmograph, trauma, and victimology.

A number of patients consented to contribute information about recovery and the treatment process to this work. Although this material was not intended for publication, or a research project, and the data was not used, the information was of great help. The information provided by these patients greatly influenced and helped in the preparation of this workbook. The authors wanted to have a work that represented clinical information—combined with thoughts and suggestions from those living recovery—and for this workbook not to be completed only by "experts" who are not walking the walk. These brave men and women work recovery. They are courageous individuals and are committed to changing their lives. However, please note all case summaries are fictional; to avoid any breach of confidentiality for addict, offender, or victim.

Sexual abuse, sexual addiction, and sexual offending have become an enormous clinical problem in the past twenty years. Some lay professionals have approached the problem in a punitive manner by advocating the building of more prisons and other harsh measures. This may be a reactionary response, but is understandable. However, one must view this as a global problem, with the goal to help future addicts, offenders, and victims for the long term. The cost of

Sex-Offender Therapy
© 2008 by The Haworth Press, Taylor & Francis Group. All rights reserved.
doi:10.1300/5753_a

building prisons is beyond many state and federal budgets. Also, the problem disorders remain, and unless the behavior is treated, are most likely to reoccur if the offender is released. Another victim will be harmed. Actually, treatment is very cost effective for those patients in the community. Also, research shows that therapy is found to greatly reduce the recidivism of sex offenders.

Certain dangerous sex offenders do not merit treatment. The only solution is incarceration. This work does not intend in any way to excuse the hurt that is caused to the victims. There is no excuse for harming others. The physical and psychological damage to victims is long-term. Instead, the purpose of this work is to limit future victims.

Nearly 60 percent or more adult offenders now reside in the community. There is no known data on how many adolescent or child offenders are in localities. It is known that approximately 16 percent of rapes and 17 percent of sex crimes are committed by minors. Also, there is no available information on how many patients exist who possess a sexual addiction and prey on others. We also know only 16 percent of all sex crimes are reported by victims (Greenfeld, 1997; Righthand and Welch, 2001).

It is the belief of the eight authors that persons with sexually aggressive behaviors can lead non-addictive and offense-free lives. Most important, there is hope for those afflicted, if treatment is provided. As one professional recently said: "How much is the life of one child worth?" As well, one may consider how much the life of one adult woman who is sexually abused is worth. Many future victims can be avoided.

For more information from the authors about sexually aggressive children, adolescents, and adults, readers may contact www.floracounseling.com.

Acknowledgments

I would like to thank JaNan again, who has now given encouragement to me through two books. Also, I would like to applaud a number of persons behind the scenes who worked hard to make this workbook happen. Angie Hall . . . who kept the home fires burning . . . and gave us the opportunity to write . . . while reading rewrites. Sheila Roark . . . you are a saint . . . for typing this workbook. We would not have made it without your help . . . thanks so much. Joyce St. John and Lori Caldwell for your fine help. In addition, I would like to thank the authors who shared in this exciting journey with me. So, thanks to Barbara, Joe, Jeff, Leroy, Michael, Sandy, and Wanda, for making this book come alive for readers. What great helpers each of you have been. Also, I want to thank the staff of The Haworth Press who supported this work. Each of you has provided a great deal of help in bringing this workbook to life. All of you are a great crew to work with on a book. So again, thanks, to Margaret Tatich, Dawn Krisko, Amy Rentner, Marylouise Doyle, and Paul Deamer. Also, a very special thanks to our editor, Terry Trepper, for outstanding advice, counsel, and support.

Rudy Flora

I would like to acknowledge the following individuals: Anthony, David, Keynan, John, David, Melvin, Don, Adam, Steve, Robert, Mike, Evan, Jon, and Roland, who have taught me that with courage, strength, commitment, and perseverance, anyone can change their life and does not have to be defined by their past experiences.

Joseph T. Duehl

I would like to thank Dr. Robert Hill, my mentor, who believed in me and encouraged me to follow my dreams and to Rudy Flora, for giving me the opportunity to work with him in this amazing profession.

Wanda Fisher

Special thanks to Margaret Bonham, Matt Verlander, and Allison Hagy—dedicated graduate students who contributed to the research effort for this project without compensation. They each proved themselves to be indispensable.

Sandra Halsey

I would like to say thank you to Rudy Flora for giving me the opportunity to increase my clinical skills and providing me this opportunity to write about a subject that I feel needs a voice. I would also like to thank Carolyn Peterson for believing in my potential and sharing her wealth of clinical knowledge and wisdom with me. Also, I would like to thank all of my teachers both in the classroom and out of the classroom, who have taught me to look deeper than the surface of a person. This section would not be complete without saying thank you to my mom, who has pro-vided me inspiration throughout my life.

Michael Keohane

My gratitude is to my wonderful mother, Helen, who gave me life, love, and the late-in-life opportunity of pursuing my education and career. To Terri, for love and support along this jour-ney. To Rudy . . . for your guidance and counsel. To Deborah . . . for seeing my potential and giv-ing me a chance in this field. To Angie . . . for always being there and for our friendship. To Mark . . . for making me "get-er done," even though I thought I was too old. To my clients and group members . . . for providing an invaluable education that money could not buy!

Bob, Deborah and, the "Grand Pooh Bah" Leroy Parson
Barbara L. Maberry

Chapter 1

Introduction

Sex offenders can be treated successfully. Study after study has documented a significant decline in recidivism of persons with sexual misconduct behaviors who stop offending. Several studies endorse the conclusion that programs are effective. These treatment programs have the elements of being empirically comprehensive and offense-specific (Lieb, Quincy, and Berlinger, 1998). Hall (1995) has researched and analyzed treatment outcomes for sex offenders. Treatment is effective. The recidivism rate has an 8 percent reduction for offenders who participated in treatment.

Hanson and Bussiere (1998) found that sex offenders who do not complete their treatment programs are at greater risk for sexual and general recidivism. Alexander (1998) analyzed the results of group therapy for sex offenders. He used a large group of approximately 11,000 in number. Seventy-nine studies were combined and reviewed on sex-offender treatment. Sex offenders who were in a relapse-prevention treatment program had a combined re-arrest rate of 7.2 percent. There was a 17.6 percent re-arrest rate for offenders who were not in treatment and a 13.2 percent overall re-arrest rate for treated sex offenders.

Treatment effectiveness is viewed by several factors.

1. Selection of treatment provider.
2. Selection of sex offenders who are in treatment. Sexual sadism is not treatable.
3. Sex offenders who are successful in treatment must accept responsibility for their offenses.
4. Offenders must also understand how their sex crime affects the victim, family, and community.
5. Patients must examine and change their beliefs, values, morals, and prejudices as well as make a behavioral change.
6. Selection of treatment modalities is crucial to treatment success.
7. Probation and parole supervision and their related intervention.

The number of sex offenders who commit sex crimes is underreported. Not all sex offenders are reported, apprehended, or convicted of their crimes. Research shows only 16 percent of all sex crimes are reported.

The criminal justice system is monitoring better than 234,000 adult sex offenders, requiring specialized treatment for this population. This figure is static and does not include persons who are released from probation and parole supervision (Greenfeld, 1997). Nearly 60 percent reside in the community.

Sex offenses committed by juveniles have increased. Barbaree, Hudson, and Seto (1993) estimate that adolescent sex offenders represent up to one-fifth of all rapes. They account for one-half of all cases of child molestation committed in a year.

Sickmund, Snyder, and Poe-Yamagats (1997) report that in 1995 adolescents were involved in 15 percent of all forcible rapes. These were cleared by arrest. Eighteen adolescents per

Sex-Offender Therapy
© 2008 by The Haworth Press, Taylor & Francis Group. All rights reserved.
doi:10.1300/5753_01

100,000 were arrested for forcible rape. Close to 16,000 adolescents were arrested for sexual offenses excluding prostitution and rape in the same year.

THERAPISTS WHO TREAT SEX OFFENDERS

Therapists who treat sex offenders are unique individuals with specialized training. One must recognize the need to protect adults, adolescents, and children from sexual abuse. In addition, the clinician must provide treatment for the offender.

As therapists, it is important to treat patients with dignity and with respect; understanding that the patients, most likely, were at some point in time themselves victims of physical, emotional, or sexual abuse. It is clinically challenging to treat sex offenders. Therapists will also treat (in sex offenders) a variety of clinical problems with patients such as mood disorders, sexual or drug addiction, post-traumatic stress disorder, depression, anxiety and panic disorders, impulse control issues, personality disorders, and developmental delays or mental retardation.

O'Connell, Leberg, and Donaldson (1990) suggested that therapists should possess certain qualifications. These are summarized as follows:

1. A formal education with a professional degree at the master or doctorate level or a medical degree.
2. Clinical experience is considered to be the single most important qualification for a sex-offender therapist.
3. Such prior clinical experience should include work with involuntary patients.
4. Clinical background should include knowledge of sexual deviancy and offender issues.
5. A therapist must be aware of the psychological impact sexual abuse has had upon victims.
6. The sex-offender therapist must be knowledgeable in the criminal justice system as in law enforcement, corrections, probation, and parole.
7. Clinicians should have an understanding of the dynamics of the court system.
8. Clinicians should have knowledge of the available resources in the community.
9. Clinicians should display the ability to be assertive and direct.
10. Clinicians should be alert to manipulation by a sex offender.
11. Therapists should have the ability to question the offender about his or her sexually inappropriate behavior in a very detailed manner.

O'Connell, Leberg, and Donaldson (1990) cite several personal traits and abilities as important when working with sex offenders. These are summarized as follows:

1. The ability to cope with stress because work with sex offenders can be especially demanding.
2. The ability to discuss sexual matters openly and without reservation is a must. The information obtained will be of a graphic nature.
3. Sexual deviancy can be unpleasant to hear about and many skilled clinicians are often deterred by this situation.
4. Be alert to issues of counter transference.
5. The ability to be precise, show attention to detail, be accurate, and have a desire to seek out information is important.
6. A therapist must be aware of certain sexual misconduct behaviors in an effort to be alert to a possible relapse situation.

7. The ability to be objective if necessary.
8. A therapist must be willing to work with a patient on a long-term basis.
9. The ability to be realistic, if needed, because sex offenders do not easily give up their sexual deviant interests.
10. Clinical insight is essential, as some offenders will oppose therapists, resist changes, and are not amenable to treatment and remain a threat to community safety,
11. The clinician must have no sexual deviant or criminal history because a therapist must serve as a role model.

TAKING CARE OF ONE'S SELF

Taking care of one's self while providing treatment is important for the therapist as well as the patient. Taking care of emotional and physical well-being is important. The following are suggestions for how to care for yourself while providing treatment for sex offenders.

- Follow code of ethics set by the state. Guidelines and standards of practice are provided. As a professional, obtain whatever education, license, or certification necessary to practice in treating sex offenders.
- Be a well-trained, reliable, and ethical professional.
- Use supervision, staff support, and consultation to debrief or process session content while working with a patient.
- Therapist's self-awareness of their own sexuality, gender identity, and attitudes toward sex and sex offenders is essential.
- Be aware of and expect to confront transference and countertransference issues in working with sex offenders.
- Do not work alone. Do not work without developing an alternative plan for safety for yourself and your patient. Frequently, therapists are expected to work and perform in hazardous situations without adequate safety measures for their personal health and safety. This is a dangerous population to treat.
- Know individual strengths and limitations as a therapist.
- Display a balance between personal and professional life. Have supportive relationships. Allow time for hobbies, humor, and vacations.
- Know the symptoms of burnout—feeling fatigued or exhausted, detached from your work and patients, cynicism, irritability, change in mood, increase in negativity, or feeling unable to keep up or cope with all the demands of your schedule. Take control of your scheduling.

PROBLEMS, STRESS, AND BOUNDARY-SETTING

While the number of sex offenders being treated in their community and in prison is rapidly increasing, there is a limited number of therapists working in this profession. Finding office space in which a therapist can provide treatment to sex offenders is often a challenge. The public in general does not understand and are often fearful or threatened when confronted with sharing office space with the treatment providers who treat sex offenders. Pressure may be brought on Realtors not to rent office space to providers treating sex offenders.

Another problem in working with sex offenders is that the clients in treatment are not there on a voluntary basis. They are there because they are court-ordered and mandated to treatment. The therapist can expect to meet resistance when beginning to work with sex offenders.

Stress may present in the following ways: fatigue, headaches, muscle pains, gastrointestinal disturbances, neglecting yourself and your physical appearance, evidencing anger, irritability, or negativity. Do not ignore symptoms of stress. Build exercise and relaxation into your personal daily routine. Do not take what the patients say or do personally. Do not take responsibility for the patients' feelings or behavior.

Boundary development is an important part of sex-offender treatment. Therapists have physical, mental, emotional, as well as ethical boundaries. Boundaries are imaginary lines we create around ourselves. These boundaries protect us and our patients from engaging in unhealthy or destructive behaviors. The purpose of these boundaries is to protect us physically (bodies), emotionally (our spirit), and mentally (our mind).

Boundaries are also set by each professional's code of ethics. Therapists must identify and know their own boundaries. The patient may initially be resistant to the therapist setting boundaries. Boundaries are as individual as the person and his or her life experience. Boundaries must inform patients that they can get only so far and no further. The consequences must be clearly identified if patients overstep or infringe on these boundaries.

In working with sex offenders, we may note that they share similar characteristics. Often the patient comes from a dysfunctional or chaotic family where violence and abuse was a family dynamic. The patient may experience problems with societal standards of setting boundaries that are acceptable behavior. There is a perception that sex offenders lack sexual boundaries. They, themselves, may have been sexually abused or have problems related to sexual dysfunction. They have problems delineating the boundaries between themselves and others.

At no time should a therapist sexually exploit a patient. This is clearly a boundary violation. Sex offenders can be quite seductive, while subtle, when interacting with their therapist. In the therapist's efforts to show unconditional regard for their patient, this may be misinterpreted as sexual. Therefore, therapists are challenged to develop treatment procedures that respond to the needs of sexually exploited patients without putting the therapist at risk.

A PERSONAL INVENTORY, TRANSFERENCE, AND COUNTERTRANSFERENCE

Therapists working with sex offenders must remain professional at all times. Countertransference issues may occur when the therapist provides treatment. Countertransference refers to the unconscious expectations, wishes, and defenses of the therapist that interferes with his or her ability to be objective, perceptive, and provide the quality of treatment needed by the client.

If patients feel the therapist is being punitive or judgmental through his or her interactions with the patient, they are less likely to engage in treatment. They will act out and may become exploitative or aggressive, reverting back to the behavior they exhibited with their victims, parents or other authority figures in their past.

Reactions of transference by patients most often are unconscious. All patients engage in transference relationships with their therapist. Helping patients recognize, experience, and understand their transference reactions to the therapist is therapeutic in the treatment process. Therapists may use transference as a positive tool in treating sex offenders. However, it is valuable for the therapist to use transference in a positive way that exhibits for patients how their emotions, feelings, and behaviors can be acted out with a person who is not the cause of the pain they are experiencing.

Patients will relate to therapists in terms of how they want the therapist to be or how they expect or fear the therapist is in reality. Patients who develop transference often experience similar feelings and act out familiar relationship scenarios with the therapist as though he or she was a part of their important relationship. Transference issues may create intense emotions—anger, rage, hostility or aggression, sexual arousal or excitement, low self-esteem, feelings of rejection, inadequacy or depression, anxiety, guilt, or shame.

In a group setting, the more people present will help patients stay focused in the moment of their present experience, decreasing transference issues.

Therapists' awareness of their own vulnerability is important when working with sex offenders. Therapists can also display defense mechanisms when confronted with difficult patients or behavior.

Countertransference and transference can impede both the therapeutic process and successful outcome in treating sex offenders. Therapists are responsible for monitoring their own countertransference issues and how it influences behavior while providing treatment for the patient. Please complete Exercise 1.1.

SUMMARY

In summary, Chapter 1 is the foundation for this workbook. The need for a workbook has been established. As a therapist who treats sex offenders you will be challenged clinically and must:

- be able to take care of yourself mentally, emotionally, and physically and be able to identify and appreciate the positive aspects of providing quality treatment for sex offenders;
- avoid stress by identifying the source of stress and setting about to decrease stressors;
- know your boundaries as well as the boundaries of your patients;
- take a personal inventory of your defense mechanisms; and
- know the dynamics of transference and countertransference in the therapeutic relationship.

EXERCISE 1.1. PROFESSIONAL SELF-AWARENESS INVENTORY

1. How do you feel about working with sex offenders?

   _____

   a. Can you work effectively with sex offenders? Yes_____ No_____ If you answered no, what is your reason?

   _____

   b. Can you work effectively with:

   Adolescent sex offenders? Yes_____ No_____

   Female sex offenders? Yes_____ No_____

   Male sex offenders? Yes_____ No_____

2. Do you have the knowledge, skills, ability, and interest to treat sex offenders?
   Yes_____ No_____

   a. If you answered no, why?

   _____

   b. If you answered yes, why?

   _____

3. When other professionals, family, or friends ask, "How can you work with 'those people,'" what is your response?

   _____

4. Do you believe sex offenders can be treated and have a positive outcome?
   Yes_____ No_____ Explain your answer.

   _____

5. Do you believe sex offenders should be returned to the community or serve life in prison? Explain your answer.

   _____

6. In your treatment of sex offenders, will you be working with:

Adult male sex offenders?	Yes_____	No_____
Adult female sex offenders?	Yes_____	No_____
Sexually agggressive adolescents?	Yes_____	No_____
Sexually aggressive children?	Yes_____	No_____

7. As a therapist, you work with a variety of patients with various diagnoses. Do you feel comfortable and skilled to treat patients with the following disorders:

Gender identity disorders?   Yes_____   No_____

Sexual addictions?   Yes_____   No_____

Sexual masochism?   Yes_____   No_____

Pedophilia?   Yes_____   No_____

Paraphilia?   Yes_____   No_____

Sexual disorders?   Yes_____   No_____

Exhibitionists?   Yes_____   No_____

Voyeurism?   Yes_____   No_____

a. Are you comfortable with your own sexuality? Yes_____ No_____

b. Do you have your own sexual dysfunction or perversion? Yes_____ No_____

c. If your answer was yes, how will this affect your ability to work with sex offenders?

_____

Chapter 2

Sexual Recovery Therapy

Sexual recovery therapy is a treatment model that is useful with sex offenders. In addition, it may be employed in treating patients with a specific sexual disorder or those who are sexually addicted (Flora, 2001).

The sexual recovery therapy format may be used in clinical settings with adults, adolescents, and children who exhibit misconduct behaviors. This therapy can be modified for individual, family, and group work. Sexual recovery therapy does not endorse group therapy for adolescents or children in outpatient settings. Many excellent inpatient programs are available for adolescents and children who use group therapy. However, since the goal for an adolescent or child usually is to be reunited with his or her family—a family therapy component is found to be more productive.

BACKGROUND

Adult sex offenders are a growing population, as well as sexually aggressive children and adolescents. Community safety is an issue. However, short-term therapies are not found to be useful with this group. Normally, a successful candidate who does not reoffend should complete at least three to five years of psychotherapy upon release from prison. Usually, children and adolescents that are sexually aggressive merit long-term treatment, lasting at least eighteen months to two years.

Research shows that patients who are treated are less likely to reoffend than offenders who are released from prison or placed on probation without follow-up outpatient therapy. A number of programs have been developed through the years, but often the focus is on "here and now" issues. This type of therapy has been proven to be successful with some patient population groups. However, the lack of in-depth work is not always useful for patients with developmental scaring. In order to change behavior, childhood experiences, traumatic events, or other life milestones need to be revisited. A number of sex offenders were sexually abused themselves. In addition, sex offenders are not always viewed by lay persons and professionals as a treatable group. This is in conflict with clinical research, which shows that recidivism is lowered by in-depth therapy.

Disturbingly, sexual disorders are not often viewed as a population that merits study. Yet, anger and countertransference only allow more victims to be harmed. In addition, many states have invested large sums of money to house sex offenders in correctional facilities—with the primary focus being punitive rather than an interest in rehabilitation.

Nevertheless, despite the lack of support by many, there have been several excellent landmark theorists and cutting-edge work globally, including Australia, Canada, Europe, the United Kingdom, and the United States, as well as some European countries.

Interestingly, a phenomenon is found among sex offenders—most do not reoffend while in treatment. The consequence for a reoffense is high for this type of patient. In comparison, a ther-

Sex-Offender Therapy
© 2008 by The Haworth Press, Taylor & Francis Group. All rights reserved.
doi:10.1300/5753_02

apist is fortunate in many other populations to still have a third of a caseload that has not relapsed as compared to a sex offender group. Yet, consequence alone is not the only cause for stabilization. A number of sex offenders tend to be very responsive to therapy once they overcome their resistance. Many have had broken lives and find that a change is merited.

SEXUAL RECOVERY THERAPY

Sexual recovery therapy is hybrid psychotherapy. Earlier treatment models were more esoteric or very simplistic. This is typical when a new patient group becomes the attention of the mental health community. All treatment models evolve as a new clinical disorder is found to exist.

Sexual recovery therapy is humanistic in form and views a person with a clinical disorder as an individual with an inappropriate learned behavior that merits treatment services. Certain developmental problems have occurred during childhood. However, sexual recovery therapy may not be useful for patients in denial or involved in sexual sadism.

The sexual recovery therapy model is a psychotherapy that provides a multiple therapeutic approach in care. It is a long-term psychotherapy, and should not be used for brief work. Acknowledgment, accounting, atonement, change, education, expression, detailing, hope, insight, reflection, and restructuring are all key elements.

Sexual recovery therapy is a process-oriented therapy that encourages patients to take responsibility for their actions. Insight is important. Directive work and confrontation are used on occasion, but as the patient makes changes, such techniques may not be a part of the work. Such a therapy is applicable to sexual addiction problems as well. And as with all hybrid therapies, sexual recovery therapy is influenced by integrative therapy.

Sexual recovery therapy shares elements of cognitive-behavioral methods, family system's theory, psychodynamic features, reality therapy, relapse prevention, and supportive psychotherapy.

All therapies are related to other previous work—sexual recovery therapy equally is a stand-alone psychotherapy—unto itself similar to other models. It is a therapy that promotes introspection and is to be used in work with sexual disordered persons.

Clinicians are encouraged to review standards of old masters of psychotherapy. Too often, a quick-fix therapy is encouraged in contemporary society. Patients who possess a sexual disorder cannot be quickly treated, and should never be, for the risk is too high.

For example, Freud's theory of personality is important. Several therapies appear to have lost sight of the significance that personality plays in reframing a patient. Personality is broken down into three parts: the *id, ego,* and *superego* (Heffner, 2001). In treating sexually aggressive adults, adolescents, and children, the id is found to have taken over a large amount of control and is encouraging impulsive behavior. The superego provides patients with a moral standard; but the superego is fractured, and is sending distorted messages to the offender. The ego is the center of personality and limits the urges of the id, while trying to please the superego. However, the ego is failing to keep a balance and is permitting sexual acting-out behavior.

Equally important in working with persons with a sexual disorder is adhering to the principles of self-actualization, developed by Abraham Maslow. A patient who is able to advance upward in the stages of self-actualization is less likely to reoffend than the individual who remains trapped at a particular point. The hierarchy of human needs, starting at the beginning, are as follows: survival, security, social acceptance, self-esteem, and self-actualization (Boeree, 1998).

CASE SUMMARY

Self-esteem was a problem for Jim, a forty-seven-year-old, single, Caucasian male. Jim was referred to treatment as the result of an offense in which he fondled the breasts of a teenage girl. In group treatment he admitted that he had committed the offense. He expressed remorse for his victim and was concerned about the psychological harm he had caused the girl. Jim reported a history of depression. Jim was sexually abused at age eleven by an adult female neighbor. He said he was afraid to tell anyone at the time. Prior to the offense, Jim said he had broken up with his girlfriend. Also, his sense of security and social acceptance were at risk. Such situations are found to be typical in the history of a sex offender. This was Jim's third incident. He had not been arrested for the previous two. He reported similar negative events prior to each assault.

In an analysis of Erikson's eight stages of development, referred to as the eight stages of man, the socialization of an infant, child, and adult is dependent upon a "psychosocial crisis" (Child Development Institute, 2005). This theory can be applied to Jim. The patient reported his sexual abuse to have occurred at age eleven. Achieving competence is important at this level. Sexual abuse at this point for a child of school age—age six to twelve—will be severely traumatized by a sexual abuse incident—a crisis. Jim suppressed his abuse and was impaired with feelings of inferiority.

Sexual addiction and offending may be examined by applying Erikson's eight stages of development (Child Development Institute, 2005):

1. *Learning Basic Trust versus Basic Mistrust (Hope).* Love, nurturing, and security are important during infancy, including ages one and two. A child who is not loved becomes mistrustful.
2. *Learning Anatomy versus Shame (Will).* This stage occurs between eighteen months and four years of age. The well-treated child will feel sure of him or her self. Children who do not succeed at this level will show anxiety, fear, guilt, and a lack of self-esteem.
3. *Learning Initiative versus Guilt (Purpose).* This stage can begin as early as three-and-one-half years of age to preschool. This level includes active play; to learn to cooperate with other children and adults; to follow or lead as needed. If developmental problems occur, the child will become impaired by guilt, fear, social impairment; will become more dependent on adults than peers; and may show problems in play and imagination. The impaired child may have a feeling of inferiority and relationship problems may show up later in life (e.g., sexually acting out).
4. *Industry versus Inferiority (Competence).* In this stage, the school-age child learns to incorporate more formal developmental skills in interaction with peers, moving from free play to structure exercises with rules and teamwork, and learning in school. Classes may include math, reading, and social studies. The child must learn to structure time to include homework and become more self-disciplined. Self-discipline is important to growth as the youth grows. Successful children are found to enjoy trust, autonomy, initiative and can be industrious. The developmentally impaired youth will show mistrust, self-doubt, shame, guilt, and feelings of inferiority. This can be a turning point for one who later becomes sexually aggressive as the result of failure to master this stage of growth.
5. *Learning Identity versus Identity Diffusion (Fidelity).* This stage begins as early as age thirteen, and lasts to about twenty. The adolescent who is successful will find out, "Who am I." It should be expected that some role diffusion will occur, including more separation from parents, interest in peers, and being a part of a social group. The young person develops self-certainty. Also, achievement is found as the youth grows and begins to develop ideas. Role experimentation may occur. Problems with this stage result in delinquency, a negative sense of self, and a feeling of self-consciousness that is counterproductive. A sex offender

does not often succeed in this developmental stage and has had contact, in some cases, with the criminal justice system. As well, sex addicts and offenders report problems of not fitting in with others, social isolation, self-consciousness, and problems with being successful in tasks.

6. *Learning Intimacy versus Isolation (Love).* At this stage, the young adult learns to be emotionally intimate with another person. Such a learning experience will later enhance future relationships and marriage. Also, this person will enjoy friendships with others that are fulfilling. Sexually disordered patients report problems with emotional intimacy, maintaining long-term friendships, difficulty with relationships, and problems in marriage and sex. The clinically disordered patient will feel unloved, uncared for by others, and seek superficial relationships to fill the void.

7. *Learning Generativity versus Self-Absorption (Care).* During the adult years, becoming creative, finding meaning to life, and being productive are important. This can be expressed successfully in marriage and by being a parent. Persons who fail at this stage can have contact with the criminal justice system, feel depressed, possess job problems, feel unworthy, report difficulty in relationships or marriage, show resistance to authority, sometimes violate the rights of others that includes sexual aggression, or become sexually addicted.

8. *Integrity versus Despair (Wisdom).* Persons who have been successful in the first seven stages find these to be happy years. One is reflective and will display a life that represents meaning and purpose. The individual has developed a concept that is positive. Persons who have failed to reach this stage continue to spiral downward, showing anger, anxiety, depression, family problems, social problems, and occupational regrets. Sexual acting out is an expression of their outlook upon life. If certain developmental stages were not met, the individual is more prone to act upon distorted thoughts.

The sexual recovery model is an in-depth approach to changing learned behaviors. The model is applicable for sexual addiction, sexual offending, and/or sexual aggression. The following discusses the three stages of the sexual recovery model.

Stage One

1. Referral

Treatment begins at the time of referral. Patients are usually referred by courts, probation, or social services. Rarely do patients with sex offending seek out therapy on their own accord. However, sexually addictive patients are found to be more proactive and will enter treatment when family, occupational, and social functioning are impaired by the problem.

2. The Clinical Assessment

A clinical assessment should be completed on each patient. If the patient is a sex offender, this format should include a clinical interview, testing, polygraph examination, and a penile plethysmograph. Sexually addictive patients will need only the interview and testing.

Stage Two

3. Engagement

The second stage should include rapport-building. Some old school prototypes believe harsh confrontation should occur at the beginning. Confrontation in the beginning will only cause the patient to manipulate. Others will offer data they believe the therapist wants to hear. Engagement permits the patient to tell the therapist why he or she is present. Rapport-building is very helpful in working with any type of patient.

4. Expression

Sex offenders have not had an opportunity to openly voice their feelings. Many have lost family, a job, and/or their home. As a result, the therapist, at this stage, should permit patients to voice their anxiety, anger, fear, grief, sadness, regret, and worry.

5. Acknowledgment

Sex offenders must acknowledge their offending in order to be treated. Sexual recovery therapy does not allow a token admission to a sexual offense. Therefore, before additional stages occur, patients will be expected to admit to their offense. Sex offenders who refuse to admit should be terminated from a program. A sexual addict tends to be less resistive and is more inclined to talk about problems.

6. Accounting

A cost analysis should be completed for each patient. A summary of what the patient's sexual acting out has cost in monetary terms should be used. The patient may have lost family, home, job, a vehicle, or have been sent to prison. The patient should assign a figure to the estimated replacement value.

7. Challenging and Detailing

An evaluation of the sexual history of the patient must be completed. During this level, the offender is to review the details of the index crime. Also, all past incidents of sexual misconduct will need to be revealed. Addicts and offenders tend to lie, distort, minimize, or rationalize their behavior. Confrontation may occur here. Sexual addicts also should offer an inventory of their affairs, relationships, and partners. A clinician will want to use a step-by-step approach to understand the patient's cycle of addiction and offending.

8. Strengthening and Hope

In this level, the clinician may encourage hope that recovery will lead to change. It is important for all persons to feel worthy and have a sense of validation, aside from their abuse. Also, the patient may have experienced despair, humiliation, and shame. Positive words of support will be helpful. The individual often will display defeat and a low self-worth. Depression may be an issue. Hope is critical to recovery and change. Insight will begin to be displayed by the patient.

9. Developing Empathy

Addicts and offenders must begin to work on empathy and remorse. Victims, family, and friends have been harmed. Depersonalization was used to rationalize the abuse or affairs. Cognitive distortions were used to offend or engage in sexually addictive behaviors. What was the physical and psychological harm the victim experienced? How did the partner of an illicit affair feel?

10. Apology and Atonement

Each person the addict or offender has harmed must be reviewed. One task that is useful is to ask patients to write a letter to themselves from a victim or someone that they sexually used. Twenty years have passed and the victim is now contacting them to recount how the sexual abuse or addiction impacted their lives. This can be a very powerful exercise. Denial, depersonalization, and rationalization are cracked as patients learn the harm another experienced. Written words have a strong impact. Addict's may want to write to someone that has been harmed (e.g., a family member or sexual partner). The letter should not be mailed. This act is symbolic and permits the door to be opened for atonement. Atonement should be started in treatment and may also include, as an example, a special trust fund created through a third party for a victim. The victim will not be informed of the person who created the account. Introspection usually occurs at this level. Atonement does not excuse sexual misconduct.

11. Past Sexual Abuse

Sexually aggressive adults, children, and adolescents may have been sexually abused and are acting out their trauma. It is important to address this abuse and the patient's trauma.

12. Detailing

Review crimes, offenses, and misbehavior with the patient. "Layering" is a process found in sex addicts and offenders in which details are revealed over a graduated period. The therapist should encourage the patient to talk about the past and those that were harmed. Additional information is often reported. Detailing allows an addict or offender to stop keeping secrets. No longer will the patient need to withhold information. This can be an important step for the recovering patient. Insight begins.

13. Sexual Education

A sexual education component must be offered to patients. Many sexually disordered patients often lack a basic understanding about sex. It is helpful to permit them to ask questions and understand what is appropriate sexual activity.

14. Changing Sexual Behavior

This part of therapy focuses on developing techniques to avoid reoffending or sexually acting out. Appropriate behavior is encouraged. Changing sexual behavior requires the patient to examine distortions, triggers, rituals, victim selection, or a person who can be seduced. Patients should identify high-risk situations and interventions. Therapists may query patients about difficult experiences and how they managed the event. Change is important to the recovery process. Patients are told they must give up old coping behaviors if they want to be successful. Insight is encouraged.

15. Sexual Restructuring

Sexual restructuring follows the change level. In-depth work on how patients started to use people in a sexual manner is explored. They explore the past. What childhood events impacted their ego and behavior? Sexual restructuring will sometimes be difficult for patients. The change process is more surface in technique. Sexual restructuring requires more introspection and insight. In order to recover, this process must be completed. Analogy and metaphors may be used here. Insight is encouraged. The id, ego, and superego should be examined by the therapist. The cycle of addiction and offending are a part of this process.

16. Sexual Recovery and Insight

Insight is now active for the addict or offender. Recovery is a part of his or her everyday life. The patient has answered questions about why he or she engaged in sexual misconduct behaviors. "What if" situations may need to be discussed. Why did addiction or offending become a part of the patient's lifestyle? How did sexual misconduct impact the patient's life? What does the future include for the patient now? As a result, a basic level of insight emerges in the patient.

17. Personal Safety Plan

A personal safety plan is recommended. The plan may include a reoffense chain, triggers, stressors, rituals, preplanning, and victim selection. Also, high-risk situations should be included. Interventions should be a part of a personal safety plan. Places to go for help may be listed. Support persons with telephone contacts may be listed.

Stage Three

18. Preparation for Termination

Termination should be completed in a gradual stage. It should begin as early as six months to one year of completion of the program in order to prepare the patient for release.

19. Review of Termination

One month prior to discharge the patient should begin the final termination phase of work. As a result, the patient spends time reviewing his or her progress and discusses the future. Goodbyes are said if the patient is in a group. Support, encouragement, and hope are given to the patient. The patient is offered booster shots if problem behaviors reemerge. If the patient is a member of a group, he or she may select to continue in the program at no cost. In large communities, a support group for graduates of a program may meet on a regular basis. No sex offender should be terminated if the patient displays problem behavior.

20. Termination

Upon termination, patients are encouraged to continue their work in recovery and to maintain appropriate behavior. Booster shots are revisited. Contact telephone numbers are given to the patient to use if a problem occurs.

SEXUAL RECOVERY THERAPY AND FAMILY TREATMENT

The sexual recovery therapy model is a useful psychotherapy for sexually aggressive adults, adolescents, and children who require family treatment. However, it should not be confused with reunification. Many times young children or adolescents are permitted to remain in the home by the court. In addition, persons with sexual addictive behaviors who have had no criminal charges will stay in a home. This type of treatment is more family-oriented than reunification-directed.

Parents should always be involved in therapy with a child or adolescent on an outpatient basis. It does little good to see the youth alone for all sessions. Remember, the problem most likely started somehow in the home, and therefore, needs to be resolved where it started.

Individual sessions should be evaluated closely. Such sessions indicate a position of power for a patient in family treatment. A therapist should tread carefully, for some patients will sexualize a situation, and the worker may be at risk. Children may prefer to have their parents present for all sessions. It is recommended that all family members be seen together.

As well, a partner should be involved in couple's work, if the person who is sexually addicted is an adult. Children should not be involved in couple's therapy in such cases—unless special occasions are merited. Adult sex offenders should first be involved in group therapy.

A family model can follow the elements of sexual recovery therapy. The goal is to stabilize the family unit that was upset by the sexually acting out adult, child, or adolescent. Sexually aggressive behaviors are often products of family systems in which sexual misconduct, physical abuse, or emotional neglect are present. Violence may also have been a part of the family. (This same approach is used for adults who are sexually addictive.)

In work with sexually abusive families, one often finds that the family is extremely enmeshed or disengaged from one another. Either they are overly involved with one another, or each member acts independent of others.

In addition to helping the patient resolve their sexual aggression, the secondary goal is to restructure the family in order to enhance everyone's quality of life.

Structural family therapy is one recommended psychotherapy when working with chaotic families (Minuchin and Fishman, 1981). Although this model was not created specifically for sexually abusive family systems, it is useful in many ways.

1. This therapy allows the therapist to join with the family in order to make change.
2. The clinician will make a hypothesis and plan to implement a change.
3. The change is started by the therapist to make new structural roles.
4. The worker starts to reframe the family to lessen dysfunctional behavior.
5. Enactment is encouraged in order to determine control, power, and how a family interacts during a stressful period.
6. The clinician focuses on interaction by selecting one problem that the family encounters.
7. It is important to raise intensity in order to produce change and restructure the family.
8. The actual restructuring process; family members' roles are changed.
9. Boundaries are examined.
10. A therapist will unbalance a family to test to how well members now are able to manage difficult situations.
11. In the complementary stage, the therapist works to help the family recognize the one member who is less important, then helps them learn to work together as a unit.
12. Realities in which the family has developed a misguided way or distorted view of seeing the world.
13. The clinician works to help the family maintain its new changes by the constructions that have been made to the system.

Sexual recovery therapy, following the structural model, requires all family members to be present for sessions when the offender is an adolescent or a child. Rules will need to be addressed. Remember, this therapy is to be used when the court has allowed the sexually aggressive child to live at home—and/or the family is to be involved in therapy while the youth is placed in a nearby therapeutic foster home.

INDIVIDUAL THERAPY

Individual therapy is considered the "goal standard" of psychotherapy. Such sessions involve only the therapist and the patient. These sessions should be held weekly if on an outpatient basis. Individual therapy is recommended for patients with a sexual addiction problem or offenders who have advanced in group therapy but merit one-on-one work. Individual therapy may also serve as an adjunct to group treatment. Work is based on the patient's progress. Adult sex offenders should be referred to a group program.

The sexual recovery therapy model is still used. Modifications are made to adhere to the style difference. Advantages may include:

1. One-on-one sessions with a therapist.
2. Work is based on the patient's progress and is not influenced by a group.
3. A patient may be a part of a group, but will see a clinician in addition for more in-depth therapy.
4. Individual therapy is recommended for sexual addiction problems.
5. Sex offenders should be referred to a group program.
6. Although a sexual addict is not court-ordered to attend treatment, the same problem behaviors may be recognized: anger, cognitive distortion, denial, deception, minimization, obsession, preplanning, rituals, and sexual fantasy.

Disadvantages may include:

1. The patient may try to emotionally seduce, groom, or manipulate the therapist.
2. The patient will not have the opportunity for a shared experience with others.
3. The patient will miss the opportunity of the group experience and being with the real "experts."

As noted in the sexual addiction section, there is a cycle of addiction. This addiction is compulsive, and the patient has been unable to stop. He or she has made promises that would cease the behavior, but the problem behavior continues. As a result, it is important for the therapist to identify the patient's cycle of addiction, and incorporate this into homework assignments.

Individual therapy is not recommended for adolescents or children with sexually addictive or aggressive behaviors. Family therapy is the choice of treatment.

SUMMARY

Sexual recovery therapy is a model that is appropriate for treating sexually aggressive patients. It may be used in a variety of formats, can be modified to the person's need, and may be used with individuals, families, or groups. Also, sexual recovery therapy may be applied to either gender—both males and females. Children, adolescents, and adults who display sexual misconduct problems may benefit from this form of treatment. A clinician should use caution if considering individual treatment for a child. See Exercise 2.1 for additional review.

EXERCISE 2.1. REVIEW QUESTIONS

1. What type of patient is appropriate for the sexual recovery therapy model? Please make a list.

   _____

   _____

   _____

2. What importance do the id, ego, and superego play in treating a sexual addict or offender?

   _____

   _____

   _____

3. What developmental stages are most likely found to have been mismanaged by the parents of a sexual addict or offender?

   _____

   _____

   _____

4. What stages in self-actualization, if missed, could produce recovery problems for a sexual addict or offender?

   _____

   _____

   _____

5. Why is the detailing level in sexual recovery therapy important in the recovery process?

   _____

   _____

   _____

6. Why is it important for sexual addicts or sex offenders to admit to their misconduct behaviors?

   _____

   _____

   _____

Chapter 3

Using Sexual Recovery Techniques

Sexual recovery can almost become a state of mind. It involves changing a distorted belief system (Carnes, 2001). Upon first entering treatment, the therapist should expect denial from patients, but extend hope. It is essential that the idea of hope be included in recovery. Without hope there cannot be lasting and meaningful recovery.

Motivation is another necessary ingredient for recovery. Without it, old behaviors may return if a patient is not supported to change. Recovery is not comfortable. It requires action on the part of the patient. Often this action involves the patient looking at him or her self in an honest manner for the first time in many years.

The patient must accept responsibility for what he or she has done. Sexual recovery therapy focuses on techniques to assist in change. The techniques used can produce a positive result when working with sex offenders. However, all sex offenders may not be appropriate for this type of therapy (e.g., sexual sadism patients).

Recovery begins before the patient realizes his or her goal to make changes. The techniques involved are geared to assist the patient in the implementation of this change. It is important that the therapist offers options and be invested in the techniques being used. The following are several different sexual recovery therapy techniques that the therapist can utilize in individual and/or group sessions with sex offenders.

JOURNAL-KEEPING

1. The patient should have a notebook that is specifically used as a journal.
2. The patient should write down his or her fears, hopes, memories, beliefs, opinions, experiences, and sexual fantasies (both appropriate and inappropriate) in this journal on a regular basis.
3. Each entry should be at least one page in length. The therapist should expect some resistance at first. Also expect that the entries display some problems in writing about feelings and experiences. As the patient continues to write and becomes more invested in his or her recovery, the journal entries will reflect these treatment issues.
4. The therapist should give specific homework assignments related to issues discussed in group that will evoke thought.
5. The therapist should randomly select patients to review their journals.
6. Journals should be brought each time that the patient comes to a group session.

TAPE-RECORDING

At times there will be patients who are unable to read or write. Certain allowances should be made to ensure that these patients have the opportunity to participate with the rest of the group.

Sex-Offender Therapy
© 2008 by The Haworth Press, Taylor & Francis Group. All rights reserved.
doi:10.1300/5753_03

The use of a tape recorder also requires that these patients are still held accountable. The following is a criteria list that will be important for these patients:

1. Patients are to use the tape recorder for the same reasons that their counterparts write in journals. Taping a session is not allowed.
2. The tapes used by patients should clearly be identified as journal tapes or homework assignment tapes.
3. Patients should verbally speak about their fears, hopes, memories, beliefs, opinions, experiences, and sexual fantasies (both appropriate and inappropriate) on their tapes on a regular basis.

SELF-READING

As part of the patients' recovery they should have a recommended reading list. The list should contain books that will educate about specific sexual offenses, the addiction cycle, as well as challenge cognitive distortions and evoke conversations in the group. The therapist should find books that will help patients move forward in their recovery.

DEVELOPING NONSEXUAL RELATIONSHIPS

The idea of developing relationships that do not involve sex can sound strange to patients. Their entire lives have revolved around sex. Oftentimes, love and sex are confused. Offenders are void of intimacy and feel that the act of sex fills their loneliness and the inner emptiness that percolates. Relationships become hollow and are based solely on sex. The partner/victim is seen not as an equal, but as a sexual object whose only purpose is to satisfy the offender. In order for patients to develop relationships that are not based on sex they must do an overhaul on their belief system and their distorted views of sex and intimacy must be challenged by the therapist, the group, and eventually by their own assessment. The following are some guidelines to assist patients in their understanding of developing relationships that do not have a focus of sex.

1. Don't go into a relationship with sexual intimacy as a desired goal.
2. Treat people with respect and not as sexual objects.
3. Develop a relationship with an individual who is not attractive to you sexually.
4. Look for qualities within the person that do not have anything to do with physical or sexual attractiveness.
5. Self-assess the values, interests, preferences, and beliefs that you hold as important.

This list may change as the patient becomes more involved in recovery.

HOPE AND VALIDATION

It is critical that patients feel that they have some success in their recovery. Validation and hope are two main elements that are needed for the recovery to go forward (Flora, 2001). Of these two, hope is the most important; without hope there will be no recovery. A patient that feels there is no hope in recovery runs a greater chance of reoffending and thus creating another victim. As the therapist, you have a major responsibility to ensure that strength and hope are intertwined throughout the treatment provided. Exercise 3.1 is for therapists to measure their ability to help patients with hope and validation.

COGNITIVE DISTORTION

Cognitive distortion is an impaired view of reality. Patients allowed themselves to believe that it was all right to harm another person. Patients gave themselves excuses. They may have started off by telling themselves that what they were doing wasn't hurting anyone; or maybe they felt that the experience would make the victim stronger; or perhaps they were so consumed by their own sexual desires and wants that they didn't think of anything. (See Exercise 3.2.)

NEGATIVE THINKING

Most often there is no one single thing that patients told themselves while they were in their offense cycle. Their distorted views allowed them to believe many different things about themselves and their role in the offense. In her workbook, *The Adult Relapse Prevention Workbook*, Steen (2001) talks about twelve different types of distorted views that rely heavily upon the negative thoughts that patients carry around with them.

1. *All or nothing*—Patients with this view see everything as good or bad, black or white, right or wrong. There is no middle ground or any room to wiggle.
2. *Negative expectations*—Patients automatically expect that anything that they try or do will have a negative outcome. People with this type of attitude decide the day is going to be bad and that nothing will work in their favor.
3. *Overgeneralizing*—Patients believe that if one person thinks something bad about them or does something to them then everyone will have the same attitude toward them. Patients try to get a job, but employers turn them down because of their criminal history, so all employers will turn them down.
4. *Entitlement*—Patients feel a sense of privilege. They feel that they deserve something just because they need or want it.
5. *Seeing yourself as a victim*—"Poor, poor, pitiful me" is the view that patients take. They play the role of victim.
6. *Personalizing*—This view creates a vacuum of negative treatment for patients that they set up for themselves. They feel that everything that happens to them is bad, even those situations that are out of their control.
7. *Jumping to conclusions*—Before having all of the information needed to make a rational decision, patients assume that something will turn out badly even if it hasn't happened yet, as in making impaired decisions. Patients with this view will assume that since a person did not return a greeting or because they are looking at them a certain way then that person is obviously thinking the worst of them.
8. *Grandiose expectations*—Patients with this type of distorted view also have a sense of entitlement. They are self-centered and see themselves above other people.
9. *Overemphasizing one detail*—Patients have the ability to hone in on a negative comment or detail and throw out anything that is good that may have been part of the same conversation. This view is similar to overgeneralizing.
10. *Rejecting the positive*—Patients discount anything that is positive, choosing instead to clothe themselves in negative belief.

11. *Catastrophizing*—Patients treat their lives like a chain reaction. Because one negative thing happens, their view is that one bad thing after another happens to them.
12. *Calling themselves names*—When things go wrong, patients verbally attack themselves through negative names (i.e., I'm an idiot or I'm so stupid; no wonder I can never get this right).

LIVING A HEALTHY LIFESTYLE

Changing one's lifestyle is necessary in order for the treatment to be successful. As the therapist, you are in charge of prompting this gradual change in the members of the group. Part of the sexual recovery therapy model is development of a healthy lifestyle.

The following are lifestyle issues that you, the therapist, can discuss with the members of your sex-offender treatment group to help them establish a productive direction in their lives.

1. Prioritize your life! As you look at your life what are the most important areas that you need to focus or refocus on?
2. Develop nonsexual hobbies.
3. Work your recovery program both inside and outside of the program.
4. Do a self-inventory. Assess your values, principles, desires, wants, and needs.
5. Take care of your physical needs, such as proper diet and sleep.
6. Change/modify your environment if it is counterproductive or becomes an obstacle to living a healthy lifestyle. Find ways to perform a community service or volunteer at a food pantry.
7. Have a plan in place in the event that you find yourself in a high-risk situation.
8. Be aware of your stressors, triggers, or anything else that can make you slip down the reoffense chain.
9. Have workable and obtainable goals in place (Daley and Moss, 2002).
10. Structure your time, so that you don't get bored (Daley and Moss, 2002).

COGNITIVE-BEHAVIORAL THERAPY

One therapeutic technique in treating sex offenders is cognitive-behavioral therapy (CBT). CBT is psychotherapy based on modifying everyday thoughts and behaviors, with the aim of positively influencing emotions. CBT is based on the idea that how we think (cognition), how we feel (emotion), and how we act (behavior) all interact together. Our thoughts, specifically, determine our feelings and our behaviors; therefore, negative and unrealistic thoughts can cause distress and result in problems (Beck, 1975; Bush, 1996).

One example could be when an offender, who is disappointed, thinks, "I am useless and worthless." This negatively impacts his or her mood, making the offender feel depressed, instead of focusing on the cause of the source of the disappointment. The offender stays focused on the negative feelings generated by the thoughts of being "useless and worthless." The problem may worsen if the offender avoids situations that could cause disappointment in the future. As a result, a successful experience becomes more unlikely, which reinforces the original thought of "useless and worthless." In therapy, this example is called a self-fulfilling prophecy—"If I think I'm useless and worthless, then I am useless and worthless." You, as the therapist, would be focused upon working to change those thinking patterns. Addressing the way the offender thinks in response to similar situations can help to do this. CBT says that the offender's core beliefs (often formed in childhood) contribute to thoughts that come up automatically in any given situation (Beck, 1975).

Thoughts are not set in concrete. People change their beliefs as they gain new understanding on a given subject. For instance, as a child you might have thought that there were monsters under your bed, but as you gained more information about life, you realized there were no such thing as monsters. Thoughts can change, but not easily, and it takes a deliberate, conscious effort to break old thought patterns. As you examine the patient's past thinking patterns what you may discover is that each time the offender was in a particular situation he or she reacted in the same way because his or her thoughts were similar each time. To help the offender to develop new, healthier thinking patterns, you may want to introduce him or her to the concepts of self-talk, thinking errors, and thinking distortions (Steen, 2001).

Self-talk refers to the things we say to ourselves to make sense of the world around us. This conversation can be either positive or negative. Negative self-talk can lead offenders to commit a crime by the negative way they feel about themselves. Positive self-talk can make offenders feel good about themselves and their future, thus making it less likely that they will want to offend. Offenders can change negative self-talk into positive self-talk by changing their thoughts about a particular person or situation. The more they are upbeat and positive about themselves the more likely they are to think through a problem before they act. Some people act before they are aware of how they are feeling or thinking. Impulsive actions can lead to very negative consequences. Offenders need to learn to slow their reactions down. Exercises 3.3, 3.4, and 3.5 will show how offenders can change their thinking from thoughts that will make them feel negative to positive, thus changing how they feel.

The next concept to address is thinking errors. A thinking error can cause problems that may lead a patient into an offending cycle. When the offender begins to make decisions based upon a faulty belief system, certain kinds of negative, wrong, or unhealthy thoughts can be formed that can be harmful to the offender and a potential victim. To assist the offender in correcting those negative thought patterns the following techniques can be used: thought stopping, thought switching, and journaling.

Thought stopping is the ability to tell yourself STOP! as the result of having inappropriate thoughts. This can be accomplished by telling oneself either by thinking or out loud to stop the negative tape that is running. It will take practice, but it can be accomplished.

Thought switching occurs when an inappropriate thought pops up into an offender's thoughts and he or she switches his or her thoughts to something more appropriate. For example, John begins to objectify a woman in shorts walking in front of him. He immediately starts thinking about the time he spent in prison.

Journaling is used when the offender cannot find someone he or she trusts to talk with. The offender can write his or her thoughts down and discuss them later with a trusted person or a therapist.

One of the problems that prevents offenders from successfully overcoming negative thought patterns are the roadblocks they set up for themselves. Roadblocks are words and phrases offenders use to prevent themselves from making positive decisions in their lives.

The following are some examples of negative thinking and positive thoughts errors:

Negative Thinking Errors	Positive Thoughts
"I can't"	"It may be hard, but I will try to do it"
"I have to"	"I want to" or "I choose to"
"I should"	"I may if I want to"
"I should have"	"I made a mistake, but it's not the end of the world"
"I don't have a choice"	"I do have a choice"
"It's your fault"	"It was no one's fault but mine based upon the decisions I made"

SUMMARY

Cognitive distortions have evolved over an extended period for a patient. In working with persons with a distortion it is important to confront the patient in an open manner, giving him or her a new reality to consider, rather than continuing to operate with misleading information. The therapist should encourage a patient to share distortions before making an intervention. As simple as this may sound, sometimes a clinician can offer an intervention when the patient has revealed only a portion of the distortion pattern of thinking. Such behavior should not be confused with a thought disorder such as schizophrenia. Distorted thinking has evolved to events in a patient's life that were traumatic or stressful to the individual and an inappropriate way of coping developed.

EXERCISE 3.1. HOPE AND VALIDATION

1. As a therapist, how important do you value hope in therapy? _____

_____

_____

_____

2. As a therapist, how important are strength and encouragement in therapy? _____

_____

_____

_____

3. As a therapist, how do you address issues of poor self-esteem as felt by members of your
   group? _____

_____

_____

_____

4. What does hope mean to you? _____

_____

_____

_____

5. Think of a time that you felt helpless. Explain the feelings and your view on the issue.

_____

_____

_____

_____

EXERCISE 3.2. COGNITIVE DISTORTION

1. Cognitive distortion is a phrase that you, the patient, will hear and at some point use yourself. In your own words, write down what you believe this phrase means.

_____

_____

_____

2. What type of excuses did you give yourself while you were committing your offenses?

_____

_____

_____

3. Are you still making excuses for yourself?

_____

_____

_____

4. Explain how you blamed your victim.

_____

_____

_____

5. Are you still blaming your victim?

_____

_____

_____

6. After the offense, how did you rationalize the offense to yourself?

_____

_____

_____

EXERCISE 3.3. SELF-TALK

1. Betty is told that she is stupid by her boyfriend. Betty believes him and feels she is useless. What can Betty tell herself to feel better?

_____

_____

_____

2. Joe has been studying for months for a part in his local theater production. He showed up for the audition and found over twenty other people trying out for the part as well. He tells himself, "They all have more talent than I do," and leaves without auditioning. What self-talk could Joe have used?

_____

_____

_____

3. George has worked hard on a project for work, but his boss does not like what he's done. George thinks, "I can't do anything right," and feels depressed. What can he say to make himself feel better?

_____

_____

_____

4. Jack's mother criticizes everything he does. Jack is thirty-one years old and decides it is not worth trying to please her, so he stops trying. How could Jack change his self-talk so that he would feel better and not give up?

_____

_____

_____

5. Elliott was convicted of raping his next-door neighbor. It was reported in the newspaper. He is sure that everyone thinks he is a pervert. What can he say to himself so he can feel better?

_____

_____

_____

EXERCISE 3.4. NEGATIVE STATEMENTS

List five negative statements you have made and the situations in which you made them. Then list positive statements you could have made instead.

Negative Statement and Situation   Positive Alternative Statement

1. _____   1. _____

_____   _____

_____   _____

_____   _____

2. _____   2. _____

_____   _____

_____   _____

_____   _____

3. _____   3. _____

_____   _____

_____   _____

_____   _____

4. _____   4. _____

_____   _____

_____   _____

_____   _____

5. _____   5. _____

_____   _____

_____   _____

_____   _____

EXERCISE 3.5. THINKING DISTORTIONS

For each of the following examples, write what the offender could have said to him or her self instead, which would have been more positive.

1. *All or nothing:* Harry trained for the state championship which he planned to win. He had to qualify by coming in at least third place in the regional finals. He came in second and was thinking of quitting the team because he didn't win. What would be a better way for Harry to think about this?

_____

_____

_____

2. *Jumping to conclusions:* Frank saw his girlfriend embracing a man he didn't know. He thinks she is cheating on him and wants to break up. What could Frank say to himself instead that might help him deal with his problem?

_____

_____

_____

3. *Overgeneralizing:* Jimmy tried out for the swim team and didn't make it. Jimmy thought, "I'm no good at sports." What could Jimmy have thought instead?

_____

_____

_____

4. *Catastrophizing:* Along with seven other guys, David was turned down to dance by Chris. He thinks, "Nobody will ever dance with me again." What should he say to himself instead?

_____

_____

_____

5. *Entitlement:* Joyce wasn't paid what she felt she earned at the beauty shop, so she thought, "I'll take a perm kit from the stock and do a perm for my neighbor." What could Joyce say to herself instead?

_____

_____

_____

6. *Personalizing:* J. D.'s girlfriend broke up with him. J. D. thought, "She thinks I'm not man enough for her." What are some other things J. D. could have said to himself?

_____

_____

_____

7. *Rejecting the positive:* Hector feels he is lazy and an underachiever because he doesn't have a big house like his older brother. His wife tells him she's proud of his work ethic and his love for the family. He says to himself, "Those things don't matter. I still don't have a house as big as my brother." What could Hector say to himself instead?

_____

_____

_____

8. *Calling yourself names:* After Kobe missed the winning shot in the game, he said to himself, "I'm such a big loser." What could he have said to himself instead?

_____

_____

_____

9. *Overemphasizing one detail:* Angel is a smart, ambitious, and friendly man with a dazzling smile. His sister makes fun of his crooked teeth, which he broke while playing football. Because of that, he said to himself, "I'm ugly." What could Angel say to himself instead?

_____

_____

_____

Chapter 4

Clinical Sexual Disorders

Clinical sexual disorders are not a new phenomena. However, due to the sensitive nature of these disorders they can be uncomfortable to discuss. No longer do members of society have the luxury of believing that the paraphilic behavior that causes harm to so many people happens in other neighborhoods, cities, or other parts of the country. These types of disorders are very real and happen in all communities.

A person with a paraphilia or sexual disorder is dependent upon specific behaviors or actions in order to become sexually aroused and/or to reach climax. The specific paraphilia has a ritualistic flavor that is needed before sexual excitement and/or orgasm can be reached.

A paraphilia disorder is much like a drug addiction. At first the drug of choice is used to make the person feel good; however, before long euphoria turns to necessity of life. A paraphilia in the same vein is very much the same way, before sexual arousal can be reached, the paraphilic behavior must be present. Just like the drug addict who generally has more than one drug that is used in his or her addiction, it is not uncommon for a patient who has a paraphilia disorder to have other types of paraphilic disorders that are present and active (Flora, 2001; American Psychiatric Association, 2000).

The following ten recognized sexual disorders, although different in their focus, share similarities in that the sexual thoughts, feelings, and/or behaviors must be ongoing for at least six months and cause significant clinical difficulties in all aspects of their lives that they deem as important.

1. *Exhibitionism* involves the desire and compulsion to expose one's genitals to another person. The victim is generally a stranger or someone not expecting to be exposed to.

2. *Fetishism* is present when the patient is aroused sexually on a repetitive basis by certain inanimate objects. The objects that the patient picks are special in their meaning, eroticized, and elicit strong sexual emotions. In addition, the fetish is not limited to female clothing or any device that delivers tactile genital stimulation.

3. *Frotteurism* involves a person that is sexually stimulated by touching, rubbing, or bumping into a nonconsenting, unsuspecting individual.

4. *Pedophilia* involves the sexual attraction and/or sexual relationship with a child. Individuals who are actively engaged in this disorder must be sixteen years of age or older and at least five years older than the child. When making the diagnosis of pedophilia it is also required that the therapist specifies if the patient is *sexually attracted to males, sexually attracted to females, sexually attracted to both,* or *limited to incest.* In addition the therapist must indicate *exclusive type* or *nonexclusive type.*

5. *Sexual masochism* involves the repeated act of being beaten, humiliated, bound, or another aggressive manner where suffering is the goal in order to reach sexual arousal or sexual gratification. Violent fantasies including being raped or bound, or administering self-inflicted pain. Seeking a partner to conduct such acts as being blindfolded, spanked, beaten, and other physical acts involving suffering are also part of this disorder. The humiliation can be either physical or verbal.

Sex-Offender Therapy
© 2008 by The Haworth Press, Taylor & Francis Group. All rights reserved.
doi:10.1300/5753_04

6. *Sexual sadism* is an individual obtaining sexual arousal and/or sexual gratification through the physical and psychological suffering and pain of other people. Always present is the need and desire to control and belittle others as well as to cause pain. As this disorder escalates, so does the emotional and physical trauma, as well as possible death to the consenting or nonconsenting person involved.

7. *Transvestic fetishism* should not be confused with an individual with a gender identity problem. This disorder is found only in heterosexual males and is present when the individual has an intense, frequent desire to wear women's clothing, which is then further escalated by having masturbatory fantasies that he is in the sexual role of both male and female and/or in a sexual situation with a woman or object of sexual importance. In addition, the *Diagnostic and Statistical Manual of Mental Disorders, Fourth Edition, Text Revision* (DSM-IV-TR) also requires that when making a diagnosis of this disorder the therapist specify if the patient has *gender dysphoria* (American Psychiatric Association, 2000).

8. *Voyeurism* derives sexual excitement from watching unsuspecting persons taking off their clothes, being naked, and/or engaging in sexual activity. This disorder is predominately found in males and begins before the person turns fifteen years old. The person engaged in the voyeuristic behavior is only interested in looking and does not want any contact with the person he or she is watching. The person will often masturbate or bring him or her self to orgasm either during or after the event.

9. *Paraphilia not otherwise specified (NOS)* is a coding set aside for paraphilic disorders that do not meet the criteria of the clinical sexual disorders already discussed. *Necrophilia* (arousal occurs through some type of sexual activity with corpses), *telephone scatologia* (sexual pleasure is derived in making or hearing obscene phone calls), *partialism* (sexual pleasure is reached through the focus on a particular part of the body), *zoophilia* (sexual pleasure is sought through sexual activity with animals), *coprophilia* (sexual activity that involves the use of feces), *klismaphilia* (sexual activity revolving around the use of enemas), and *urophilia* (sexual activity involving urine) are but a few examples of this category. Currently, there are more than forty known types of paraphilias.

10. *Sexual disorder not otherwise specified (NOS)* identifies sexual disturbances that do not meet diagnosis for any particular sexual disorder and also do not meet the criteria for a sexual dysfunction or a paraphilia. Examples of this category include feeling inadequate about one's sexual performance as it relates to self-imposed masculine and feminine responsibilities; clinical distress through having a series of sexual relationships with the primary focus of treating the partners as sexual objects to be discarded after sexual exploration; and recurrent clinical distress about one's sexual orientation.

SUMMARY

The DSM-IV-TR recognizes a number of sexual disorders. It is important for a therapist to also be aware that other clinical disorders may exist that are nonsexual but may influence the patient and his or her problem behavior. The clinical community recognizes eight separate sexual disorders, in addition to *sexual disorder NOS* and *paraphilia disorder NOS*. Many therapists consider *rape* as a clinical disorder as well, but it has not been recognized by the formal clinical community. *Sexual abuse of a child* or *sexual abuse of an adult* may be used to represent rape. Some clinicians also use *impulse control disorder NOS* for rape.

Chapter 5

Acknowledgment

Taking full responsibility for the sexual offense is one of the major treatment principles of sexual recovery therapy in working with sex offenders. During the first session, older members will identify their first names, how they harmed their victims, and the offense charges. Rules of the group are also reviewed. New members are asked to offer information about their problem behaviors.

A new patient may or may not admit to the offense. He or she is given eight sessions to acknowledge the offense or be terminated from treatment. The patient is on probation during this time. Upon completion of a truthful polygraph admission of the crime, and a stand-up presentation (see Chapter 6, this volume), the patient enters Phase I of therapy.

The new patient who admits to his or her crime must offer a detailed report of the incident. The patient cannot say that he or she was charged with rape and offer no additional information. Also, in order to lessen depersonalization, an offender must begin to talk about the incident and the harm he or she caused the victim. Victim empathy work begins at the first session.

The therapist may model behavior that is open and honest during the acknowledgment process. The guidelines also give professional information about the group leader and demonstrate how knowledge about yourself helps others get to know you better. In a therapy group, members have to give very intimate personal details about themselves in order for the therapeutic process to begin. Group leaders often have to give professional knowledge about themselves to serve as role models of self-disclosure.

TALKING ABOUT FEELINGS

Sex offenders need to learn how to identify and talk about their feelings throughout the treatment process. In the early stages of treatment (or Phase I), sex offenders often experience problems finding words to articulate their feelings.

One way to assist the sex offender in identifying his or her feelings is to let him or her pick a few feeling words from a written list (see Exercise 5.1). It is often helpful at the beginning of each group session to have group members identify three feelings that they have experienced in the last eight to twenty-four hours. If he or she has trouble identifying any feelings, he or she can look at a list of feelings and pick three from the list. Group members can also pick words off this list that they are not familiar with and ask the group members about this particular feeling word. What does it mean?

In Phase II of the program, the sex offender will be expected to write many details about his or her feelings in regard to sex offense. If he or she has trouble expressing or talking about feelings then the written assignments will be difficult. This exercise can be utilized to teach the offender about his or her feelings as well as to provide him or her with the tools for expressing and describing those feelings.

Sex-Offender Therapy
© 2008 by The Haworth Press, Taylor & Francis Group. All rights reserved.
doi:10.1300/5753_05

Group leaders should participate by choosing three feelings that they have experienced in the last twenty-four hours. This is an optional exercise, and depends upon how the group leader feels about sharing this information. If there is some reason for not wanting to share this information then this exercise can be done by the therapist before the group meets. Take a few moments to sit by yourself and write down three feeling words that come to mind to describe how you felt in the last twenty-four hours. If you cannot identify any feelings at this time then look at the feeling words on the feeling list in Exercise 5.1. Another activity is to concentrate on what you would like to happen today in the group. What would make this group special for you? What is often lacking in the group and is there a way to make this happen? This is often a good warm-up for the group leader prior to leading the group, when identification of emotions is the goal.

IDENTIFYING EMOTIONS

Sex offenders have intense feelings as a result of the consequences of their sex offense and as a result of being forced into treatment. Common emotions are anger, rage, guilt, and shame. The first step in learning how to deal with emotions is identifying what they are. Sex offenders have spent much of their time using defenses such as denial, projection, and justification as a means to ignore their emotions. As these emotions come up in the group, it is appropriate to identify them and begin to teach the sex offender appropriate ways of dealing with these emotions. The most common and difficult emotion is anger. If anger is not identified and dealt with it will often sabotage treatment goals. If the sex offender gets angry enough he or she might adopt an "I don't care" attitude and this will serve to defeat any progress made in treatment. It is very important, at some time near the beginning of treatment, to introduce the sex offender to a basic course of anger management. There are many such courses on the market and it is advisable to pick one that is suitable to your population and treatment approach. A good anger management course should include the following:

- A definition of what anger is and several ways of identifying the emotion by its patterns.
- An exploration of how anger affects the individual and any system that this individual comes into contact with.
- An explanation of different ways that anger is expressed.
- Introducing the individual to a comprehensive system of managing anger.

SUMMARY

Acknowledgment, or taking responsibility for one's actions, is the keystone to the recovery process. Using feeling words that break down emotions can often lead to the patient admitting to the sexual harm of another in therapy. Clinicians are encouraged to study feeling words that may be of help to patients. Patients who refuse to admit to their offenses are not appropriate for therapy.

EXERCISE 5.1. FEELINGS

abandoned	choked-up	impotent	rejected
accepted	close	impressed	rejecting
accused	cold	incompetent	relieved
aching	comforted	incomplete	removed
adventurous	competitive	independent	repulsed
affectionate	complete	insecure	repulsive
aggravated	confident	innocent	resentful
aggressive	conflicted	insignificant	resistant
agony	distrusted	insincere	stubborn
agreeable	dominated	inspired	stunned
alienated	domineering	insulted	stupid
alluring	doomed	intolerant	subdued
alone	down	involved	submissive
aloof	dreadful	irate	successful
amazed	eager	irresponsible	suffocated
amused	ecstatic	irritated	sure
angry	edgy	jealous	sweet
anguished	elated	put-down	sympathetic
callous	embarrassed	puzzled	tainted
capable	empty	quarrelsome	tender
captivated	enraptured	quiet	terrific
caring	enthusiastic	raped	thrilled
cautious	enticed	ravished	ticked
certain	esteemed	ravishing	tickled
chased	exasperated	real	tight
cheated	exhilarated	refreshed	timid
cheerful	important	regretful	

Chapter 6

The Stand-Up Presentation

In Phase I of any treatment program, clients have to learn the rules of the program and what is expected of them. This process usually takes anywhere from six to eight weeks.

After this initial period, sex offenders need to admit to their offense and take full responsibility for their actions. This is demonstrated in a stand-up presentation before the group. If the sex offender is able to demonstrate full responsibility for his or her actions, then he or she is ready to enter into Phase II of the treatment process. Rules for the stand-up presentation are as follows:

My group members will decide how well I present, so I must take this very seriously.

1. I will remain on probationary status in this group until I do my stand-up presentation. I need to present my stand-up by the eighth week of the group. It is my responsibility to ask for group time in order to make my presentation.
2. If I try to avoid doing the stand-up presentation, then I will be at risk of termination from the group for noncompliance.
3. I must stand before the group and remove items such as coats or hats that I can hide behind.
4. I must present my offense in an honest manner, and with a humble, remorseful, and sincere attitude.
5. I must describe my offense in behavioral terms—telling what I did, not what I was charged with. I must do a good job of helping others understand what really happened. I should not withhold any information.
6. My emotions must come across as sincere and my feelings should match my facial expressions.
7. I must describe how I hurt my victim—physically, emotionally, and mentally. I must discuss the short-term and long-term effects of the abuse upon my victim.
8. If I am successful, and the group accepts what I presented, then I can be promoted to the next phase and have all of the rights of a full group member.
9. If I fail to meet the group's standards for my stand-up, then I will remain on probationary status for another eight weeks, or be discharged from the treatment program. My group leader will lead the discussion about my status, after I present my stand-up.

After the stand-up presentation, the group leader will instruct group members to discuss the presentation with the presenter in attendance. After the discussion a vote will take place by all group members who have already passed the stand-up presentation. If accepted by the group, the presenter will be accepted into Phase II and will be a voting member of the group. If the presenter fails, he or she will be given feedback on why he or she failed and will have another six to eight weeks to pass another stand-up presentation. If the sex offender fails the second time, he or she will be terminated from treatment until such time that he or she takes full responsibility for the offense and must be readmitted to the process.

Sex-Offender Therapy
© 2008 by The Haworth Press, Taylor & Francis Group. All rights reserved.
doi:10.1300/5753_06

The group leader needs to be very active during the stand-up presentation. Certain leadership skills in this phase of the treatment process are essential.

1. All the facts of the incident must be clearly stated.
2. All of the thoughts and feelings associated with the incident need to be clearly stated. These should be the thoughts and feelings at the time of the incident as well as what the sex offender is feeling in the here-and-now while he or she is speaking about the incident.
3. At the end of the stand-up presentation, the group leader can use this time for teaching the group about responsibility and accountability for their actions. One way to practice these skills is to utilize them in experiences in your own life. This can be accomplished with Exercise 6.1.

VICTIM EMPATHY

Once sex offenders are admitted into Phase II of the program, they are given the outline in Exercise 6.2 for developing a victim empathy statement. This should be completed by the end of Phase II. It is crucial for sex offenders to learn victim empathy in order to complete a relapse-prevention plan. At the time of their offenses, the victims were just objects of their desires. With the victim empathy statement, sex offenders can learn to go back and treat their victims as individuals with dignity and respect. If the role reversal is complete, this can be the first step toward learning true empathy, respect, and intimacy with other human beings.

Another way for the therapist to understand victim empathy is to go through a very simple exercise such as 6.3.

CYCLE OF OFFENDING

The sex offender should be taught that there are four phases to the deviant personal cycle (Bays and Freeman-Longo, 1989). They are as follows:

1. Pretend normal phase
2. Build-up phase
3. Acting-out phase
4. Justification phase

Case Example

Mr. Q was a loving, caring father to his teenage daughter. He was promoted in his company and started to work long hours. He was soon getting very distant from his wife and his daughter would make special efforts to be with him. He began to see his daughter very differently than he did previously. However, he pretended that everything between him and his daughter was the same. This was the start of the pretend normal phase. He would go up to her room each night to give her a kiss. Sometimes she would be sleeping; sometimes she would be awake. As Mr. Q changed his perception of his daughter, this innocent, normal bedtime ritual became the continuation of the pretend normal phase. In the build-up phase, he began to treat her differently. He started to cave-in to what she wanted and suspended many punishments. He let her get away with things and tried to be more like a friend than an authority figure. In the end, he looked at her in a different way. It was no longer a father's love. In the acting-out phase, Mr. Q would go into his daughter's room and begin touching her inappropriately and later use these images of his daughter for the purposes of masturbation. He would later justify his behavior by telling himself that he did no harm.

A personal cycle worksheet can be utilized by the group therapist in order to understand this process for the sex offender. A very simple outline can be constructed, using four headings: (1) pretend normal phase, (2) build-up phase, (3) acting-out phase, and (4) justification phase. Each sex offender is expected to take their offense and plot it out on the worksheet using these four headings. Under each heading, the particular associated thoughts, feelings, and actions are listed. This can be presented to the group for discussion and rewriting, which is frequently needed. (See Exercise 6.4.) In Phase II of the treatment program, Mr. Q was asked to fill one of these worksheets out, in detail. The group assisted him in filling in all the blanks and understanding his personal deviant cycle.

SUMMARY

The stand-up presentation is very important to the recovery process. The patient must tell his or her story to the group in detail. The stand-up presentation is used in adult groups. A patient is required to explain his or her cycle of offending and relapse-prevention plan. Also, each person is expected to give a complete story of his or her history dating back to childhood. Emotional, physical, or sexual abuse is expected to be told during the stand-up if the patient was a victim. The person is on probation until he or she completes a stand-up. Upon hearing the story, senior voting members may ask questions. Some stand-ups take up to three sessions. Basically, a group will need to learn if the patient admits to the offense, has taken responsibility for his or her sexual misconduct, and is able to show some victim empathy or remorse. After the stand-up is completed, members may vote the patient into the group. On occasion, voting members may request that the patient work more on certain issues and present additional information to the group. In some situations, a noncompliant patient will not be permitted to continue in treatment and is returned to his or her probation and parole officer. The stand-up can be modified for individual and family sessions, but the setting and structure is changed.

EXERCISE 6.1. RESPONSIBILITY AND ACCOUNTABILITY

1. Recall the sequence of events of a recent incident:

_____

_____

_____

_____

_____

2. What time did this event occur? What day of the week? What was the weather like? What were you feeling and thinking at the time?

_____

_____

_____

_____

_____

3. Go over the sequence again and this time, add information of all five of your senses. Were there any smells? Did you touch anything or anyone? What did you hear? Did you taste anything? What did you see?

_____

_____

_____

_____

_____

Repeat this sequence several times until you have a final version that contains all of the facts of what happened. This is what is needed when a sex offender does his or her stand-up presentation. During the actual presentation, the group leader should be taking very detailed notes so that afterward the process can be discussed with the presenter and other group members. It would also be helpful to have group members write down what they hear in the stand-up presentation and give that feedback to the presenter. The feedback may be both positive and negative, thus creating a learning environment for the presenter.

EXERCISE 6.2. DEVELOPING VICTIM EMPATHY

Describe Your Sexual Offense from the Standpoint of Your Victim

1. What might your victim have been doing or thinking about just before the offense occurred?

   _____

2. What do you think your victim might have thought and felt when you made your approach to offend him or her?

   _____

3. What do you think your victim might have been thinking and feeling while you were actually committing your offense?

   _____

4. What do you think your victim might have been thinking and feeling immediately after the offense?

   _____

5. What sort of questions do you think your victim may have had about the offense?

   _____

6. What questions do you think your victim may still have about the offense and him or herself?

   _____

Describe Your Victim

1. How did you know your victim?

   _____

2. How do you think your victim felt or thought about you prior to your offending him or her?

   _____

3. Do you think your victim's attitude, thoughts, and feelings have changed in any way toward you? If so, how? If no, why not?

   _____

EXERCISE 6.3. THE THERAPIST AND VICTIM EMPATHY

1. Think of a time when you hurt someone physically, emotionally, or spiritually.

   _____

   _____

2. Consider what this person was thinking or doing just before this incident occurred.

   _____

   _____

3. What do you think this person was thinking or feeling when you first encountered him or her?

   _____

   _____

4. What do you think this person was thinking and feeling immediately after the incident?

   _____

   _____

5. What kinds of questions do you think this person has about what happened?

   _____

   _____

6. What do you think this person feels about him or her self after this incident?

   _____

   _____

7. How did you know this person?

   _____

   _____

8. How do you think this person felt about you prior to this incident?

   _____

   _____

EXERCISE 6.4. PERSONAL CYCLE WORKSHEET

1. List personal habits that are good or bad for you that you do on a regular basis. For example, it could be some form of exercise or something you eat.

   _____

   _____

   _____

2. Choose one of the activities that you listed above.

   _____

   _____

   _____

3. List all of the activities that are considered part of the build-up phase. This part should include the thoughts, feelings, and actions under the build-up phase. What kinds of behaviors, thoughts, and feelings are you experiencing that are leading up to executing this activity?

   _____

   _____

   _____

4. From the beginning, list all of the activities that are part of the acting-out phase. This part should include thoughts, feelings, and actions under the acting-out phase.

   _____

   _____

   _____

5. After the exercise or behavior is completed, list all of the activities that are part of the justification phase. This part should include thoughts, feelings, and actions under the justification phase.

   _____

   _____

   _____

Chapter 7

The Four-Phase Program

Certified sex-offender treatment providers must use a relapse-prevention format when treating sexually aggressive adults. According to Laws (1989), using a phase program provides a structured format in a group setting to be completed within an estimated period of three to five years of treatment. For many counselors specializing in brief therapy, three to five years may sound too long for third-party payment; however, the clients are required to pay the weekly costs. Many probation districts will provide financial assistance; however, should those contributions not be available the offender is mandated to pay the entire amount.

Using a four-phase program offers clients the opportunity to become acquainted with all aspects of the expected curriculum of the program. Phase I acts as the initial stage of therapy; Phase II maintains that structure, further encourages the required reading and assignment material, while teaching appropriate, constructive confrontation, communication, and feedback skills; Phase III provides the more advanced group members the chance to utilize their skills and take a leadership position within the group; and Phase IV operates as an aftercare/maintenance program without the aid of a counselor for those members who have completed the program, as well as the ultimate initiation for new treatment members prior to joining Phase I.

PHASE I: LEARNING TREATMENT LANGUAGE

In the first phase of group work, offenders learn and develop using the appropriate language of sex-offender treatment. Offenders are required to obtain a three-ring notebook (at least three inches in diameter) to keep weekly handouts, homework assignments, monthly progress reports, their copy of the program contract, payment receipts, and a journal. This notebook also initiates personal responsibility and allows patients to utilize skills for daily bookkeeping. Clients use the notebook on a weekly basis and the sections continue to grow over the full duration of the program.

It is important for the offender to begin using "I" statements in the very beginning of treatment, which encourages accountability and responsibility for his or her inappropriate thoughts, deviant behaviors, and the resulting consequences of the offense. Self-awareness is the center of this phase, as the offender looks at the basic concepts of his or her personal cycles of offending behaviors, errors in thinking, seemingly unimportant decisions, and reframe how they think about self and others. The offender must learn empathy, which is a deep, emotional understanding of the victim's perspective. This skill must develop throughout the first and second phases of the program.

Learning appropriate sexual language and behaviors will be a majority of the skills learned during the first phase, as many offenders have admitted not knowing the appropriate and correct anatomic terminology or actions. The program contract states that verbally abusive or offensive language will not be allowed, so having the offenders learn the appropriate jargon of sex offender treatment is imperative. It is equally important for clients to learn what sexual behaviors

Sex-Offender Therapy
© 2008 by The Haworth Press, Taylor & Francis Group. All rights reserved.
doi:10.1300/5753_07

are considered the "norm" to society and the law. The group discusses many of these inappropriate behaviors in order to educate everyone without the chance of embarrassing anyone within the session.

Through using the cognitive-restructuring theory, offenders learn to use victims' names, which will enable them to see the victims as people and not objects for sexual gratification. Teaching interpersonal skills during this phase of the treatment group, the clinician encourages offenders to develop skills for challenging and confronting other members. As an important aspect of this phase, the offender must submit to a full disclosure polygraph, which provides the clinician with vital information sighting the offender's sexual history, level of truthfulness, offense accountability, and possible degree of pathology. It is recommended this phase last approximately sixteen weeks in duration. Each client requires different amounts of time to learn the initial methods of sex-offender treatment and all three phases of the program may require more than the average three-year estimation. Incorporating a behaviorist model at this early point, the clinician would encourage extremely interactive group exercises, presenting positive behavior changes through group role-playing and role modeling. Combining both theories provides extremely effective group activities and teaches cohesion in the early stages of the first processes of Phase I.

PHASE II: COOPERATION WITH AUTHORITY AND SOCIAL RULES

In the second phase of treatment, offenders learn to develop an increased cooperation with authority (the court system) and social rules. The clients learn proper social skills and develop a better understanding of society's norms. They learn to have personal acceptance for their potential to reoffend (a treatment milestone), which will act as a key component of increasing dedication to program participation and treatment accountability. Developing skills to manage their emotions and personal relationships teaches offenders suitable skills necessary to maintain healthy daily functioning and age-appropriate intimacy. These techniques will provide the clients with useful resources for the future. Offenders begin to develop the next levels of accountability and responsibility of acceptance regarding their sexual misconducts, as well as replacing maladaptive thinking and cognitive distortions with more appropriate decisions.

As these steps are achieved, offenders develop a greater degree of victim empathy, learning to appreciate the destruction they have caused to others. Creating a personal relapse-prevention plan is the key to this second phase, as offenders establish a list of their stressors. Then they develop appropriate alternatives to these triggers, while defining how to prevent previous deviant thoughts and behaviors. Within this plan is a list of support systems and these people will be who the offenders contact to provide emotional assistance during high-stress and high-risk times. The plan contains information providing offenders with well-detailed, pre-planned activities and thoughts warding off future offensive stressors and thoughts. Offenders must submit to maintenance polygraph, any offense since the first full-disclosure test, every six months during treatment. This phase is recommended to last approximately twenty-four months.

PHASE III: RESPONSIBILITY

The third phase focuses offenders' responsibility for their actions. Clients must demonstrate a commitment to a life focused on having no more victims, while displaying daily personal relapse prevention and appropriate behavior modifications. Offenders must maintain high levels of personal responsibility in daily life, including financial obligations, close relationships, community safety, and program compliance. Each group member is responsible for active involvement in challenging and assisting others in group treatment, by confronting them about inconsistent and maladaptive thoughts and behaviors. However, if one member confronts another, he or she should provide options and solutions to the group.

Clients contract to the required six-month maintenance polygraph(s) during this phase of the program. This third phase also represents their final financial obligation to the program, as Phase IV work is voluntary and free-of-charge. The third phase is recommended to last approximately twelve months.

PHASE IV: AFTERCARE AND MAINTENANCE

There are few aftercare programs providing long-term maintenance utilizing the most important aspect of offender's lifelong responsibility and accountability. During this phase it is expected that the client demonstrate total commitment to an ongoing life of having no more victims. A Phase IV group allows recovering offenders to attend weekly meetings with no cost factor, providing continual structured group support with leadership from advanced and former group members who successfully completed the program, without the aid of a counselor. Phase IV members may attend voluntarily for as long as they like.

Phase IV is also utilized for being the initiation process of every new offender to the program. New members attend approximately four, weekly sessions prior to entering Phase I, which familiarizes them with group rules, weekly protocol, and developing a personal introduction. This introduction states the offender's victim(s) by first name and age, weekly admittance of guilt for the offense, and ends by saying "No more victims." This empowering statement is the focus of relapse-prevention therapy for the sex-offending population and is the ultimate goal of each recovering offender.

SUMMARY

Progressing through a four-phase program provides the offender with many beneficial aspects of treatment, including structured reading and assignments, weekly therapy sessions, role modeling by advanced group members and the clinician, personal and professional skills, understanding sexual addiction and abuse cycles, gaining insight, and developing constructive adult relationships with other adults. The structure of this program also offers clients a tentative deadline for the treatment to be concluded, which intensifies their accountability and responsibility levels to their treatment. Many offenders share personal histories of having learning disabilities, because of limited resources for assistance in completing assignments and reading. By working from a group setting, the clients share information and work together to help each other through these phase progressions.

Chapter 8

Working with Difficult Sex Offenders

As a sex-offender therapist you will encounter numerous challenges—keeping the group on task, paperwork, hierarchical attitudes within the group, and fear and anxiety over new members. The list is endless, but none is more challenging than working with the difficult sex offender.

Difficult sex offenders are defined as individuals who use various defense mechanisms to avoid being accountable/responsible for the crime(s) they have committed. There are numerous defense mechanisms that an offender can use to keep from facing the impact of their actions. For the sake of our purposes, we will focus on the following three: *anger, passiveness,* and *over compliance.*

If offenders with any of these defenses arrive in your group or practice, they can disrupt the group process, challenge your authority, or give you a false sense of progress. Remember that the motivation of offenders is power and control over people and things in their environment. Just as they controlled the environment to commit their crimes, they will try to control the treatment environment as well. By examining these defense mechanisms, we will be able to get an overall perspective of offenders' willingness to manipulate the environment they are in to their distorted way of thinking.

ANGRY OFFENDERS

Angry offenders distinguish themselves by acting as if they are raging bulls in a group. They blame, justify, minimize, and rationalize their actions. It is everyone else's fault they are in treatment—the judge, the probation officer, the courts, their families, and their victims. They have a million and one excuses for the offense, "I was just teaching them about sex," "They were already sexually active," "They touched me first," and "They wanted me to do it." Now that they must come face-to-face with their deeds, they will try to deflect any and all responsibility.

Regardless of your skill level, beginner or experienced, the challenge is not to get *"hooked"* by the offenders. Being *"hooked"* means you are reacting to the offenders at an emotional, rather than a cognitive level. The goal of difficult offenders is to control their environment and those who are in it.

Case History

Terry came into treatment after spending fourteen years in prison for molesting his step-daughter. As a condition of his treatment, he had to attend sex-offender treatment. He was not pleased with having to attend the group; he felt his time in prison was payment enough for his crime.

Needless to say, his first session was difficult. As a part of the orientation to the group, group members had to introduce themselves and describe their crime. Immediately, Terry began to impose his will upon the group. He verbalized his displeasure with the unfairness of his prison

Sex-Offender Therapy
© 2008 by The Haworth Press, Taylor & Francis Group. All rights reserved.
doi:10.1300/5753_08

sentence, the incompetence of his lawyer, the money he had to spend for his defense (or lack thereof), and the fact that he didn't really hurt his victim. His verbalization was so intense that some of the group members literally drew back from the group circle.

Recognizing that he was intimidating the group, Terry got to his feet and started lambasting the program for not caring about the offenders, but just being in it for the money. Because of his large stature, he seemed to loom over the group, literally and figuratively. The group leader, realizing that no one was going to confront Terry's inappropriate behavior, asked Terry to be seated and stated that his behavior was very inappropriate. This further infuriated him. He turned the full measure of his fury upon the group leader and cursed, postured as if he would assault the group leader. Watching the reaction of the group, which was a mixture of fear and anticipation, and Terry's body language, which was intimidating, the group leader realized that several things were going on simultaneously. Terry's need to control both the group and the group leader, his need to vent his frustration, his need to establish himself as a leader within the group, and the group leader's need to protect the group and access the immediate danger to his person.

After Terry had completed his tirade, the group leader reemphasized that it was his crime that had brought him into treatment. He acknowledged Terry's frustration but stated that if he couldn't control his temper and behavior more appropriately he would be terminated from treatment, which was an automatic probation violation with the likelihood he would be sent back to prison. It was the group leader's intent to make Terry aware of his responsibility for being in treatment, the consequences of his actions, and to let the group members know that they would be protected from unsuitable behavior. After firmly establishing the boundaries of the group process with Terry and remaining consistent with those boundaries, he became a model group member.

How to Work with Angry Offenders

As a group leader working with angry sex offenders, there are a few things to know to make working with them more effective.

1. Never get into a power struggle with the offender.

You are the standard of appropriateness within the group. Regardless, if you get angry offenders to comply with treatment and participate in group discussions, you are using the same technique they used to commit their crime—power and control.

Angry offenders are masters of controlling their environment through intimidation and fear. When they cause a therapist to focus on them and their reactions, they establish themselves as unspoken leaders of the group, undermining the purpose and direction of treatment.

To avoid getting into a power struggle with angry offenders, focus on the issue at hand, not how they are reacting. Often their motivation is to manipulate and control.

The purpose of anger is to place a hostile barrier between persons and angry offenders are masters of using that defense. By attacking other group members, usurping the group leaders' credibility, creating alliances, or refusing to participate in group activities, their sole purpose is to manipulate their environment to their will.

2. Establish and maintain firm boundaries.

Angry offenders are used to having their way, usually through intimidation, whether real or perceived. As the group leader, you must establish the norms of the group, although confrontation is important to break denial, rationalizations, and other defense mechanisms. At no time can it be the norm to "beat up" (verbally assault) on a group member. If you do not establish firm boundaries, angry offenders will not see that their behaviors are inappropriate and the weaker group members will not confront anyone in the group for fear of being verbally attacked.

3. Keep the focus on the offense and its effects.

Many offenders, especially angry offenders, dislike focusing on the details of their crime. They would rather admit to their crime, and discuss the lessons they've learned, and the person they want to become, but they don't want to talk about their crime. Their crime forces them to face an aspect of themselves that is selfish, cruel, and ruthless, which isn't congruent with the person they see themselves to be. They will use various ways to avoid the subject, from saying, "It was so long ago I can't remember" to "What's the big deal, they (the victim) wanted me to do it." These attempts to avoid accountability/responsibility for their actions can be frustrating to a group leader or counselor. One way to prevent avoidance is to keep the focus on the offense and its effects by maintaining these perimeters.

PASSIVE OFFENDERS

Passive offenders are those in the group who just show up. They don't contribute to the group process, they rarely speak, agree with whatever the group decides, and never offer an opinion without being asked. They are like crocodiles. They float along in the group until something disturbs them, then they strike out with the viciousness of their counterpart. Their goal is to control, through silence and disengagement. When that has been upset, they must restore things back to the status quo. Because passive offenders say little, they carry more authority within the group. The problem with not expecting passive offenders to actively participate in group discussions is that they will seize control of the group from a position of quiet resolve. Because most passive offenders are very observant, they know what to say and when to say it. Their judgments regarding group member behaviors are so insightful and penetrating that it intimidates and frightens the group. When this level of ascent happens, groups will become superficial and meaningless. No one will be willing to share at an emotional level for fear that their vulnerability will be used against them.

Case Study

Fred had come into a group; this was his third group since being in treatment. Each of the previous reports on him basically read the same: Fred is quiet and causes no trouble in the group, although he shares little about himself. When confronted regarding his behaviors or beliefs, he will listen to the feedback as if he is contemplating what is being said. It is done in a way that is appropriate, but the underlying feature is to put the person in his or her place and to leave him alone. Each time he has done that to a group member, the group ceases to be open and honest with each other; they act as if they met together and agreed to not be "real" with each other.

Fred was sent to his second group and the same thing happened. When the group leader confronted him about his controlling behavior he replied, "I am doing what I am supposed to do, confront 'stinking thinking,' and that's what I'm doing." Because Fred's interactions with the group were appropriate, it was difficult to point out what he was doing. Although the group leader could see the effect Fred was having on the group process, the leader could not see the erosion of the process. The impact of Fred's persona was so insidious that the group leader sought to have him terminated from treatment.

When Fred arrived in his third, possibly last, group there was little expectation for his progress. The group leader laid out the expectations for the group process and the consequences for noncompliance with those expectations.

Initially, Fred assumed the same posture, as in his previous groups, observing, allowing others to speak and share, and responding only when necessary. Instead of allowing Fred to establish his pattern of quiet control, the group leader pressed him for his thoughts and suggestions. When he tried to withdraw, stating he did not know the group member long enough to have a valid opinion, the group leader confronted Fred with the fact that he had been in previous groups where he had seen these patterns of behavior and his excuse of not knowing the group member was unacceptable. This set up an expectation that Fred would no longer be allowed to manipulate the group from the sidelines. He was expected to participate.

How to Work with Passive Offenders

These offenders can easily slip through the cracks of treatment because they blend into the background and cause little outward difficulties. Because they are accustomed to information-gathering and know how to use that information for maximum effect, it becomes the therapist's task to keep them involved in the process.

1. Establish the expectation for their involvement while in the group.

Passive offenders use distance and silence to control their environments; the same is true when they come to treatment. They don't want to be seen or acknowledged thus opening them up to be more vulnerable, hence taking away their control.

When you establish what is expected while in treatment and remain consistent in the expectation, you are informing passive offenders that no excuses will be allowed for their lack of involvement. That level of expectation continues to keep them accountable for their progress in treatment.

By addressing unacceptable actions promptly and consistently, you send the message that nonparticipation is not an option, which is the life's blood of passive offenders. If they say they don't know how to participate in the group, this becomes your chance to model what you expect from them and the other members of the group (e.g., appropriate confrontation, how to accept unpleasant feedback, or whatever is needed to make significant progress while in treatment and beyond).

2. Establish what is reasonable and acceptable.

Passive offenders see their environment as places where they can shape and mold things to their will. Oftentimes, that shaping and molding serves no one purpose but the offenders', who are unconcerned how their vision of the environment affects others. That distortion of reality has placed them outside of seeing what is "normal." As the group leader/counselor, one will have to assist in problem solving with them, what a reasonable person would do if he or she were in your place.

3. Establish what is in their best interest.

Some passive offenders are so internally driven that the only way to get them to adhere to the treatment protocol is to have them determine what is in their best interest. Trying to get them to feel empathy and understanding for others is inconceivable. The challenge is to look into the passive offenders' environment and find what's important to them and use it as an incentive to progress through treatment.

Case History

Fred's significant progress fell off and he reverted back to his "old ways." In spite of heavy confrontation from the group and the group leader, he would not respond. After a few weeks of nonprogress, the group leader told Fred that if he didn't see some major progress posthaste, he would recommend Fred for termination from the group.

Within a few weeks Fred completed his relapse-prevention plan, confronted inappropriateness in the group, and terminated an unhealthy relationship (which was the cause of his dramatic change). When asked why such a turnaround in his attitude, Fred replied, "I was involved in this on again-off again relationship. A relationship I knew the group would not approve of.

"When I first came into treatment, I didn't care if I got locked up or not. You must understand I was convicted when I was nineteen years old and I spent the next fourteen years of my life behind bars, so I learned not to trust. Since I've been out, I have a trailer, a car, and was recently promoted at my job. The thought of losing all of that because of my desire for this relationship isn't worth it."

Once Fred realized it was in his best interests to follow the requirements and expectations of the treatment program, rather than go back to prison, he made substantial progress in treatment.

OVERCOMPLIANT OFFENDERS

Overcompliant offenders come into group/counseling sessions expressing regret and a strong desire to learn what caused them to commit such a terrible crime. They become emotional when describing the pain they have caused their victims, their families, and all those whom their crimes have had an impact upon. They are so convincing that you can believe them and their willingness to change.

Case History

Jeff came into the group confronting, accusing, and challenging established members. He quickly made an enemy of the group. But the group leader was excited to have someone willing to address some important issues. Jeff was always the first to share his relapse-prevention plan, self-disclose, or whatever was needed to move the group along. Without realizing it, the group leader had elevated Jeff to the level of co-leader, a role he relished. For months these exploits went on, until a substitute leader came into group.

During the substitute's tenure he confronted Jeff regarding the superficiality of his description of his crime. Immediately, Jeff became defensive and stated that if the regular counselor had no problems with his description of his offense, why should he? The more the substitute confronted Jeff's insincerity the angrier he became, resulting in the substitute group leader being cursed.

When the regular group leader returned, he met with the substitute leader. As the substitute related his encounter with Jeff, the regular became upset and started to defend Jeff. As the conversation began to disintegrate, the substitute asked, "Why are you defending Jeff?" The regular group leader had to stop and think about the question; Why *was* he defending Jeff? The conclusion he came up with was that he took Jeff's pseudosincerity as a true desire to progress, but in actuality he had been fooled by Jeff's compliance to the group expectations, when others in the group were not.

How to Work with Overcompliant Offenders

These offenders take advantage of groups that are stuck, by confronting and sharing (although it's superficial). It allows them to see the "good offender" and garner favor with the group leader by "demonstrating" what is supposed to be done during the group.

1. Regulate the amount of time the offenders speak.

Compliant offenders' strength is their ability to direct the flow of what they decide to self-disclose. By mixing a little truth with a lot of falsehoods, they'll be able to control the process of their treatment with misdirection. By controlling how much they share in the process, you minimize their impact on the group and the process.

Case History

Jeff stated that when he sodomized his sixteen-year-old victim, he was unsure of his sexual preference. He felt he was gay, but he wasn't sure. He had seen some gay porn as well as straight porn; both excited him. "I was confused. I was just as excited by breasts as a penis. I spent hours looking at gay as well as straight sights. My hormones were all over the place. Looking at a naked woman was a big turn on. I masturbated to various fantasies. But when I saw a naked male, I did the same." The group leader realized that Jeff was controlling the group through misdirection.

By regulating compliant offenders you will limit the amount of time lost by discussing irrelevant issues.

2. Accept feedback without responding.

Because overly compliant offenders are looking for ways to defend their actions, they are prepared to respond to whatever is said to them. The key to making progress in treatment is to get them to listen to others' assessments of their behavior without responding.

3. Journal their thoughts.

Overcompliant offenders have a self-centered quality that needs to be fed, which is why they try to dominate the group process. By having them journal their thoughts and feelings you can get them to share more about themselves than in regular group sessions.

SUMMARY

The challenge of working with difficult sex offenders is to break through the anger, passivity, and overcompliance. Be alert to both process and treatment. Offenders can respond to treatment. It is important for the therapist to allow expression, but also to set boundaries.

Chapter 9

Trauma

SEXUALLY AGGRESSIVE CHILDREN AND ADOLESCENTS

When sexually aggressive children or adolescents experience a trauma in life, it is like a switch that changes day into night. Most have been sexually abused. Others were physically abused, severely emotionally neglected, or traumatized. A new perception of the world is created that is directly opposite from the previous one. If life was safe, predictable, and happy before, then after the trauma experience, life is experienced as dangerous, unpredictable, and sad. From that moment on, life takes on a single goal that is to protect one's self from experiencing the trauma or anything like it again. Entire sets of defenses begin to emerge to combat the thoughts of anything to do with the traumatic experience.

As a result, in the initial session, traumatized patients might show a restricted affect or a resistance to feeling and thinking. In the initial stages of treatment, it is easy to label this behavior as resistance or uncooperative when it is actually the client's attempts to defend against the feelings of the trauma. Such behavior is found to be typical in working with the sexually aggressive youth.

It is important in the first stages of treatment to educate the traumatized patient about the therapeutic process. At this juncture, the patient is given information about the therapy used in treatment and what is expected of the youth. The sooner this information is given to the traumatized client the better so that he or she will be able to deal with the unknown more effectively. Remember it was the unknown circumstances that traumatized the client to begin with and many of the defenses are created to deal with the unknown.

In the second phase of treatment, we begin to work intensively with the trauma. Patients are asked to complete Step One of the relapse-prevention plan. In this stage, such an assignment may read as follows:

Describe the sequence of THOUGHTS, FEELINGS, and ACTIONS that led to your offense. Use your own language, and demonstrate that you know the difference between thoughts, feelings, and actions. Give examples of your old "stinking thinking" that contributed to the offense.

The sexually aggressive child or adolescent is instructed at this point to trace back from the past to what led up to his or her sexual offense. The following is an example:

Tommy was ten years old when his uncle sexually molested him. Tommy trusted his uncle and did many things with him. He often slept in his uncle's bed because of crowded conditions in the home. On one of those nights, his uncle pulled down Tommy's briefs and placed his erect penis between the cheeks of Tommy's buttocks. His uncle moved his penis back and forth without penetration in the anus until he ejaculated. Tommy felt confused, frightened, and was full of shame afterward. Nothing was said between the two of them and Tommy never told anyone because he was afraid that he would get in trouble.

Tommy was very defensive and resistive when he was first referred for therapy. He had low self-esteem, feelings of guilt, ineffective communication skills, emotional numbing, anxiety, anger, and isolation. He had many symptoms associated with trauma victims. However, he never

Sex-Offender Therapy

doi:10.1300/5753_09

considered that he was sexually traumatized himself and had never talked to anyone about the incident with his uncle. He first mentioned this incident with his uncle when he was writing Step One of his relapse-prevention plan. In session, he asked many questions, and he finally wrote about the entire incident. During the reading, he was very anxious and cried. He also realized exactly how his victim felt since he had done the same exact thing to her.

The traumatized youth has to understand his or her own trauma in terms of thoughts, feelings, and actions before he or she can understand what happened to his or her victims. The traumatized client is much more willing to invest in treatment once he or she has dealt with his or her own trauma in the group. Common symptoms associated with trauma are: nightmares, flashbacks, anger, depression, anxiety, intrusive thoughts, insomnia, emotional numbing, low self-esteem, feelings of guilt, and ineffective communication. As the client begins to deal with the trauma, it is often helpful to give an outline of what can be expected in writing about the trauma incident. Some clients might need to talk about the incident in the group before writing about it on their own. Some of the guidelines are listed in Exercise 9.1.

The traumatized child or adolescent can be very difficult and resistant at the beginning of the treatment process. However, once the traumatized youth begins to deal with his or her own trauma, the process becomes a gift of healing. While processing the youth's own trauma, he or she will begin to learn about victim empathy. For example, in Tommy's case, he talked about the confusion of love for his uncle after being sexually molested by him. This opened the door for other issues to talk about regarding abuse and offending. By being asked many questions about what he was thinking and how he was feeling at the time, Tommy gained insight into how he was really feeling. In the process, family members learned how to care more and empathize about a youth that really represented their victim's story. While learning about victim empathy, family members can examine their own journey. They now know what it's like to have power taken away, and to feel helplessness, anger, depression etc., just like their victims.

ADULT SEX OFFENDERS

In helping sex offenders deal with their own trauma, the therapist often has to help them tell their story first. It is very difficult to write about the trauma as a way of initially telling the story. The reason for the difficulty is the process of writing is done alone and the sex offender has to deal with all the emerging feelings by him or her self. It is advisable if this the first time of telling about the incident, that it be told verbally in the group. Telling the group about what happened can bring a wide range of very strong emotions. Typically these emotions are fear, anger, guilt, helplessness, panic, numbness, disassociation, etc. The emotions present or absent at the time of the disclosure will give the therapist a good idea of how emotionally intense this trauma was for this individual.

In many cases, panic and helplessness are expressed. When this happens, the entire group may mirror the same exact symptoms. If this occurs, then the entire group experiences panic and helplessness. Unless this is dealt with, the message to the individual telling about the trauma will be to only share in group material that can be easily handled. Groups that mirror this type of reaction are often called resistive and filled with denial and fear. One person in the room can and must be a role model for what needs to be done—the group therapist.

THERAPISTS

The most important role of the group therapist is to direct the flow of information in the group. It is his or her job to insure that each member gets a chance to be heard; that feelings are expressed appropriately; and that the group is safe emotionally, physically, and spiritually. In order to direct this flow of information, the group therapist has to remove him or her self by being objective. One way of being objective is to think more than to feel. This is not very easy to do when group members are dealing with very intimate, emotionally charged material. However if the process is going to be one of healing as opposed to defensiveness and resistance, it is essential that the group therapist be the leader and role model of this group process.

It is highly advised that a relatively inexperienced therapist obtain the appropriate training before taking individuals through an intense traumatic event. Encouraging individuals to deal with their trauma incidents without structured guidance can often traumatize them all over again. At the foundation of most trauma incidents is helplessness and if an individual feels that helplessness again in telling of the event then it only reinforces in them the idea that they are hopeless and helpless with this incident. For example, a patient finally has the courage to tell the group that he was violently raped. After this revelation, the group is silent and the process moves on as if this revelation had not been expressed to the group. The following week, this offender comes back to group and states that he has been extremely depressed and upset during the past week. In questioning this young man further, it is revealed that he told the group that he had been raped because he wanted some empathy and caring from the group. Instead he felt ostracized and lonely, the same exact emotions that he felt after his rape except now it was being experienced from this group. An experienced group leader would have elicited some type of feedback from group members about this experience. How are they feeling after hearing that this young man was violently raped?

Experienced therapists have to learn not to get involved in the intense emotional content so that they can do the job of thinking about what needs to be done at any particular time during the therapeutic process. When a sex offender has shallow breathing as a result of panic in telling a story then he or she needs to be stopped and concentrate on his or her breathing until it is normal again. Group therapists can learn several skills that will help in doing trauma work. The first is learning how to ground oneself in order to teach this technique to clients. Grounding helps keep you in the present time when everyone else is in some other timeframe (e.g., the past or the future). The basic principles of grounding are as follows:

1. Sit straight up and put both feet on the floor. Imagine that there are actual roots coming out of the bottom of your feet, anchoring you to the ground.
2. In your mind say who and where you are. For example, I am John so and so and work in this blankety blank agency in anytown, USA.
3. Look around the room and name out loud in your mind three objects that you see.
4. Listen and name out loud three sounds that you hear.
5. Focus on your feeling level and name three feelings that you are experiencing.

The therapist should now be thoroughly grounded. This exercise can be used for clients as well. As soon as the person feels grounded, the sequence can be stopped. So if client A feels grounded after Step Two, there is no reason to continue with the grounding process. Also for clients who suddenly lose their sense of time and place, the following is a more basic way of grounding:

1. Say the client's name repeatedly.
2. Have the client look around the room and identify people by their names.
3. Have the client state where he or she is (the actual physical space).
4. Then add Steps One through Five above if still needed.

When the group is going to listen to trauma incidents, members should be prepared in advance by being told about the grounding techniques in case they lose their sense of reality so that they won't panic if it happens. If necessary, group members should be encouraged to reposition their seats, so that no one is isolated by sitting alone. Ask group members to remove any barriers to communication such as hats or dark glasses. Now the group is ready to listen.

As the group begins to deal with trauma issues, it is essential that the group leader not get emotionally involved in the trauma material. Group therapists are often trained to be empathetic, and in trauma work this can really work against you if the leader is not careful. Since it is extremely difficult to think and feel at the same time, it is helpful for the group leader to keep thinking while leading a trauma group.

1. Prepare the group by teaching grounding techniques and other precautions for trauma work. This will help the group worker to stay in his or her thinking mode.
2. As the sex offender begins talking about the traumatic incident, imagine what else is going on in the environment. For instance, if the description is that I am entering the bedroom; ask questions like How big is the bed? What does the room feel like etc?
3. In every scene described ask for feelings, thoughts, and actions by the sex offender.
4. In every scene described, ask for experiences that are perceived by the five senses of sight, hearing, smell, touch, and taste.
5. Be vigilant in observing the other group members for their reactions or nonreactions to what is being said.

By doing these exercises and keeping one's mind active, the group leader has the best chance of staying objective and not letting the traumatic material render him or her helpless.

Working with traumatized sex offenders and constantly hearing details about incidents that were filled with violence and self-centeredness can often skew the group therapist's view of the world. The group therapist can often experience feelings similar to or just like their clients' such as feeling hardened, noncaring, and/or just trying to get through the day. Brenda Collins (2001) states the following, "My goal is for my clients to experience my optimism instead of my experiencing their trauma" (p. 23). One way to accomplish this goal is to be very cognizant of the process that goes on in the group each week, especially being aware of what is happening to the group therapist. Collins recommends that rituals need to be created that can help the therapist stay centered in the midst of the storm of the client's emotions. Exercise 9.2 offers ways to accomplish this.

It is essential in working with traumatic material that the group or individual therapist have an entire arsenal of skills to combat the effects of secondary trauma. Without these rituals or ceremonies, the therapist can run the risk of creating a world similar to that of the client's that he or she works with, rather than the opposite. For example, after a traumatic session, it is not a good idea to read upsetting stories in the newspaper or view movies that are depressing and demonstrate the negative side of life. Before the group starts, the therapist should always check in with him or her self and determine what his or her thoughts and feelings are. If the group therapist is tired or depressed then energizing the self with stretching exercises and/or looking at quotes can bring back much-needed energy for motivation. After the group, a ritual can be created of writing down any bad thoughts or feelings on a piece of paper and then throwing it in the trash. By doing this ritual, the therapist symbolically releases these feelings. If the therapist cannot discharge these feelings, talking to someone that evening or the next day can often be a great help in restoring energy and balance to the therapist.

EXERCISE 9.1. QUESTIONS FOR THE CLIENT

1. How old were you when the trauma occurred?

_____

_____

2. What was going on in your life and who was living in your household?

_____

_____

3. What was the perpetrator's relationship to your family and yourself?

_____

_____

4. Where were you when the incident occurred?

_____

_____

5. Describe in detail what the perpetrator did and said.

_____

_____

6. What were you thinking, feeling, and doing during the trauma incident?

_____

_____

7. What happened after the incident?

_____

_____

8. What did you feel, think, and do after the incident?

_____

_____

EXERCISE 9.2. RITUALS

1. Find a quiet place where you will not be interrupted and take several deep breaths. As you begin to relax, write down images, thoughts, and feelings that are pleasant and relaxing to you.

_____

_____

_____

_____

2. Take those images, thoughts, and feelings and think about how you can create a ritual or ceremony each day before the session to ground yourself. Write your ritual here.

_____

_____

_____

_____

3. It is very important at this time that a ritual is followed at the beginning and at the end of each session. It is also helpful to have a variety of written materials or quotes on hand that can inspire you to look at the more positive side of life. List some of your meaningful quotes.

_____

_____

_____

_____

4. There should also be a list of friends or colleagues that you can call for supervision to discuss very upsetting material. The goal is not to continue to think about these thoughts on your own. List the people that you can call.

_____

_____

_____

_____

Chapter 10

The Cost of Offending

Sexual Offending Costs. Sexual abuse is one of the few crimes in which monetary gain is not the primary goal of the crime. Still, there are emotional, family, financial, psychological, and occupational consequences that follow sexual misconduct behavior. Many of these issues end up costing the patient money.

By cost we are referring to financial and emotional cost. Sexual acting out costs money for the offender. The patient has high attorney fees, court costs, and court fines. He or she, if jailed for a short period, will experience a loss of wages. On other occasions the stigma of the offense will result in a job loss. Sometimes, personal property has to be sold or is repossessed. A house mortgage may go unpaid and the patient has to move. Also, he or she may experience divorce. What is the cost value to a companion? Family estrangement may occur. Parents and extended family distance themselves. Contact with their own children is prohibited. Friends are uncomfortable in maintaining a relationship. What is the monetary value to the patient of these relationships? Restitution may be ordered. Finally, the court may determine a prison sentence is merited, sometimes lasting many years.

The cost of sexual addiction behaviors can be extremely high. If the patient has been involved in sexual addiction behaviors, it may be helpful to have a cost analysis list made of expenses. For example, if the individual was involved in affairs, how much was spent on food, lodging, and travel? If the patient was involved with prostitutes, how much would the total cost be for these encounters? What is the cost to the patient if the spouse learns of the behavior and decides to divorce? How much will a divorce cost the patient? What value does the patient place upon the relationship? Does the patient have children? What will be the monetary costs to the patient if he or she loses custody and has to pay child support?

Crimes involving sex include at least two persons—an offender and a victim. A sexual offense occurs if the act is forced, the person is a minor, or the person is mentally incompetent to grant consent.

USING THE COST OF OFFENDING IN THERAPY

In the beginning stages of therapy, a patient who has been referred for sex-offender treatment may display resistance. One quick icebreaker to be used by the therapist during this phase of treatment is to request that the patient complete an inventory of how much the offending has cost in dollars (Schwartz and Canfield, 1996). Use this exercise early in the psychotherapy process. It is helpful to ask patients to bring their journal writing materials to each session. A blackboard or other similar type of writing stand is recommended.

It is important to promote victim empathy in the cost analysis section for an offender. Request the offender to complete an expense list of costs for the victim. It should include attorney fees, job losses, inability to hold a job, medical costs, problems in parenting, psychological problems, psychiatric hospitalizations, relationship or marital problems, and substance abuse. A therapist should inform the offender that all victims do not recover quickly. Many have long-term problems that impact their ability to enjoy a normal life with a spouse and children. Ask an offender what would

Sex-Offender Therapy

doi:10.1300/5753_10

the cost of fear for the victim be estimated in dollars. Does the victim leave a light on each night? Does the survivor avoid experiences that would be fun? What about sex? Does the offender believe the victim will have a normal sex life? Will trauma of the sexual abuse be long term? Will the victim require therapy? All of these things should be included in the victim's detailed expense list created by the offender.

The most important loss (as noted in the addiction paragraph) for sexual addicts and offenders, is a marriage or significant relationship. In many cases, this is a surprise to the patient. Many sexual addicts and sex offenders report that the relationship was very important to them. If the patient was involved in a relationship or marriage, and separation or divorce may occur, a cost analysis should be encouraged.

The second item of concern for a sexual addict or offender is shame. The secret lifestyle they have been living is now exposed. Employers, family, and friends learn of the patient's inappropriate behavior. If the behavior results in a criminal charge, the local newspaper may do a story on the offense. In most states, persons who commit certain sex crimes are now listed on the Internet and are sometimes harassed or discriminated against in some fashion.

The third loss is primary loss, as in employment, personal property, emotional, or physical losses. Sexual addicts or sex offenders have exceeded their earnings to fuel their addiction. As a result patients will experience problems paying a home mortgage, keeping an expensive car, and maintaining a lifestyle they once enjoyed. Such patients will often require the services of an attorney. In some cases, both addicts and offenders will lose their rights to have contact with their children or have limited or supervised visitation rights only. An employer may discharge an employee as the result of his or her sexually inappropriate behavior. Friends, family, and acquaintances will distance themselves from the patient.

It is always attention-grabbing and insightful, first, to ask a patient how much money he or she would accept to go (or return) to prison for one year. No crime is to be committed. The person is to serve a sentence to earn money. Be rather creative at this point. Perhaps even have a token representation of a check or checkbook available. This exercise should not be used to humiliate the patient, but to help him or her evaluate the seriousness of the offense.

Some patients report no amount of money would be worth the cost of staying in prison for one year. Historically, most sex offenders do not like jail or prison, for they held a rather low status among other inmates in the general population. Also, it is dangerous in some prison population groups if it is learned that a patient was incarcerated for a sex crime. Some patients report that they have fabricated a story about their offense to avoid harm. A charge of armed robbery, drug trafficking, or car theft carries more clout in a prison setting. Some offenders report beatings, harassment, sexual abuse, and stabbings. Therefore, the fear is not imagined and is very real.

Patients who possess an antisocial personality disorder are the most-likely group to name an imaginary dollar figure for a return to prison. However, even among this group, the cost of stay for one year is usually set at a high figure. It is not uncommon to hear that a person would be willing to return to incarceration for at least $250,000. Other patients will report higher estimates that exceed $500,000 or even a $1,000,000 for a stay in prison.

Most patients with a pedophile disorder will not agree to return to jail or prison for any amount of money. The therapist should encourage a discussion among those persons who would return to prison for a set amount of money—and patients who are opposed to returning to a structured setting. This conversation should then lead to the start of Exercise 10.1.

SUMMARY

The purpose of this exercise is to illustrate to patients how much they have lost as a result of their inappropriate behavior. This exercise can be very insightful to many patients who have experienced loss because of sexual offending. A therapist uses the information to help patients see how much another offense would cost them.

EXERCISE 10.1. COST OF OFFENDING

1. Calculate the cost of your lost wages while in prison or jail.

   _____

   _____

2. How much did you incure in attorney fees and related court costs?

   _____

   _____

3. The cost of sex offending can be high. List any costs that may have resulted as the outcome of your offense (e.g., the loss of a home, car, personal property, etc.).

   _____

   _____

4. The loss of a loved one while in prison. Did a significant family member die? Did you experience a divorce or estrangement by parents or relatives?

   _____

   _____

5. What was the cost of a marriage, if a divorce occurred?

   _____

   _____

6. If you have children, calculate in dollars the loss of time spent with sons and daughters. Do you have visitation rights? Does a no contact order with your children exist as a result of the offense?

   _____

   _____

7. What is the cost of a job loss?

   _____

   _____

8. What is the cost of finding a new job if your former position was lost as a result of your offense?

   _____

   _____

9. What is the cost of shame that you have experienced as a result of your offense? For example, have you lost friends or are others reluctant to talk to you?

   _____

   _____

10. Do you have neighbors who pretend they no longer know you? What is the estimated cost to you for those lost relationships?

    _____

    _____

11. What other costs have occurred as a result of your sexual offense?

    _____

    _____

12. What is the total of all of the expenses listed in items one to ten?

    _____

    _____

13. What monetary value do you list if your son or daughter was your victim, and a no contact order has been issued?

    _____

    _____

Chapter 11

Adult Male Patients

Treatment providers for sex offenders include social workers, psychiatrists, psychologists, correction personnel, nurses, and community case managers. These individuals require specialized training in order to treat and help the patient as well as protect the community from further victimization.

Providing treatment for male sex offenders in a community-based, outpatient treatment program is appropriate for the patient who is willing to work within the limits placed on him or her by the program, society, and the correctional system. When the offender is assessed and found to be an appropriate candidate for the treatment program, he will be placed in a specialized sex-offender treatment group. Treatment issues addressed in a group relate to the offender's sex crime, sexual deviancy, and taking responsibility for his sexual deviancy.

Engaging male sex offenders in therapy is challenging and occurs over an extended period of time. The therapist has a dual role to provide therapy and protect the community. As mandated reporters, the duty to warn is present to protect the community. Engaging the offender after advising the patient of our mandated reporting often requires quality clinical skills. Traditionally, sex offenders share the same traits. They will withhold information, leave out details of their sex offense, lie, and misrepresent their sex crime and sexual aggression.

CHARACTERISTICS

Male sex offenders share common characteristics. (This is by no means an all inclusive list of characteristics.)

1. They are skilled at manipulating people and will attempt to manipulate the therapist.
2. They are not in sex-offender treatment on a voluntary basis. Their attendance is court-ordered and they are held accountable for their attendance.
3. The sex offender will pick up on and exploit any conflict between co-therapists.
4. They are intuitive individuals who recognize conflict.
5. Male offenders traditionally have one or more disorders: mood, affect, thought, cognitive impairment, substance abuse, impulse control, and/or sexual disorders. Male offenders have prevalent personality traits such as antisocial, narcissistic, borderline, or paranoid. This plays out in a group through their resistance to treatment and change.
6. A majority of male sex offenders who are arrested and incarcerated come from a category of most-suspected individuals: fathers, stepfathers, grandfathers, uncles, close family friends, other biological and extended-family relatives, trusted neighbors, and others—teachers, clergy, and scout leaders.
7. Only a small percentage of male sex offenders abduct their victims out of their homes or drag them off the streets. A majority of offenders have direct access to their victims and

Sex-Offender Therapy
© 2008 by The Haworth Press, Taylor & Francis Group. All rights reserved.
doi:10.1300/5753_11

their homes on a regular basis. They are in a position to have authority, power, or control over their victims.

8. Male sex offenders are hard to identify. They do not have physical traits or signs that make them look like a child molester. They come from a variety of economic, educational, and professional backgrounds. They appear to be normal people who have jobs, families, go to church, pay taxes, and vote. They go about their daily activities like ordinary people.

9. They are often sexually addicted—typically after being polygraphed it becomes evident there have been multiple partners and/or victims.

10. They may be, and most often are, alcohol and drug abusers.

11. They manipulate their victims, and often the victim's family members, in order to gain access to the intended victim.

12. They have low self-esteem or are overly self-confident in their sexual prowess.

13. They have relationship problems including anger management, or physical or verbal abuse of wife, girlfriend, or other family members.

Male sex offenders have distorted thinking (Steen, 2001), which allows them to sexually offend or reoffend. Through distorted thinking, they minimize or deny the harm to their victims. These thinking distortions include:

1. *Projection*—they believe their victims want to have sex with them. The victims, in fact, are not asking for sex and don't want it. For offenders, their perception is that the victims are willing participants.

2. *Rationalization*—making excuses for their sexual offenses. For example, they may say, "It's OK to molest a child; I was molested as a child." or "Their parents don't love them the way I do. I can do more for them."

3. *Minimization*—minimizing what they do. For example, "It did not hurt me when it happened to me, so it won't bother my victim." or "He'll just have to get over it; it wasn't that big a deal."

4. *Denial*—not being responsible for their sexual offense, but blaming their victims or other people who were there. For instance, "I told her mother she was coming on to me. Her mother knew and didn't try to stop her." or "She came on to me. I didn't start it. She dressed like that knowing it turned me on. What was I supposed to do?"

Thinking errors, also known as cognitive distortions, are shared by sex offenders (Kahn, 2001).

1. Blaming or placing the responsibility for their sex crime onto their victim or someone else in order to avoid exposure, embarrassment, or legal consequences.

2. Minimizing the significance of what they do. "Why are they making such a big deal of it?" "It did not nurt me when it happened to me. So, why would it hurt my victim?" "He'll just have to get over it; it wasn't that big a deal."

3. Justifying or making excuses. "I just came from work so I don't have my group homework." "I didn't know how to do it, so I didn't." "My probation officer said you'd help me do it."

4. Being arrogant, self-centered, narcissistic, and self-indulgent. The offender only thinks about his wants and needs without regard for his victim.

5. Being the victim and drawing attention to themselves in an effort to get other people to feel sorry for them, not hold them accountable for their actions or to get others to do things for them that they can/should do for themselves.

6. Not thinking about the consequences of their actions in advance. Acting impulsively, avoiding responsibility for not controlling their impulses. Thinking the offense is "no big deal" until something happens to expose their offense, then the fear sets in.
7. Denial. When the offender tells himself something isn't true when it really is.
8. Lying. There are three types of lies: (1) *Omission*—deliberately leaving out or holding back information and telling only the part that they want you to know; (2) *Commission*—saying something that you know is not true; (3) *assent*—pretending to agree with someone when you really don't. Offenders lie for several reasons: to avoid facing the consequences of their actions, not wanting to hurt someone's feelings, or some lie out of habit or fear of getting caught doing something that's wrong.
9. Avoidance or "I don't know" statements. This is used in an attempt to change the subject, avoid telling the truth, or to avoid sharing information that offenders feel embarrassed or ashamed of. This is used in an effort to not take responsibility for their behavior.
10. Magic thinking or super optimism. Thinking, "I'll never get caught." or "I'll never offend again." Magical thinking is wishful thinking that everything will work out if we want it enough. This thinking error is used to avoid the responsibility of working to correct mistakes and taking the steps we need to make our lives the way we want them to be.

In order to take responsibility for and change their behavior, these thought distortions and thinking errors must be addressed in treatment, therefore helping offenders break the cycle of sexual deviancy.

Sex offenses and deviant thinking transpire almost exclusively in isolation. No sex offender wants attention drawn to his sexual deviant behavior. Nor does he want an audience. Situational offenders are perhaps the largest group of child molesters. They select victims where there is little environmental hindrance to prevent them from getting to their victims.

RITUALS

Sexual rituals involve the repeated engaging in an act or series of acts in a particular manner due to sexual need (Hazelwood and Burgess, 2001). Before the sexual offender can become sexually aroused or experience sexual gratification he must engage in the act in a certain way. Rituals may be motivated by psychological, cultural, or spiritual needs. Rituals are erotic imagery and fantasy. They may be bizarre in nature. Ritual is necessary to the offender, not to the successful commission of the sex crime. Ritual is need-driven.

The ritualistic offender is unlike the impulsive offender. He invests his time more in the pursuit of his fantasies. Ritualistic offenders are fewer in number than impulsive offenders; however, this type of offender is typically more criminally sophisticated. He is the most successful, yet he is the most difficult to identify and apprehend. He plans and spends a great deal of time, thought, and energy into rehearsing his offense. Ritualistic offenders are motivated not by love for the victim, rather their motivation for committing sex crimes is for the power or anger or a combination of both.

Barbaree and Marshall (1991) indicate that the ritualistic offenders experience a cue response to the control and aggression contained and provided within the rape. Their perceptions contribute to the level of their sexual arousal. This indicates a response style reflective of paraphilic interest in coercive sexuality.

A ritualistic offender's personality style is varied. This offender is less generically exploitative. They may be withdrawn or inept in their social interactions. Some are outgoing and charming. Respected community members may be involved in some of the most extreme cases of sadistic violence. Therefore, their position allows their perverse sexuality to remain hidden for the most part. Sexual sadists are considered a highly ritualized group of offenders who act out their sexual fantasies with wives and girlfriends.

Case Study

A twenty-seven-year-old white male was convicted and served seven years in state prison for aggravated sexual assault, sodomy, and rape of a minor. He had ten victims, both male and female. They ranged in age from a five-year-old girl to a fifteen-year-old boy. The offender has rituals incorporated into his sex crimes. He cross-dresses, wearing his sister's used undergarments. He also dresses in his aunt's dresses, bra, panties, slip, and hose. He "loves to feel like a woman." He randomly selected his victims based on his ability to physically dominate and control them. He doesn't think he's committed a sex crime with the five-year-old, stating, "I was teaching her about sex. She needs to know about sex and who will teach her if I don't?" The rape was brutal, resulting in physical problems which may prevent the girl from having children as an adult. The sex offender lacks social skills and is considered "odd in appearance and behavior."

FANTASIES

Sexual fantasies are perfect. Reality is never perfect. Fantasy for the sex offender is played out in his mind. Sex offenders have a rich fantasy life. For most offenders, fantasy is sufficient to satisfy psychosexual desires. There is no impulse to enact it in reality. The ultimate goal of a fantasy is to derive some form of sexual gratification and satisfaction. For some, fantasy is not satisfactory.

Fantasy plays a small role in the impulsive offender's sex crime. His criminal behavior is designed to accomplish two things: to obtain and control his victim. He lacks the criminal skills to control his victim without using violence.

Fantasies of the ritualistic offender are complex. Hazelwood and Burgess (2001) identified five common components in the ritualistic offender's fantasy life: relational, paraphilic, demographic, situational, and self-perceptual. The ritualistic offender's fantasy is the relationship he perceives between his victim and himself. Ritualistic offenders act out their fantasies with inanimate objects, prostitutes or paid partners, or the partner may be consensual. Ritualistic offenders commonly use three inanimate objects to act out their fantasies: dolls, clothing, and pictures.

Fantasy does play a role in the ritualistic offender's crimes. He uses theme pornography. The theme does influence how he interacts with his victims. The type of pornography used may possess bondage or torture, soft core, and nonviolent pornography. He may create his own pornography. This involves cutting and pasting images from out of the desired scenario or having victims or consensual partners act out erotic behaviors that are then photographed or videotaped.

Fantasies may involve the use of the following methods (Hazelwood and Burgess, 2001):

1. Use of nonliving objects for fantasy or playacting. These items are nonthreatening and present the least precipitator to criminal acts toward a person.
2. Female dolls have been used in sex crimes. Dolls may be used in bizarre ways. They may be burned, slashed, stabbed, bound, amputated, or have piercings.
3. Photographs are altered as a means to acting out fantasies. Pictures may be taken from pornographic or nonpornographic magazines. Changes made to photographs include drawings, sexual bondage, mutilation, guns, knives, wounds or blood, or replacement of favorite pictures in photo albums.
4. Fantasies may be acted out through having female clothing, lingerie, or other seductive articles of clothing.

5. Sex offenders often act out their sexual fantasy with spouses, girlfriends, prostitutes, or their victims.
6. Sexual fantasies may involve verbalization of sexually explicit words or acts that excite the offender's imagination or fantasy, leading to masturbation.

Other factors involved in sexual fantasy are:

1. Sex offenders become sexually aroused when reporting their current or past deviant behavior. They reenact their fantasies during masturbation (Abel, 1989).
2. Sex offenders typically receive some pleasure from the sexual deviancy, which may affect or impair sex within their current relationship.
3. In time, sex offenders see a change and exacerbation in the type of deviant fantasies. This results in an increase in high-risk behaviors.

CRUISING

Offenders seek out places where they hope to find potential victims. They may drive by schoolyards, playgrounds, arcades, or gamerooms specifically specialized for children. Offenders go to malls, sporting events, school functions, and children's favorite eating places in order to make contact with their victims. Offenders cruise the Internet in their search for sex. They scan for pornographic images on the computer or illicit children who lack the experience to know their intent.

Cruising may be more subtle. For example:

1. Using religion as a cover while attending church to select victims.
2. Insist on having their children have friends stay overnight instead of their children staying with a friend.
3. Using sex talk around children. Talking about sexual acts with children or telling off-color jokes to children to test their response and interest.
4. Unusual interest in young children in public places.
5. Staring at one or more children who are engaged in normal activities.

Case Study

The victim, age thirteen, was a cheerleader who practiced after school on the football field. Her sexual abuser was nineteen. He'd been a high school athlete who lettered and was popular with the girls at his school. After going to a local community college, he learned he was just another guy on campus. To appease his ego, he started watching junior varsity cheerleaders practice in the afternoon.

His victim, after finishing cheerleading practice, then walked with her girlfriends to the ice cream parlor. There she'd leave her friends and walk home. The sex offender watched her and knew her daily routine after school. After dark, he'd sit in his car and watch her in her bedroom. After practice one day, the sex offender wore his letter jacket to watch her at school. He followed her to the ice cream parlor where he went in, ordered a milk shake, and talked small talk with her and her friends. When she left to walk home, he offered her a ride. He seemed harmless enough; after all, they had gone to the same school. After getting her into his car, he took her to a well-known hangout for athletes. No one was there. He fondled her, digitally penetrated her, and performed oral sex on her. He made her perform oral sex on him, and then he raped her. This sex offender is serving eleven years in prison.

GROOMING

Grooming is paying special attention to someone that you have already made the decision that you are going to sexually victimize. Kahn (2001) indicates grooming is like flirting or checking out the other person to see if they are interested in you. Sex offenders are trying to get the victim interested in them and gage how the victim will react to their sexual acting-out. Grooming behavior is the "setting-up" process and is often called the ritual. Grooming involves making promises to the potential victim, often through the use of rewards, games, or bribes, to get a victim to comply (Kahn, 2001). The use of coercion, force, threats, or intimidation may also be part of the grooming process. Its purpose is to make victims afraid, therefore eliciting their cooperation in the sex crime. Sex offenders use some of the following grooming behaviors:

- Pornography or pornographic magazines, allowing the children to see them or laying them about casually allowing the children to look at them.
- Taking advantage of the natural affection and trust that they have established with the victim.
- Paying more attention to one child over another.
- Providing monetary gains.
- Allowing the child to do things in their home that the parents do not allow.
- Wanting one child in the family to stay home while the others go out.
- Offering to babysit with children while the caregivers complete an errand.
- Roughhousing with children and "accidentally" touching the private parts of their body.
- Being inappropriately dressed around children.
- Having a child sit on their lap.
- Playing with children whose parents work and do not have time to spend with children.
- Becoming actively involved in sports or activities where they have access to children.
- Letting a child know that they are sexually aroused by letting them see their erection.
- Threatening the child, by saying that if he or she doesn't have sex with the offender, the offender will harm the child's family member.
- Threatening a child with the loss of his or her parent(s).
- Using threats of violence against the family as well as friends.

SUMMARY

Adult male patients are the largest patient group being referred to treatment. The therapist should be aware of the sexual misconduct behaviors that these patients bring to the clinical setting. (See Exercise 11.1.) Distorted thinking, rituals, fantasy, cruising, and grooming are common behaviors found in this population group. Interventions should reflect these problem behaviors. In addition, an outpatient sex offender treatment provider has a dual role: to provide treatment to adult male patients who have sexually offended, and to protect the community by sharing information with supervising probation and parole officers, social service workers, courts, and other professionals involved in the case.

EXERCISE 11.1. ADULT MALE PATIENTS

In this exercise, please check yes or no when appropriate. Check all that apply to you.

1. List your sex crime charges—all of them since age twelve.

_____

_____

2. How may (total) victims do you have? Do not give names, just numbers.

   Number of male victims_____ Number of female victims_____

3. What age range did your victim(s) fall into? Check all that apply.

   ____ 1-5 years of age
   ____ 6-9 years of age
   ____ 10-12 years of age
   ____ 13-15 years of age
   ____ 16-18 years of age

4. Which category do you fall into with your victim(s)? Check all that apply.

   ____ family member
   ____ extended family relative
   ____ close family friend
   ____ neighbor
   ____ babysitter
   ____ person in authority (teacher, group leader, clergy)
   ____ stranger

5. Which method did you use to gain access to your victim(s)? Check all that apply.

   ____ Manipulated the victim or the victim's family members to have access to the intended victim.
   ____ Saught out employment where contact with children was part of the job.
   ____ Volunteered to work where contact with children was part of the job.
   ____ Cruised areas where children were known to be (e.g., playgrounds).
   ____ Coerced, bribed, or tricked the victim.
   ____ Threatened or physically harmed victims or their family members.
   ____ Intimidated by verbal or nonverbal behaviors, in a position of power over the victim. Implied harm was certain if the victim didn't comply.
   ____ Groomed the victim with the use of money or favors.

Chapter 12

Adult Female Patients

Literature on female sex offenders is limited. Female sex offenders for the most part go unnoticed. They do not come to the attention of the court or criminal justice system as frequently as males. Female perpetrators, until now, have been underreported.

Current data indicates that female sex offenders are increasing as a clinical population. In 1990 the number of female offenders and the number of female defendants convicted of felonies in state courts had grown two times the rate of increase in male defendants. Furthermore, we know that in 1998 there were approximately 3.2 million arrests of women, resulting in 22 percent of all arrests that year. By self-reports of victims of violence, women account for 14 percent of violent offenders. This is a yearly average of about 2.1 million violent female offenders. Approximately 16 percent of all felons convicted in state courts in 1996 were women. Women account for 8 percent of convicted violent felons, 23 percent of property felons, and 17 percent of drug felons. According to the Bureau of Justice Statistics, in 1998 more than 950,000 women were under supervision through the correctional system. This is approximately 1 percent of the U.S. population.

Female sex offenders may be underreported for a variety of reasons:

- The average person does not want to believe that women offend in society.
- Society in general has the preconception that women are nonviolent and nurturers.
- Children, when dependent on their parent, are more reluctant to report inappropriate sexual contact.
- Mother-child incest is more difficult to detect for health care workers as the mother frequently accompanies her child(ren) to the doctor's office.
- In women offenders overt sexual behavior may be disguised as care-taking.
- Boys sexually abused by adult females are reluctant to report an offense.
- Females who commit incest are reported less than those who offend others in a sexual manner outside of the family.
- Female offenders may conceal sexually deviant action through socially appropriate behavior.
- Culturally, females are stereotyped as physically and psychologically incapable of committing acts of sexual abuse.
- Females are perceived by society as vulnerable individuals who are incapable of harming others.
- Females are not typically thought of as sexual offenders.
- Female sex offenders do not end up in court or the criminal justice system as often as their male counterparts.
- Female offenders often receive less time and fewer consequences than men who committed the same offenses do.

Sex-Offender Therapy
© 2008 by The Haworth Press, Taylor & Francis Group. All rights reserved.
doi:10.1300/5753_12

TYPES OF FEMALE SEX OFFENDERS

Matthews (1998) has researched and observed that female sex offenders are placed in the following categories or typology:

Teacher/Lover

The teacher female sex offender is involved in a relationship with a child/student. The result of this interaction will eventually lead to a sexual relationship. She acts as the initiator of the sex abuse of her victim. Her victim is usually male. As a teacher, she acts in a position of power based on her age and role in the victim's life. When victimization occurs, she most likely does not see her behavior as criminal. These encounters usually are not forced. She has no hostility toward her victim, in fact she is seeking a loving, sexual expression in her interactions with the victim. She minimizes the negative impact of her actions on the victim. Her reaction to exposure of her sex crime is to be defensive, denying any sexual abuse of her victim. This type of female offender is historically a victim of severe emotional and verbal abuse as a child. She may have been in a sexually abusive relationship with a lover. The initial sexual contact may not be planned. Later on, her actions are organized and scheduled. In fact, the victim usually becomes supportive of the relationship by attempting to prevent or help avoid detection of the sex crime.

Case Study

The victim is a fourteen-year-old male. He received tutoring after school in order to continue playing football. His female teacher, age twenty-four, felt good that she was helping her victim. His grades improved with her tutoring. The sessions after school become longer. She suggested he come to her home to "grab a snack" while studying. Her victim was popular with the girls, but did not have a girlfriend. He was shy. After weeks of tutoring, the teacher and student engaged in fondling. This led to a rather intense sexual relationship. The teacher was more sexually experienced, and the victim was receptive to her and flattered by her sexual advances. The victim kept the relationship a secret. His parents overheard a telephone conversation between their son and his teacher. They become suspicious, reporting their concerns to the principal and school board.

Male-Coerced/Male-Accompanied

This female sex offender is involved in a relationship with an adult male, either a husband or a companion. She is influenced by the male to participate in sexual abuse. She may be exposed to the threat of physical punishment by her partner. Often the female will join in the sexual abuse with her partner, which the partner has previously committed on his own. The adult male will observe the offense or engage in the sex crime during a part of the sexual assault. The male and female are likely to endorse traditional roles in a relationship. The female is the homemaker, wife, and mother. The male performs his role as the provider. Most often the victim of abuse by a male, the coerced female sex offender is the offender's daughter. This type of female offender fears her husband or companion. She feels powerless in interpersonal relationships.

The male-coerced sex offender may exhibit the following characteristics:

- Low self-esteem
- Low or average intellectual functioning
- Underassertiveness and passiveness
- Drug and alcohol problems
- Anger and antisocial traits

Case Study

The female offender was released from prison after serving twelve years for incest and aggravated sexual battery of a male under the age of ten. The victim was her son. Her husband had sexually abused their son from age five to age eleven. He threatened to take their son and leave the state. She would never see their son again. She believed him as he had moved to her state after being released from prison for malicious wounding of his second wife. Initially she was forced to watch her husband molest their son. Then she joined them after her husband threatened to kill her if she didn't participate in the sexual abuse of their son. She felt stuck in the relationship. No one else would want her or her son if the husband left her. Who would support them if he left?

Predisposed Sex Offenders

Predisposed sex offenders were victims of sexual abuse in childhood. Typically they have been victimized by family, strangers, or acquaintances. They come from families where sexual abuse can be traced back throughout generations. Their victims frequently are family members, often their own children. Their victims may be female and can be preadolescent or adolescent. Not only do these offenders sexually abuse their victims, they may also neglect or be physically abusive with their victims. Predisposed sex offenders often are in abusive relationships with their male partners. They commit offenses that are violent in nature. The abuse may involve young victims who may be chronically suicidal or have self-injurious behavior or have low self-esteem. During their sex crimes, female offenders may reenact or relive their own abuse.

Other traits shared by predisposed female offenders is their psychopathology. Predisposed offenders may display paraphilia traits or have sadistic fantasies that may be triggered by anger. They have low self-esteem, are passive, and evidence extreme and acting-out behaviors. They initially sexually abuse independently.

Case Study

The abuser is a sixteen-year-old female. She was sexually abused by her biological father from age three to age nine. The father was incarcerated for drug-related charges. The abuser was then placed with her grandparents. The grandfather began molesting the girl. The girl was angry and at times violent with her younger brother. She began to sexually abuse her younger brother. The grandmother caught them one evening while they were in their bedroom. They were supposed to be working on homework. The granddaughter told her about her father (her son) and her husband's sexual abuse of her over the years. Her response was to call her a liar. She sent both of them to live with another relative. Shortly afterward, that relative had them put in the custody of the Department of Social Services. The violent behaviors continued with additional aggressive behavior with teachers and peers. The girl and her brother were placed in a residential treatment program.

Mentally Ill Female Offenders

Treatment needs for female offenders who are mentally ill, or have developmental delays or mental retardation require skilled therapists who are willing, experienced, and well qualified to work with this population.

The offenders may also be victims of domestic violence, or have a long history of sexual abuse. Female offenders may have increased suicidal ideations or homicidal ideations. They are more likely to have unstable relationships, which may be intense, or they may devalue their victims. Female offenders often have impaired impulse control, poor judgment, and limited insight. They may suffer from neurosis or psychosis. Alcohol or drug use, predatory behavior, history of sexual or physical abuse, former use of physical force or use of a weapon, difficulty controlling anger, and feelings of abandonment are factors to be considered when assessing and treating female offenders.

Mental health diagnosis for female offenders may include, but are not limited to, personality disorders, post-traumatic stress disorders, and identity disorders. They often have mood instability and or affective disorder, depression, anxiety, or eating disorders. Mood disorders are commonly observed in female child molesters. Sexual dysfunction, sexual aversion, or abnormal sexual behavior is found in this population of female offenders.

The following are clinical features or common characteristics of female sex offenders in treatment:

- Female offenders are more likely than men to have a history of being sexually abused or experiencing other significant trauma.
- Women are much more likely to have a shared relationship with the victim. Men are more likely to treat the victim as an object rather than a person.
- A large number of offenses involve same-sex sexual molestation.
- Society views men as physically incapable of being sexually abused by females.
- Adult males are less likely to report sexual abuse by a female due to pride, embarrassment, and actual or perceived social consequences.
- Female offenders use control and manipulation with their victims.
- Female offenders express anger different from male offenders. Female offenders internalize their anger, male offenders externalize emotions.
- Defense mechanisms for female offenders include: devaluation of self, disassociation, isolation, repression, displacement, and undoing.
- Female offenders have a lower recidivism rate than male offenders.
- Female offenders have addictive behaviors including sexual addictions and/or using alcohol or drugs at the time of their offense.
- Hislop (2001) indicates that female offenders may experience emotional difficulty with sex. They may feel sexually incompetent, feel sex is too intrusive, and feel frightened, not being present during sexual activity and have difficulty setting boundaries. Other sexual problems include sexual dysfunction, gender identity, and body image issues. Anxiety during sex as well as the inability to reach climax are also characteristics faced by female offenders.

Females share similar dynamics in group therapy. The therapist must engage with the patient prior to effective treatment, establishing a therapeutic rapport may be complicated. This may be accomplished by giving the patient unconditional positive regard. The relationship between the therapist and patient may be nurturing rather than threatening or coercive. A skilled therapist will be a role model of appropriate behavior for the offender during the group process.

Role modeling may be in the form of:

1. Assisting the female offender in setting her boundaries while respecting the boundaries of her peers.
2. Teaching the female offender to be a more effective communicator.
3. Assisting the female offender in developing assertiveness skills, therefore empowering her to be involved more effectively in her treatment program.
4. Teaching social skills.
5. Role modeling how to solve problems.
6. Through positive interaction with the female offender, the therapist will address maladaptive relationship problems, a behavior in the use of defense mechanisms as a protective

method of avoiding pain or preconceived fear of harm or to receive the most benefit from the treatment program.
7. Role modeling how to safely release emotions without fear of losing control or being ridiculed.

Female offenders may initially have similar responses to treatment, including:

- Not wanting to disclose their sexual offense.
- Fearing they will have to self-disclose their own history of sexual abuse and relive the trauma resulting from the disclosure.
- They may be embarrassed about having sex with both male and female victims.
- Female offenders may be defined or passive in the group until they establish trust and feel comfortable with self-reporting.
- Female offenders must feel physically safe in the group environment. Confidentially is essential to establishing a feeling of safety and trust.
- Female offenders have histories of poor self-esteem and poor social skills.
- The offenders may have intellectual deficits, learning disabilities, or developmental delays, which influence their ability to learn from group sessions.
- Female offenders will use defense mechanisms learned from their past to decrease anxiety and emotions surrounding their own victimization and offending.
- Female offenders share some common characteristics with male sex offenders. Traditionally, sex offenders share the following traits:

  1. They withhold information.
  2. They leave out details of their sex offense.
  3. They lie or misrepresent their sex crime and sexual aggression.

- Female offenders are skilled at manipulating people and will attempt to manipulate the therapist.
- They are not in sex-offender treatment on a voluntary basis. Their attendance is court-ordered and they are held accountable for their attendance.
- Sex offenders will pick up on and exploit any conflict between co-therapists. They will attempt to exploit, at any opportunity, any perceived conflict or mismatching of therapists providing treatment in a group setting.
- Female offenders traditionally have Axis I and Axis II disorders.
- The clinical assessment addresses in detail the diagnostic criteria, primary diagnosis for sex offenders with antisocial, narcissistic, or borderline personality disorders.
- Female offenders who are arrested or incarcerated, come from a variety of different societal backgrounds.
- Female offenders are hard to identify. They don't have physical traits or signs that make them appear to be child molesters. They come from different economic, educational, and professional backgrounds. They are seen as normal people who have jobs, families, go to church, pay taxes, vote, and are actively involved in community activities.
- They have sexual addictions.
- They may, and most often do, have alcohol and drug-abuse issues.
- They manipulate their victim and often the victim's family members in order to gain access to the intended victim.
- Female offenders seek employment where they will have contact with children as part of their job.
- They have low self-esteem or are overly confident in their sexual prowess.

- They have relationship problems, including anger problems dealing with their own victim-ization by males or females in their past.
- They may feel more comfortable associating with children than with adults based on their history of victimization.
- They may gain access to children by treating them more as adults.
- Female offenders may evidence a diminished interest in their husband, paramour, or in their marital sexual relationship.
- They may or may not have a prior conviction of nonsexual or sexual crimes.
- Female offenders have thought distortions. They deny the harm their victimization has caused their victim. They project their thoughts and desires onto the victim. They minimize how the victim is affected by their victimization. They rationalize or make excuses for their sexual offending.

Male and female sex offenders are different. They have different issues and dynamics, including:

- Women are more open about their sex crimes in group therapy.
- Women take responsibility for their sex crimes much earlier in the treatment process.
- Women self-report abuse more often than men do.
- Women develop victim empathy earlier in the treatment process than men do.
- Women are goal-directed in treatment, therefore they are invested in completing group as-signments in a timely manner.
- Women provide more emotional support through group therapy.
- Female offenders engage more in positive group interaction with peers.

Matthews (1998) identifies additional factors. Women typically do not use others as accom-plices in their sex crimes. Force, violence, and threats are used less often than by their male counterparts. Men become abusive at an earlier age than women. Males start around the adoles-cent age, women start in adulthood. Men forgive themselves for their sex crimes quicker than fe-males do. Women remain ashamed of their sexual misconduct/behavior longer than males who sexually offend.

Hislop (2001) writes about female sex offenders who are perpetrators engaging in ritualistic sexual abuse. Little research or literature is available on ritualistic aspects of female offenders. This most often takes form in the context of satanic rituals. Satanic rituals do not commonly oc-cur in isolation. The offender has a partner or another family member or co-offender. The female offender may sexually victimize children and then make them available through force or duress to another person. The victim may be asked or forced into sexual activity with a child, animal, or another adult.

Ritualistic sexual abuse is a bizarre behavior. The abuse by the female offender and co-offender may involve exhibitionism, pornography, photography, and sexual penetration. Pene-tration may be sexual contact or with an object such as knobs, dolls, or animal parts. Ritualistic paraphernalia such as swords, candles, or altars may be used. Drugs may be used on the victim and/or by the sex offender. Fear and torture is most often the theme of ritualistic sexual abuse.

FANTASIES

Female sex offenders may fantasize about same-sex or sexual activities with adolescent males, females, or children. Female offenders who have been sexually molested may have fantasies where punishment is the theme to reach orgasm.

According to Lane (1991), fantasies in some females are related to love, sexuality, or hostil-ity. Female offenders may have fantasies that are sexual and sexually abusive, violent, or retaliatory in nature. Domination fantasies may be present, not related to power or force, but to inflict harm or sexual humiliation on their victims. Fantasies related to sexual abuse are often followed by masturbation. Female offenders become aroused by fantasies of their current or past deviant sexual activity, which they reenact during sexual molestation (Abel, 1989).

CRUISING

Female offenders are often in the position of having contact with their victims in a place of employment. For example, day care workers, teachers, coaches, or stay-at-home moms that carpool several children to school or activities. Female offenders may be less obvious in their cruising activity. They are viewed by society as caregivers as well as protectors of children.

GROOMING

Female offenders groom often under the pretense of nurturing their victims. They will use coercion, threats, or intimidation. The ultimate goal is to have sex with their victims.

TREATMENT

Group therapy is the preferred treatment model for female offenders. This may present a problem for service providers since a limited number of female offenders are referred to treatment. Therapists may have no option but to offer individual or family therapy services.

Therapists should never consider placing a female offender in a group with male offenders. This type of treatment is inappropriate, placing both the female offender and the group at risk. Female sex offenders are often victims of sexual abuse. Placing female offenders in a group with males would be clinically harmful for the patient.

Exercise 12.1 can be used by the therapist to assist the female offender in better understanding herself, why she abused, and how she selected and gained access to her victim(s).

SUMMARY

Adult female offenders possess many clinical features found in other sexually aggressive patients. However, one significant behavior that is different for adult women is the reported number of victims. Women are often found to have an emotional relationship with their victims. In addition, adult female offenders, in most reported cases, have a low victim total. Another feature is that adult female offenders often show more victim empathy and remorse for their sexual misconduct than male offenders.

EXERCISE 12.1. ADULT FEMALE PATIENTS

Be honest in this exercise. Check yes or no when appropriate. Check all answers that apply to you and your sex crimes. When asked to explain your answers use more paper if necessary and attach it to this exercise.

1. List the sex crime(s) you were legally charged with. List all crimes you committed from age twelve to the present.

   _____

   _____

2. How many total victims do you have? Do not give names, just numbers.

   Number of male victims _____ Number of female victims _____

3. Were you related to your victim? Yes _____ No_____

4. If you answered yes to question 3, check all categories your victim falls into:

   _____ biological   son _____   daughter _____

   _____ a stepchild   male _____   female _____

   _____ adopted child   male _____   female _____

   _____ foster child   male _____   female _____

   _____ family member's child   male _____   female _____

5. If you answered no to question 3, which of the following categories does your victim fall into:

   _____ The victim was a friend of my child.

   _____ The victim was my friend's child.

   _____ The victim was a student of mine.

   _____ The victim was a patient of mine.

   _____ The victim was a member of a group I worked with (coached, led, or sponsored).

   _____ The victim was a stranger.

6. Were you married when you committed your sex crimes? Yes _____ No _____

7. If you were not married, did you have a companion? Yes _____ No _____

8. If you answered questions 6 or 7 with a yes, check all that apply:

   ____ My spouse/companion knew of my crime.

   ____ My spouse/companion forced me to participate in the sex crime with him.

   ____ My spouse/companion coerced me.

   ____ My spouse/companion watched me have sex with my victim.

9. I acted alone without my spouse or companion knowing about my sex crimes.
   Yes ____ No ____

10. Which of these situations apply to you? Check all that apply.

    ____ I was a victim of incest.

    ____ I was raped/molested/stalked by another family member, neighbor, friend, or stranger.

    ____ I have been involved in a male-coerced sexual relationship where there was a threat of physical harm to me or a family member.

11. Did you deny or acknowledge your sex crimes initially?

    _____

    _____

    _____

12. Do you feel you harmed your victim in any way?

    _____

    _____

    _____

13. If so, in what ways has your sex crime(s) affected or influenced your victim's life?

    _____

    _____

    _____

Chapter 13

Antisocial Disordered Patients

Clinically, the antisocial disordered patient is one of the more challenging, complicated, and difficult populations to treat. As therapists, we see our professional goal as assisting patients with identifying their personal relationships, their interactions within society, and learning how to change behavior for a more positive outcome.

Seldom do antisocial personality disordered (APD) patients seek treatment on their own. Most often, APD sex offenders are in treatment because they are required to be there by some person in authority. They are referred to treatment by the following resources: the criminal justice system, human services, or mental health providers. Referrals may also come from residential treatment facilities, detention centers, or advocacy groups whose goal is to protect children not able to protect themselves.

Risk factors in the development of APD patients include both genetic and environmental factors (Law and Psychiatric Institute, 2000). Having a first-degree biological relative with the disorder, and/or a history of child abuse or neglect, unstable or erratic parenting, or inconsistent parental discipline may increase risk. Genetically, having a first-degree biological relative with the same disorder may also increase the risk of developing an antisocial personality disorder.

Consider the following:

1. Was the patient victimized?
2. Was the patient a victim of child abuse or neglect?
3. Did the patient have emotionally distant parents?
4. Were the patient's parents absent due to divorce, work, or simply an inability to connect with the patient?
5. Was the patient's lifestyle in the home dysfunctional, chaotic, or unstable?
6. Did the patient have the opportunity to see or experience erotic materials in the home?
7. Was there inconsistent parenting?
8. Did the patient's basic needs go unmet due to the parent using alcohol or drugs?

If the above factors are present, an APD person's risk factors may increase significantly. Other factors to consider in developing an APD would be the patient's degree of social compliance or juvenile delinquent behavior as a youth under the age of eighteen, which is viewed as an indicator of adult antisocial behavior. Patients with narcissistic personality disorder or borderline personality disorder from a clinical perspective are indicators of the possibility of an existing antisocial personality disorder.

Sex-Offender Therapy
© 2008 by The Haworth Press, Taylor & Francis Group. All rights reserved.
doi:10.1300/5753_13

As sex-offender treatment providers, we know the following about sex offenders who have an APD:

1. Sex offenders with APD represent a large population of individuals referred for sex offender treatment.
2. APD is more prevalent in males than in females (American Psychiatric Association, 1994). The ratio may be 3 percent males to 1 percent females in the community. However, in the clinical setting, there is a higher estimate, possibly from 3 percent to as high as 30 percent.
3. There is a higher prevalence rate of APD patients who are associated with jail, prison, forensic, and substance-abuse settings.
4. Seldom do APD sex offenders act on impulse. Their sex crimes are premeditated.
5. Approximately 29 percent of all men charged with rape alone have APD (Knopp, 1984; Able, Rouleau, and Cunningham-Rathner, 1986). When averaged out, this equals to a population of about one third of all rapists exhibiting some form of an APD. Berger and colleagues (1999) indicate that APD can be found in approximately 42.2 percent of individuals with sadistic personality disorder.

CASE STUDIES

Male

The sex offender is a forty-two-year-old male. He served nine years in the state prison system for aggravated sexual battery and sodomizing a thirteen-year-old female. His victim was physically impaired. She had impaired vision. She was emotionally immature as well as intellectually limited. The victim was made fun of by her peers. She was not asked to attend social events or activities with her age group. The sex offender "traded services" with her parents to gain access to the victim. He sold her parents drugs, moonshine, and prescription pills at a "reduced price." He took the victim out to eat, bought her gifts, and let her friends drive his car. She refused his sexual advances, but he forced her to have sex with him several times a week.

Female

The sex offender is a twenty-year-old female. Her victim was a thirteen-year-old male. She served three years in prison for child molestation and sexual use of pornography to entice her victim. She then returned to the community. Sex offenders cannot have contact with their victims. When she was released from prison, her victim was sixteen years old.

She began to contact him by telephone through a mutual acquaintance. He agreed to meet with her and they began having sex. She told herself she wouldn't get caught. He enjoyed the sex as much as she did, so who was getting hurt? He wasn't the one who went to prison, so how was he hurt? After all, she was the victim. If he didn't want to, he wouldn't be meeting her. He told one of his friends how "cool" it was to have an older woman interested in him. Eventually word spread in the community, getting back to her probation officer. She is back in prison to serve her full term of ten years. The sex offender blames her victim. There is no guilt or remorse for the affect she's had on his life.

Aggressive behavior is often seen in sex offenders with an APD. They, like most sex offenders, most often evidence resistance to treatment services. Resistance may be subtle or overt in nature. Resistance may be in the form of denial, rationalization, minimization, manipulation, or indifference. Whether treating an APD sex offender individually or in a group, the therapist will experience patient resistance to treatment.

Therapists who treat sex offenders with an APD often have to be hypervigilant in monitoring and tracking the therapeutic interaction with this population. APD sex offenders often "con" themselves into believing what is clearly not true. They are skilled at manipulation or diverting attention from their behavior. APD sex offenders are interesting individuals who are articulate, intelligent, and engaging. These are the same characteristics that allow them to victimize children and adults.

A questionnaire that assists in recognizing the sex offender with an APD may be helpful to the therapist (see Exercise 13.1). Have the patient complete this questionnaire then compare his or her answers with your clinical assessment, testing results, court records, and referral information provided by the referral source. Major discrepancies will be found in information given by the patient to professionals who are involved in his or her course of treatment.

TREATMENT

Treating sex offenders with an APD requires the therapist to quickly establish expectations for these patients as well as set boundaries. Remember that these patients are skilled at "conning" themselves and others. They may present for treatment as hostile, indifferent, manipulative, or attempt to align themselves with the therapist (Flora, 2001).

The following guidelines are recommended for treating sex offenders who have an APD:

1. Before starting a treatment program with APD it is recommended that a thorough clinical assessment be completed.
2. Once the clinical assessment is completed the APD patient should be court-ordered for treatment or on probation or parole.
3. A written treatment contract outlining the rules and expectations of the treatment program should be signed by the patient, his or her probation/parole officer, and the therapist.
4. By the eighth group session APD patients should be able to acknowledge their offense, discuss their sex crime(s), identify their preferred target population, admit harm to their victim, accept responsibility for their actions and verbalize remorse.
5. While in treatment the patient will not reoffend, commit a new sex crime, or engage in other criminal activity.
6. The use of drugs or alcohol is not permitted while in treatment.
7. If the group develops slowly, group members may develop a sense of cohesiveness.
8. Use peer pressure, as it is effective in working with APD sex offenders.
9. The therapist should set boundaries at the initial phase in treatment.
10. Modeling by the therapist is effective in the treatment process.
11. When possible, and in the appropriate setting, humor can be used as an effective therapeutic intervention.
12. Be fair with group members. Any perceived favoritism or slight will be noticed by the sex offenders in treatment.
13. Be realistic in your expectations of group members.
14. Be direct when discussing group material.
15. In treatment use therapeutic interventions such as providing education, encouragement of journal-keeping, and requiring special readings, and self-study.
16. Encourage discussion on values, thinking errors, and deviant arousal patterns.
17. The use of privileges is effective for sex offenders who are inpatient or in a correctional facility. They may be more willing to attend treatment.

SUMMARY

Therapists treating APD patients must always remain hypervigilant. This population of sex offenders will use several methods of resistance, both subtle and overt. Never allow the APD patient to engage you on a personal level. Be aware of and expect to confront transference and countertransference issues. Remain professional at all times. Do not allow boundaries to become blurred, as this would jeopardize your effectiveness as a therapist and the APD patient's recovery in treatment.

EXERCISE 13.1. SELF-INVENTORY QUESTIONNAIRE

Read the following questions. Answer yes or no. Check any and all that apply to you.

1. Did you ever cheat or lie in school?

_____

2. Were you ever in after-school detention, in-school detention, suspended, or expelled from school? Did you skip or miss classes altogether?

_____

3. Did you get into physical fights while in school with your peers, teachers, parents, or family members?

_____

4. Were you ever on probation? List the offenses.

_____

5. Has any mental health professional, department of social services staff, probation officer, school personnel, parent, or family member made the following comments, observations, or statements about you?

_____ You don't obey rules or follow requests made by adults. You defy or refuse to follow instructions or requests by adults or society.

_____ You don't accept responsibility for your own behavior but blame others.

_____ You are angry, argumentative, annoying, moody, vindictive, resentful, or spiteful.

6. After the age of eighteen, have you exhibited the following behavior? Answer yes or no on the blank line. Check all that apply to you.

_____ Have you ever been charged with a sex crime, driving under the influence (DUI), drunk in public, assault and battery, destruction of property, possession of illegal drugs or paraphernalia, or the manufacturing or distribution of an illegal substance?

_____ Have you served time in a local or regional jail, prison, or any department of corrections program?

_____ Have you had more than one incarceration? If so, how many times have you been charged with a crime?

_____ Have you been found guilty of child abuse, child neglect, or reckless endangerment of a child?

_____ Have you insulted, been aggressive, or fought with your family, wife, husband, children, friend, or persons in authority (police)?

_____ Have you been accused of or charged with stealing, giving false information, armed robbery, or stolen identity from someone?

_____ Do people who know you use the following terms to describe you or your behavior: irresponsible, immature, irritable, hostile, deceitful, reckless, uncaring or have they called you a liar?

_____ Do you act on impulse without regard or remorse for having hurt or mistreated another person?

_____ Do you regret having hurt another individual or are you empathetic with their feelings?

_____ Have you used aliases for personal pleasure or personal gain, profit, or to "con" your victim or others?

_____ Do you have a poor work history? Do you frequently get into disagreements with your employer? Do you refuse to do your job description? Do you frequently change jobs?

Chapter 14

Triggers

Although each sexual offense is unique in the harm done to the victim, there are similarities in how some offenders commit their crimes. In this chapter we will look at what triggers offenders, how they choose their victims, and how they create an environment for offending.

Oftentimes when the elements of an offense are closely looked at, there are specific things that lead to offenders committing their crimes: stress, loneliness, fear, anger, losing a job, false beliefs, infidelity, and a host of other issues. When these difficulties occur, the offender who is not always psychologically equipped to address the problem appropriately, may resort to self-soothing methods that have worked in the past (e.g., masturbation, viewing pornography, or engaging in inappropriate sexual acts). The desire is to feel better, unfortunately, at the expense of someone else. (See Exercise 14.1.)

CASE STUDY

The following case study will demonstrate the elements of an offense from the perceived stressful conditions (triggers), to the internal dialogue (choosing a victim), to the manipulations of environment (creating an environment to offend the victim), to the acting-out of the offense. (See also Exercise 14.2.)

Mr. Mansion was the stepfather of three; his wife worked the midnight shift as a registered nurse. He worked in a minimum-wage job and they had one vehicle. As Mr. Mansion revealed the story of his offense, it became apparent that his inability to cope with anger, frustration, and hurt lead him to commit his crime of fondling his fourteen-year-old stepdaughter.

According to him, eighteen months prior to his offense he was the primary caregiver of the children. He cooked, cleaned, and cared for the children. His wife, when not asleep, went out with her girlfriends. This initially did not bother him because he felt that due to his wife's stressful job, she needed time to relax.

As once a week turned into three or four days a week out with the girls, their time together was compromised. When he complained, she stalled him and promised that they would spend more time together, but that never happened. This created feelings of hurt within himself. He believed his wife's need to be with her friends was more important than being with him. He also suspected she was having an affair. His anger began to manifest itself in continuous arguments and accusations of infidelity, which further decreased their time together.

Their sex life, which according to Mr. Mansion was once a daily event, now was reduced to two or three times a month. A month prior to his crime, it was reduced to once a month. This convinced him that she was having an affair. Instead of finding a peer to share his problems with, he turned to his fourteen-year-old stepdaughter who was having her own difficulties with her mother.

She became his confidant, sharing all of his suspicions and concerns about his wife with her, including his lack of sexual satisfaction. As the sexual frustration grew, he shared his frustration with his stepdaughter/victim and she would ask questions about their sex life. At first he was re-

Sex-Offender Therapy
© 2008 by The Haworth Press, Taylor & Francis Group. All rights reserved.
doi:10.1300/5753_14

luctant to talk about the things he and he wife did sexually, then he thought, "Whom else could I talk to?" Feeling justified, he answered every question she had about sex and those conversations became the fuel for his fantasies.

He reported masturbating as many as six times a day prior to his offense. Using his stepdaughter as the primary stimulus for his masturbatory behavior, he stated that on the rare occasions when he made love with his wife he thought about his stepdaughter. When asked, "Why did he share such a private matter with her?" his response was, "She was the only one that understood the problems in the house. Besides, when my wife took the car, I was miles from anyone I could talk to and she was right there." Because the stepdaughter's response to him was "sympathetic," they created an alliance against his wife. Whenever Mrs. Mansion tried to discipline or censor her child, Mr. Mansion usurped his wife's authority by telling his stepdaughter that she didn't have to do whatever her mother said. This lead to several huge arguments where the stepdaughter sided with Mr. Mansion, causing the wife to mention possibly divorcing him.

This possibility greatly concerned him, fearing that his stepdaughter would be taken from him. To ensure that his wife would stop talking about divorce, he stopped his complaining and allowed her to come and go at her leisure. Oftentimes, he would encourage her to go out, giving him more time with his stepdaughter/victim. By now Mr. Mansion had elevated his stepdaughter to peer status in his mind; he was using her physically developing body as the source for his fantasy. He reported using those images to masturbate several times a day and thought of marrying her when she became of age. He became so comfortable with the way things were going he encouraged her to wear her mother's "baby doll" nightgowns, stating that she filled them out better than her mother. To maintain the aura of secrecy, he told her not to wear her mother's gowns until her siblings were in bed, fearing that they would tell her mother and she'd forbid her from wearing them. They fell into a routine of waiting until the younger children went to sleep and the stepdaughter would parade around in the gowns. These actions went on for weeks. He had asked her not to wear panties on a few occasions, but she refused and he never pushed the issue.

One summer night she complained of it being hot. He suggested she sleep in the living room where the fan was. While going to the restroom later that night, he passed by the living room and saw her bare bottom out from under the gown. He slipped into the living room and watched her bottom for a while and then he began to masturbate. Prior to ejaculation he started fondling her bottom and vaginal area. She woke up, screamed, and ran into her sibling's room where her mother was sleeping and told her what happened.

SUMMARY

When looking at the elements of a sexual offense, there are precursors specific for every offender. Whatever those precursors are, they all start with a trigger that sets into motion thoughts and feelings of a sexual nature. These thoughts and feelings center on a particular person and events that "drive" offenders into acting out their fantasies. Once the fantasies are created in their minds, they will look for a victim to fulfill them and create an environment conducive to the offense.

EXERCISE 14.1. THERAPISTS AND STRESSORS

As a sex-offender therapist, what stressors might you encounter and how would you address those stressors?

TRIGGERS   WHAT TO DO

_____   _____

_____   _____

_____   _____

_____   _____

_____   _____

_____   _____

_____   _____

_____   _____

_____   _____

_____   _____

_____   _____

_____   _____

1. A common trigger for a patient is anger. What factors may influence a patient to sexually abuse another person to relieve anger?

   _____

   _____

2. What would you recommend as an alternate to sexual aggression, if anger is identified as a trigger for a patient?

   _____

   _____

3. Stress is often a trigger for a sexually agressive patient. What factors may influence a patient to sexually abuse another person to relive stress?

   _____

   _____

4. What would you recommend as an alternative to sexual aggression, if stress is identified as a trigger for a patient?

   _____

   _____

5. Depression is listed many times by sexually aggressive patients as a trigger to acting out behavior. What reasons may cause a patient to become so depressed that he or she would harm another person to cope with this clinical problem?

   _____

   _____

6. Can you list four alternative suggestions for patients who identify depression as a trigger?

   _____

   _____

7. Can you identify at least five other triggers that may influence a sexually aggressive patient to act out?

   _____

   _____

EXERCISE 14.2. TRIGGERS, VICTIM CHOICE, AND CREATION OF ENVIRONMENT

Using the case study, let's look at the triggers, victim choice, and the creation of an environment for the offense:

1. What were the triggers that moved Mr. Mansion to molest his stepdaughter and how would you help him avoid those triggers in the future?

_____

_____

_____

_____

_____

_____

2. How did Mr. Mansion decide that his stepdaughter would be his victim?

_____

_____

_____

_____

_____

_____

3. What elements of the family dynamic did Mr. Mansion use to create an environment for the offense and how could he have prevented himself from creating that environment?

_____

_____

_____

_____

_____

_____

Chapter 15

The Clinical Interview and Report-Writing

The clinical interview of sex offenders is unique in structure as compared to other types of patient evaluations. By structure, this implies the actual location of the meeting, who may be involved in the session, the content of the clinical questions, and interview style. Certainly, a clinical interview should include basic background history. In addition, the interviewer must address the attack and the prior sexual history. Also, the clinician should gather information about the patient's potential to reoffend and a community safety risk assessment. This places an added burden upon the writer to follow a protocol that is fact-finding as well as objective.

In this context, no other type of clinical report resembles such an evaluation. The sexual recovery therapy model is used in gathering clinical and sexual history for a psychosexual evaluation. Basically, this format is as follows: Identifying Information, Childhood History, Marital History, Education, Religion, Military History, Medical History, Substance Abuse History, Criminal History, Psychiatric History, Mental Status Examination, Testing Results, Diagnoses, Risk Assessment, and Summary and Recommendations. (See Appendix I for a sample evaluation. Appendix II is a sample juvenile psychosexual evaluation.)

WRITING STYLE

In writing a psychosexual evaluation, the word "alleged" should be used if the patient denies the offense. Also, the word "alleged" is always recommended for use in pending cases. Remember, the patient is innocent until proven guilty.

However, if the patient has pleaded guilty or the court has found him or her guilty of the offense, the word "alleged" is not used. Many offenders who plead guilty to an offense will report in the interview that their plea was recommended to them by their attorney, or they feared if they fought the charge the sentence could be worse.

In writing the report, some clinicians take notes but later dictate their clinical findings. Others write notes during the interview processes, but type their own reports. Sometimes, it is more time efficient to begin writing the report during the interview. This style of report-writing often helps the interviewer present a "here-and-now" clinical picture of the patient in a more accurate manner. This form or model is used by many journalists, and is very applicable to the use of clinical report-writing.

Nothing is more irritating to a judge who must make a decision on a patient based in part by a report, than using an evaluation that is filled with clinical jargon. Also, page after page, the author rambles on and on, with only a limited understanding that a patient's life hangs in the balance. This type of clinical distancing is not appropriate for writing a psychosexual evaluation. Some person was hurt by an attack, another is on trial for the offense. If found guilty, the remainder of his or her life will be impacted. Also, the psychological ramifications for the victim are long-term. Therefore, a readable document is expected.

Sex-Offender Therapy
© 2008 by The Haworth Press, Taylor & Francis Group. All rights reserved.
doi:10.1300/5753_15

Any diagnosis should always be explained. Clinical terms should be explained in a lay fashion. Few courts understand what the terms "rule out" or "not otherwise specified" are intended to represent. Any sexual disorder or other clinical disturbance should include an explanation of the features of the problem.

The writing style should be presented in a building-block sequence that leads the reader along section by section, in narrative fashion, to a clinical conclusion. In order to bring the patient to life in a document, it is helpful to use quotes whenever possible.

It is not uncommon to see a judge, prosecuting attorney, and even the defense attorney flip to the last page of the report where the risk assessment and recommendation sections are located.

THE INTERVIEW

To begin, a comfortable setting should be arranged if possible. If the interview occurs at the therapist's office, the patient may be escorted from jail by jail staff. Jail staff will be expected to remain in the building near the room until the session is completed in privacy.

Inform the patient that the interview is not a treatment session, and that one is not acting in the capacity of a therapist. Also, privilege for sex offenders is not recognized in many states. Therefore, confidentiality may or may not apply. All appropriate release forms should be completed before each session is to begin.

The clinician should be prepared to schedule ninety minutes to two hours for an interview. A patient should be informed of the clinician's qualifications. Also, the interviewee should be told that note-taking by the therapist will occur throughout the meeting.

As a common courtesy, offer your hand at the beginning of the interview. Also, upon completion of the session, again a handshake is appropriate. This approach may not be applicable to certain dangerous patients or those with a chronic mental illness. However, in all cases the patient should be treated with respect and dignity.

Use Mr., Ms., or Mrs. during interaction with the patient. If the individual says that he or she prefers to be addressed by first name, this is allowable.

Some time should be dedicated to rapport-building. Most patients are ordered to undergo the evaluation. As a result, their defense system is up. A professional may want to first spend a few minutes talking about minor things such as the weather, local events, sports, or whatever topic appears to help the patient feel more relaxed. Gentle humor can be a stress buster.

Safety is always an issue for the interviewer. As a precaution, the interview should be completed near other support staff. The evaluator should always sit next to the door in sessions. No weapons should be allowed in the building. Some centers use a metal detector, locked door, or alarm system security before entering the main facility. If inappropriate behavior is displayed by a patient, the interview should be stopped. In certain cases, the gender of the clinician may be an issue. As an example, it may be easier for a woman to be the interviewer of a sexually aggressive adolescent female than a male interviewer.

If the interview involves a sexually aggressive child or adolescent, a parent or other third party should be in the room at all times. Even the most seasoned clinician can sometimes be mislead or at-risk.

An offender may be cooperative with the evaluator. Other patients may be manipulative and attempt to distort or lie about their history. The psychopathology of a sex offender is different than a patient of any other type of mental disorder. Sex has become an obsession for the patient. It has interfered with his or her social, family, and occupational life. These themes will be displayed by the patient.

Many sex offenders lie, distort, minimize, or qualify inappropriate behavior. Some will even lie about items that have no relationship to the offense. Insight and judgment is often found to be impaired in a sex offender. Intellectually, the person may be very bright, but possess many cognitive distortions that interfere with his or her interpretation of an incident.

Preparation

To prepare for a clinical interview, the evaluator should request information in advance of the interview. The data should be reviewed carefully and some notes taken if certain questions need to be asked of the client. The following information should be sought:

1. A police report detailing the crime.
2. The patient's version of what occurred at the time of the incident.
3. All court orders.
4. The victim's written account of the sexual offense.
5. Any information that has been gathered by the prosecuting attorney.
6. A presence report or probation report, if available.
7. Social service investigative reports if the case involves child sexual abuse, or an adult abuse in which the victim was mentally incompetent or elderly.
8. A criminal history report, which is usually provided by the prosecuting attorney or a probation or parole officer.
9. Any previous psychiatric hospitalization or outpatient therapy reports.
10. A copy of the written complaint, if completed, depending upon the state of the incident, and a copy of the arrest warrant.
11. School records if applicable.
12. Medical records if applicable.

Interview Techniques

Remember that a sex offender has a strong fantasy system. Sex has become a way of life for the patient. And the job of a sex-offender evaluator is to interview the patient about his or her sexual history.

The initial approach by the worker during the interview is always evaluated by the offender. One should be professional and straightforward. Anxiety or fear is quickly picked up by an offender.

It is recommended for the novice that he or she discuss the case in advance with a supervisor. (See Exercise 15.1 for interviewing preparation.) Also, role-play is helpful. Dress and appearance is important, but should not be overdone. Again, the sex offender is an individual who has a distorted belief system. The following is recommended:

1. Be genuine and establish rapport.
2. Sex offenders are very artful in misunderstanding information. Therefore, use words, phrases, and terms that are easily understood.
3. Remember, you are writing a clinical report. The clinician is not vetted to determine guilt or innocence.
4. Sexually explicit details must be asked, but you should be very professional during questioning. No appearance of sensationalism of an incident should occur.
5. Sometimes with the borderline intellectual or mildly retarded patient you may have to adjust jargon to a level the patient understands.
6. Be prepared for defense mechanisms such as anger, denial, depersonalization, idealization, projection, and rationalization.

7. The "Colombo" approach is very useful when you believe the patient is being less than truthful. Acting confused or repeating the question several times, several different ways, can reveal new information.
8. How does the offender feel about harming another person? Does he or she show victim empathy and remorse?
9. A therapist should be willing to reframe a question to help the patient fully understand what type of details are being sought.
10. It is always important to look at the interview as a series of building blocks. One block is completed, leading to the next section for more data.
11. Use quotes as often as possible, by the patient as much as possible.
12. Be prepared to be tested. This may be carried out in a covert and passive manner, or in an overt and aggressive form by a patient.
13. Be prepared for the layering effect. Offenders do not always reveal all information quickly. As a result, in layering, questions may need to be repeated again to secure more data.

Sexual History

In gathering sexual history, you will need to know if the patient admits to the offense. If the individual does admit to the crime, the next sequence of questions should involve the incident. However, many offenders will initially deny or distort information about the incident. Usually, it is helpful to have other reports of the incident available to review with the patient.

Gathering a sexual history is difficult. You must be prepared to ask a number of items. This should include the patient's first sexual experience. Also, sexual abuse may be needed to be reviewed again. You will need to know how many child or adult victims have been harmed, and what type of offending was used.

In addition, ask if the individual has been involved with prostitutes or had sexual affairs. Questions should include all the sexual disorders, but avoid using clinical terms. Ask about pornography and the use of the Internet. Do not appear to be judgmental. It is helpful to skip around, rather than follow a sequence during the sexual history questions. The offender may be trying to hide information and is being deceptive. Most patients will try to limit information. The patient's sexual history may be extensive.

The following information will also be useful:

1. What are the patient's psychological triggers that start the cycle of offending?
2. What are the patient's sexual fantasies?
3. What rituals does the patient use?
4. How does the patient groom a potential victim?
5. What is the patient's target population group?
6. What is the patient's usual style of attack in an offending situation?
7. Was the attack premeditated or impulsive?

SUMMARY

Clinical interviewing for report-writing of sex offenders can be challenging. The interviewer must be aware of many nuances of behavior displayed by offenders. Questions about specific sexual behaviors are a major part of the report. Some patients will admit to the offense, others will deny. Remember, the report will have a major impact upon the outcome of the patient's trial and future.

EXERCISE 15.1. INTERVIEWING SEX OFFENDERS

1. What questions do you expect will be more difficult for you to ask a sex offender?

_____

_____

2. Why should a second person be present when interviewing a sexually aggressive child or adolescent?

_____

_____

3. How would you structure an interview if the offender is female?

_____

_____

4. How would you structure an interview if the offender was a sexually aggressive child?

_____

_____

5. What clinical questions are important in the mental status section for an adult sex offender?

_____

_____

6. What questions are important in the sexual history section for a sexually aggressive adult, adolescent, or child?

_____

_____

7. What should be included in the summary and recommendation section for a sexually aggressive adult, adolescent, or child?

_____

_____

Chapter 16

The Penile Plethysmograph

Phallometry can be utilized with the sexual-offending population in several areas of intervention. The use of a phallometric measurement can be a portion of the initial assessment; a confrontational tool to assist the client in facing denial; help in determining progress prior to the completion of a treatment program; and as a means of conditioning therapy to control deviant thoughts. There are currently two forms of phallometric measure, including the penile plethysmograph (PPG) and photoplethysmography. As a part of gaining a physiological arousal assessment, these testing methods provide vital insight into the secret deviant sexual arousals and preferences of sex-offending patients. Specialized training is required to administer and interpret the results of these measures. The information is combined with other assessment tools in order to predict deviance and possible likelihood of recidivism. The ultimate goal of phallometric measure is to locate clinically significant scores, which notate a client's deviant sexual arousal.

According to Byrne (1998), history indicates the first phallometric method was designed by Kurt Freund in the 1950s as a means to measure sexuality. The military utilized the PPG to locate potential homosexuals or sexual deviants in order to keep them from entering the service. Later, a group known as Behavioral Technology, Inc. (BTI), in Utah, took Freund's concept and developed more standardized procedures, ethical nonpornographic stimulus, event markers to locate and attempt to fake results, measure attention spans, and processing information, while assisting in locating the nonresponders to the test. The PPG now provides valid research while using the devices on patients and has proven to be a forerunner in the field.

Phallometric devices record three physical components, including sexual arousal, galvanic skin responses (GSR) (heart rate and perspiration), and respiration (RESP) readings, as both the brain and body are used to process arousal. The clinician is trained to look for abnormalities and extreme scores, which dictate the outcome of the test. Originally, stimulus was pornographic and leading, as the clients watch pornographic movies while being measured, which produced less-reliable results. Other manufacturers believed the client should read scripts, hear stories over earphones, and then attempt to imagine themselves in the same sexual situations. In recent years, designers have created audio recordings and used photographs (visuals) stimuli of minor children with no nude depictions, while the only nude photos are of adult males and females. Having arousal to no actual physical movement or obvious sexual acts proves the client has the same amount of deviant thought regardless of the type stimuli, thus demonstrating that deviance is not motivated by pornographic image alone. The BTI PPG is approved by the Food and Drug Administration (FDA) in order to be considered a medical device and gain acceptance as a useful assessment tool. It is the only known FDA approved PPG in the United States. The researchers note that only approximately 10 percent of all males will not register a GSR reading, which may be due to having calluses or rough, thick skin on the fingertips or there are some people who do not produce these bodily responses. Should a technician detect these readings, the information is highlighted and the clinician includes this in the report. This type of research has proven beneficial to sex-offender treatment agencies across the nation, as they can rely on the validity of the results and standardization of the stimuli for consistent, accurate measurement of deviant sexual arousal.

Sex-Offender Therapy
© 2008 by The Haworth Press, Taylor & Francis Group. All rights reserved.
doi:10.1300/5753_16

As a component of psychosexual assessment, the penile plethysmograph results provide the clinician with valuable information about the offender's deviant sexual interests. The technician discusses the Informed Consent specifically designed for the PPG test, which explains the reasons for using the test in the evaluation, benefits of taking the test, and requires the client to acknowledge having been provided a detailed explanation of testing procedures.

As many researchers remind us, the penile plethysmograph and photoplethysmograph are not lie detectors and cannot confirm the guilt or innocence of the client. These devices were created to be only one part of an overall psychosexual evaluation, providing more defined, specific information about measuring arousal levels unavailable by other means of testing. The stimulus should include age ranges of infants through adults and both genders. Some developers of PPG systems believe it is necessary to gain data demonstrating the client's understanding comparing friendly, persuasive story lines versus angry, more violent scripts depicting each age group and gender. This research is beneficial to interpreting the focus of the client's sexual arousals and sexual preferences and the triggers provoking those arousals. Sexual preference refers to the age range of the client's desires, not their sexual orientation, and is recorded in the gender acknowledgment section of the PPG information forms.

This test can be utilized in inpatient and outpatient treatment facilities; however, the equipment can be quite expensive to purchase. Current models of the PPG range in price from $8,000 to $15,000 and require the technician to have extensive training in order to properly administer the test and maintain the PPGs. The interpretative clinician is also required to complete hours of intensive training to understand the elements of the procedure and the resulting scores. It is necessary for the clinician to have the client's sexual history, sexual dysfunctions, list of current medications and dosages, documented convictions, and victim information, as these pertinent pieces of information are combined with the PPG test results to formulate an accurate picture of the client and his deviant sexual interests. All of this information is put together with the other evaluation components in order to consider the client's need for possible sex-offender treatment.

PHOTOPLETHYSMOGRAPHY

Female sex offenders have become more visible in recent years; however, these offenders have been in existence just as long as the males. According to Carich and Mussack (2001), manufacturers designed a device, much the same design and size of a tampon, which measures the sexual arousal by recording changes of vaginal vasoconstriction. Research presents that female arousal is not computed as easily as male reactions. A male arousal is more physically based and the female arouses to more emotionally based stimuli. Thus, for the technician performing the test and the interpretive clinician, it is more difficult to decipher the accurate level of female deviant sexual arousal toward stimulus of specific gender or age groups. This information is then processed by a computer, scored, and given to a clinician for interpretation.

PENILE PLETHYSMOGRAPHY

Male offenders have been proverbial guinea pigs used for phallometric research studies for many years. The first designs for the PPG included styles of measuring devices. Carich and Mussack (2001) stated technicians used an adjustable rubber-band style gauge or transducer, which contains mercury, named Barlow for the designer. Currently, there have been other models created to offer a more accurate measurement for the circumcised penis and using the Barlow for those clients who are not circumcised or are obese. The PPG is used to assess a client's arousal levels and specific focus of gender and age preference. Again this information is processed using a computer to record and score the data. (See also Exercise 16.1.)

FACING DENIAL

It proves very difficult for a client to continue denying his deviant interests after completing a PPG, where he is able to see his results on paper. As mentioned earlier, the scores are presented on graphs showing the PPG, the GSR, and RESP readings. There are pre- and posttest forms, which the client must complete in order to provide data for testing. Some questions covered on the pretest include age and gender of the victim, number of offenses, and types of deviant behaviors involved in the offense.

According to Laws (1989), this self-reported information provides the client a chance to admit guilt or deny his conviction. There are pretest questions about substance abuse, current medications and medical conditions, history of sexually transmitted disease, history of erectile dysfunction, and history of psychiatric counseling and sexual orientation. The posttest inquires about the client's responses to the test. The client discusses his history of sexual orgasm, including the most recent occurrence and how he experiences orgasm. The posttest also asks the client to indicate different types of paraphilic interests he may have participated in or fantasized about including sadomasochism, cross-dressing, threesomes, coprophagia, urophilia, necrophilia, and other such deviant paraphilic behaviors. This information also allows the clinician to present the client's self-reported sexual interests in his evaluation.

MONITORING TREATMENT PROGRESS

Using the initial PPG during the evaluation provides the treatment provider with data to use in future comparisons determining the client's progress or lack thereof from treatment. Laws (1989) referred to the initial test as the "pretreatment baseline assessment," which gives the treatment provider the base to judge the client's development from the beginning to the final phases. Should this information indicate no progress has been made, the client's treatment may be extended until he can demonstrate control of his deviant arousal. Laws also reported that only 73 percent of all treatment agencies had access to the PPG compared to today. Having this valuable information tells the provider how to assess the client's treatment progress.

AVERSION CONDITIONING THERAPY

In the 1970s movie *A Clockwork Orange*, Malcolm McDowell was a sex-crazed deviant, who tortured, raped, pillaged, and murdered. The character was shown participating in aversion therapy, where he was made to watch horrific stimuli in order to satiate him with deviance and break him of future behaviors. Society reacted to this movie by stating that the intervention was inhumane.

According to Laws (1989), the stimulus consists of seven categories of molesting behaviors. As mentioned earlier, each age group is represented in persuasive and coercive suggestions. The depictions include fondling a child, both consensual and nonconsensual intercourse with a child, rape version for adults and children, sadistic intercourse on a child, assault of a child, and consensual and nonconsensual intercourse with an adult. Hearing these stimuli, should the client begin to react, he is instructed to smell a foul odor, such as ammonia, in order to deactivate the arousal. During a training course, Byrne (2005) stated rotten moose liver could be used as a deterring odor. The client is also encouraged to monitor his own inappropriate arousal at home, using the same deterrent, and report the information to the clinician. There have been ethical considerations pertaining to this style of therapy; however, many clinicians are firm believers in this intervention, but use it only with extremely dangerous clients.

According to Dr. Robert Card (2000), using the PPG as a means of aversion therapy with a sex-offending client is necessary to create change in treatment progress. Though he stated knowing the PPG is no "cure" for the sex-offending behaviors, he believes using it for aversion would certainly act as prevention for future recidivism and throughout the recovery process as needed. Card (2000) says the PPG is one of the most important treatment tools to modify the patient's deviant sexual urges.

USING THE PPG WITH ADOLESCENTS

Administering PPG testing with adolescents has a few limitations, including ethical considerations of stimulus, legalities concerning informed consent, liability of viewing risky materials, and the risk of pornographic material creating a pansexual response, which would render the results useless. As mentioned earlier, BTI has created nonpornographic materials, which include no nude photographs; however, the storylines provide more explicit vocabulary describing sexual situations. Utah, considered conservative and provincial, adapted state policy and approved these stimulus to be included in psychosexual evaluations for adolescents. The state noted the importance of reaching youth prior to adulthood in hopes of addressing problematic behaviors and thoughts early in life; however, not every adolescent committing a sexual offense is a candidate for a PPG test.

The clinician must obtain a lengthy sexual history, evidence of sexual preoccupation and/or obsessions, and the age and number of victims. The presence of having more victims is more of a major risk factor for recidivism and displays more deviant arousal on the PPG.

THE PENILE PLETHYSMOGRAPH EVALUATION

After the technician completes administering the test and printing the data the information is given to the clinician, who composes the evaluation. The technician explains any anomalies he or she observed and provides the clinician with valuable information gathered from the PPG interview. This report may be used as one portion of the psychosexual evaluation or it may be a separate assessment.

The client's demographics are listed at the beginning of the report, followed by a referral source if available, which is necessary information for identification purposes. An explanation of the test and its probable finding is listed, which provides others with details of what the testing process entails. The agency must list the information regarding standardization of stimulus and sexual content, as well as explain the three guidelines used for the test including the PPG, GSR, and RESP scores. Sex-offending clients use a monitoring button during the audio recordings as "cue-ins" for the visual portion of the test.

Every evaluation should clearly denounce using the PPG as a lie detector. PPG testing is to measure arousal patterns and not used in legal proceedings to determine guilt or innocence. The results may be used in sentencing and disposition decisions, as a part of an overall sexual risk assessment. This section should also indicate how the technician and clinician were trained. It is important to list the description of the stimuli used, their similarities or differences, and who the test was developed to serve.

The victim information and sexual contact history should also be included, which provides the reader with valuable data about the client. This information should also highlight substance-abuse history, other possible victims, current medical conditions and medications, a description of the offense behaviors, and the charges or convictions. The clinician should make sure to present an accurate account of the immediate offense and offense history in this section.

A special section should note the validity of the test, which includes listing the client's current mental status, cooperation in test-taking, attitude, sexual orientation, and other information compiled from the pretest. This section also explains the test's abilities to measure the client's attending processes, where the technician is able to observe and monitor the client's test-taking behaviors, and cognitive abilities of processing information. The clinician also explains any abnormalities he or she saw in the PPG, GSR, and RESP readings. All of this data allows the clinician to state whether information gathered is an accurate representation of the client's sexual arousal pattern.

The clinician is given the chance to make professional interpretations of the data and offer potential hypothesis for the arousal reactions. As an example, if the client self-reported a history of sexual abuse at age eight and reacted on the PPG to that same age category, then one hypothesis could be the client's history of sexual abuse could be that arousal. However, the next hypothesis could discuss the same PPG reading and question if the client actually has more sexual attraction for that age range than is self-reported. Moreover, the next hypothesis could consider the client history of watching his seventeen-year-old cousin rape his eight-year-old cousin, as a possible reason for his reactions. The clinician has the client's interview information available to utilize what information was given about the client's history in order to question the full scope of possibilities for deviant sexual arousal.

The final section of the report discusses the clinician's recommendations for the client. Should the test be used to determine the client's appropriateness for sex-offender treatment, the clinician must present the pertinent data to support his or her hypotheses. This section also discusses the client's attitude in test-taking and information gathered from the test results.

SAMPLE REPORT

MONARCH 21 System Penile Plethysmograph
RE: Doe, John

Sexual Arousal Test Interpretation

It should be noted that the MONARCH System (Penile Plethysmograph) is not a lie detector. MONARCH measures an individual's sexual arousal patterns in response to the sexual stimuli to which he is exposed. MONARCH results should never be used in legal proceedings to determine an individual's guilt or innocence, but may be used in sentencing or disposition decisions as part of a sexual risk assessment. Persons using MONARCH as part of a sexual risk assessment should be trained as to the strengths and limitations of MONARCH data. The test does not reveal the degree or the extent to which an individual is likely to act out on the basis of his response patterns.

MONARCH PENILE PLETHYSMOGRAPH RESPONSE (PPG), a behavioral technology system, is a standardized, nonpornographic, penile plethysmograph system designed to assess sexual responsiveness to a variety of stimulus objects across gender, age, and sexual activity. Simultaneously with his penile response, the subject's galvanic skin response (GSR) and respiration (RESP) are sampled to attempt to detect faking. MONARCH stimuli begin with approximately one minute of audio presentation followed by four stimulus pictures presented at ten-second intervals. The audio materials are designed to "cue-in" a sex offender to visual stimuli, while the nonoffender is unlikely to "cue-in" and respond to the visual stimulus.

Description of the Testing Stimuli

MONARCH penile plethysmograph (PPG) testing uses stimulus materials especially developed for use with the adult male population that features nonpornographic projective audios and visuals. Segments of a violent nature have been labeled "coercive," while scenarios involving a persuasive approach (more playful, talking the victim into participating in the activity) have been labeled "persuasive."

Validity

Mr. Doe presented for the evaluation as quiet, polite, and calm. The client stated having only two hours of sleep prior to his testing, as he worked third shift. His affect was flat and blunted. He was very compliant with the testing process. During the pretest, the client indicated no history of sexual abuse. He is a twenty-one-year-old male, who works in a furniture factory. The client endorsed being exclusively heterosexual and being circumcised. He endorsed never being married. He also endorsed graduating from high school.

Mr. Doe stated being born by cesarean section. He reported no vision problems or hearing problems and wears glasses. He also reported no erectile issues and stated being circumcised at birth. Mr. Doe reported experimenting with drugs and/or alcohol when he was thirteen years of age. His drug history included smoking marijuana for two to three years, taking methamphetamines for two to three years, snorting cocaine for three to four years, smoking crack cocaine for two years, and taking recreational pain killers and nerve pills for one to two years. Mr. Doe stated the last time he had done any drugs was two years ago when his parents got divorced, which he stated was a painful experience. According to the client, both parents had many affairs during their marriage. His father was in the military. His mother used drugs and alcohol whenever she left the house and he stated, "She'd leave us [he and his little brother] at home alone while Dad was working."

Mr. Doe stated, "I was always sick when I was a kid with high fevers." Childhood medical conditions included having hypothermia, tonsils and adenoid removal, and tubes in his ears. The hypothermia happened while he was in the care of a local children's home. While he was rafting the rapids, he fell out of the boat and ended up unconscious for a few seconds. Regarding this experience, he stated, "I was completely blue, looked like I was dead. I almost died that day." During the interview about any possible head injuries, he stated when he was less than one year old, he fell down a flight of steps in his walker and at age four or five he hit his head on a dresser while playing. He stated at age thirteen he was sexually molested by an adult female, approximately twenty years old, who he stated got him drunk, gave him oral sex, and had intercourse with him on one occasion.

At age sixteen or seventeen he was prescribed Zoloft and Celexa, he stated, "They said I was real depressed." When discussing his medications in his childhood, he also stated, "I was in DSS [Department of Social Services] custody. I was in detention twice [truancy] at ages fourteen to fifteen years." The client also reported at age fifteen he was placed in a children's home. He was moved from home to home of each parent and the families moved around a lot. He had also been placed in a boy's home for two years and stated, "I didn't like it at first. But I liked it better than my parents'. My house parents were more like parents than my own. My mom grew up in DSS custody after her mother died at birth."

The client stated feeling dizzy and fainting a lot as a child, until having ear tubes placed in his ears. He stated still experiencing dizziness on occasion. He stated never having any sexually transmitted diseases. He reported his juvenile convictions included unauthorized use of a vehicle and possession of marijuana. His adult convictions included two counts of misdemeanor sexual battery and a violation of probation, where he received twelve months each, with all suspended but ten months and was released on good behavior. He self-reported having one, twelve-year-old victim, who was a neighbor. The offense happened in his home. Mr. Doe stated fondling the girl's breasts and vagina, her touching him, and the girl performing oral sex on him. He also stated, "I put my finger in it and around it, but I didn't pop the cherry or anything. She was still a virgin."

Currently, he reported residing with his girlfriend, who is pregnant, and stated, "We've been together two years and she says it's my baby. She's having a boy in December. She says she's had no affairs. It's scary."

During his posttest, he reported he did not attempt to suppress his arousal. He stated experiencing orgasm at least one time per week with the last one being within one week of the test. On testing, he stated that he reached approximately 5 to 10 percent of full arousal. He stated that in real life he was most attracted to females in the "twelve to thirty" age range. He endorsed being most aroused by both the audio stimuli of teen and adult females. He stated experiencing sexual orgasm five to seven times a week, with his last orgasm being within one week of the test. Mr. Doe's victim was a twelve-year-old female, with whom he had oral sex. His paraphilic interests included participating in dressing in female clothing and/or smelling and touching female undergarments; using a phone-sex line; looking at pictures of naked women in magazines, videos, or computer graphics; looking at hard-core pornography women in videos; participating in talking dirty to someone through a computer; and participating in a threesome with two women.

Examination of his responses to the built-in event markers found that, while he was attending to the stimuli, there did appear to be some problems with processing. He scored 96 percent on attention and 55 percent on a process, which was obvious in his lack of understanding the difference between the coercive versus persuasive version of the stimuli. Visual inspection of the analog PPG, GSR, and RESP traces revealed a rather inconsistent pattern of anomalies with the GSR and RESP traces. The problem on the RESP trace included significant movement from baseline, along with amplitude changes, as his RESP responses were so flat that in interpretation, one would believe he was making attempts to control his breathing in order to suppress his arousal levels during several of the segments. There were significant GSR reactions toward Child Violent, Female Teen Coercive, Male Preschool Coercive, and Female Challenge, which supported the theory of suppression. Taken together, the validity observations from this testing suggest that this administration of the MONARCH PPG, although valid, is likely a complete underrepresentation of Mr. Doe's arousal patterns.

Clinical Interpretation

Mr. Doe's responses on this measure were clinically significant with his greatest response being toward Female Challenge, Female Grammar Persuasive, Female Infant, and Female Teen Persuasive. He experienced other trending responses toward the Female Preschool Coercive, Male Grammar Coercive, Female Preschool Persuasive, Male Adult Coercive, Male Preschool Persuasive, Female Teen Coercive, Female Adult Coercive, Female Grammar Coercive, and Male Preschool Coercive, respectively, which would support the age and gender of his victim. The information pertaining to the males is sometimes an indicator of childhood sexual abuse or exposure to adult male sex; however, the client did not admit to having that type of history. As the test continued, his responses endorsed other trending arousal levels, denoting several areas of deviant arousal responses. He did not respond to an adult female category until his third most prominent arousal level, which was the Female Violent segment.

Mr. Doe's detumescent levels were also a concern to the interpreter. Detumescent time is the length of time it takes for the client's penis to once again become flaccid (without arousal) after the audio and visual stimuli end, thus indicating his level of fantasy use. This further highlights his sexually deviant interests in addition to the actual prominent arousal levels listed on the PPG. Considering his overall results were clinically significant, all categories of detumescent times were quite varied, as opposed to being equal in length, indicating a lack of deviant concern. This client displayed a number of lengthy detumescent times toward Preschool, Grammar, and Adult segments, no matter whether female or male. His most prominent detumescent times included Female Challenge, Female Adult Normal, and Female Teen Coercive, respectively.

During the pretest, Mr. Doe's responses toward both female and male segments were in complete contrast to his endorsement of being exclusively heterosexual. During the posttest, he also endorsed that he was most attracted to teen and adult females in the "twelve to thirty" age range. The PPG readings are in complete contrast to this information, as he responded to Female Challenge, Female Grammar Persuasive, Female Infant and Female Teen Persuasive, Female Preschool Coercive, Male Grammar Coercive, Female Preschool Persuasive, Male Adult Coercive, Male Preschool Persuasive, Female Teen Coercive, Female Adult Coercive, Female Grammar Coercive, and Male Preschool Coercive, respectively. He did react toward both aspects of stimuli for female teens, which does support the ages of his self-reported "real-life" sexual attractions and his PPG responses.

Mr. Doe displayed noted detumescent times toward several categories of stimuli, which supported a hypothesis of his deviant sexual-fantasy based processing abilities. He reacted toward Female Challenge, Female Adult Normal, and Female Teen Coercive, respectively. This information also provides evidence of his attraction toward more categories depicting minors as opposed to adult females.

Mr. Doe's arousal toward both minor males and females was a concern. The client displayed numerous lengthy detumescent times, which indicated the client was contemplating and fantasizing about the content of the stimuli. One of his most prominent detumescent times was toward Female Teen Coercive. As previously mentioned, there are two types of stimuli: ones of a violent nature have been labeled "coercive," while scenarios involving a persuasive approach (more playful, talking the victim into participating in the activity) have been labeled "persuasive."

In final hypothesis, his reactions toward males cannot be supported by having a history of childhood sexual abuse, as he clearly indicated there was none. He was reactive to Male Grammar Coercive, Male Adult Coercive, Male Preschool Persuasive, and Male Preschool Coercive, respectively, which suggests there may be more to know about Mr. Doe. This would certainly be information necessary to cover in treatment, should he be considered.

In summary, Mr. Doe did produce a clinically significant response on this measure; however, the trending responses to segments depicting sex with minors were also very prominent. His level of detumescent times were also most notable areas of concern. Examination of these hypotheses may shed further light on some of Mr. Doe's motivations for having engaged in sexual behavior with a minor female; however, during the PPG he also experienced sexual arousal toward adolescent and adult males, as well as adolescent and adult females.

According to these results, Mr. Doe would make an appropriate candidate for sex-offender treatment.

The administration of the PPG is part of a full psychosexual assessment and the results should be used in conjunction with other data to determine Mr. Doe's risk factors and recommendations.

Sally Hudson, PhD
Licensed Clinical Psychologist
Certified PPG Clinician and Technician
MONARCH 21 System Certified Clinician and Technician

SUMMARY

When using phallometry during an evaluation, assessment of progress in treatment, or in prevention, the clinician is responsible for providing an accurate measurement and interpretation of a client's sexual arousal levels. In evaluation, it plays only one of at least four components in establishing the possible necessity of a client needing treatment. When used as a means to monitor the progress and/or lack of change of a client's deviant sexual arousal, the PPG displays specific scores used to develop a true picture. As a means of prevention, the combination of using foul-smelling odors/tastes while seeing stimuli and experiencing arousals, the PPG can prove useful in curbing inappropriate stimulations. This form of prevention is taught to be self-administered when a client is not in the office to assist him or her in discontinuing the same inappropriate deviant sexual arousals when they occur. The most important factor to consider is the information obtained by highlighting the client's clinically significant deviant sexual arousals.

As a component of the evaluation, the clinician uses all of the client's test results to formulate if he or she has a need for treatment. Along with several psychological tests, the PPG is used to figure the red flags highlighting the need for psychoeducational group therapy using relapse-prevention theories. The psychosexual evaluation is composed of an overview of all results. The PPG provides the treatment provider a way to assist the client in facing denial of his deviant sexual arousal and desires. Allowing him to visualize his responses on paper provides more tangible proof of his behaviors and sexual thoughts. The clinician discusses the test and gives the client a chance to respond to the results, which can be a useful intervention prior to beginning treatment to combat denial. The self-reported answers from the pretest and posttest questionnaires are compared to the client's results, thus giving the clinician something on which to base his or her hypotheses.

Administering the test and completing the penile plethsmograph of the photo-plethysmograph report requires specialized training that teaches specific areas of concern to utilize in the test summation. Focusing on the client's clinically significant and trending scores, the report provides information necessary to discover deviant sexual arousal and to explain those reasons through interpretation. The report provides detailed accounts of the client's responses or lack thereof, by looking at the PPG, GSR, and RESP reactions and determining possible attempts at suppression or locating the client's areas of sexual preference and fantasy-based thoughts through recorded detumescent times. By having a PPG evaluation, the treatment provider is given a very detailed overview of the client's sexual desires that no other test offers.

Finally, using the phallometry in sex-offender treatment is detrimental to understand the full scope of an offender's problem areas of deviant sexual arousals and sexual preference. To discover the age group of the client's preference provides the necessary information to help the client through denial and pinpoint his or her demons, while also illuminating specifics for intervention needs. Clients can visualize their subconscious sexual desires and learn how to control these areas of deviance in their lives. Whether using phallometry as an assessment for evaluation, a method of monitoring progress in treatment and recovery, or as an aversion to deviant sexual arousal, these unique measurement devices act as the proverbial looking glass into the client's secret world of deviance.

EXERCISE 16.1. USING THE PPG

1. What is phallometry and who is an appropriate candidate?

   _____

   _____

2. What are the differences between and limitations of the penile plethysmograph and the photoplethysmograph?

   _____

   _____

3. Can adolescents be candidates for the PPG? What are the limitations?

   _____

   _____

4. What ways can the PPG be utilized and what are the ethical concerns?

   _____

   _____

5. Discuss the advantages and disadvantages concerned for use of aversion conditioning therapy.

   _____

   _____

6. What is the necessary information required on penile plethysmograph evaluation?

   _____

   _____

7. What must you know before considering a client for a PPG test?

   _____

   _____

Chapter 17

The Polygraph

The use of the polygraph has become a significant factor for both clinicians and probation and parole officers in the treatment and monitoring of male and female sex offenders. The effective treatment of sex offenders can be significantly increased when clinicians and probation and parole officers have enough factual information about the behavior and activities of the offenders in their daily lives.

Sex offenders are usually very much on the defensive in regard to their sexual lives and activities. They consider the polygraph as an intrusion. Both men and women are very reluctant to discuss in detail any activity that involves their personal sexuality. And, their first defense is to lie, to their probation officers, their therapists, and their treatment groups. They want to avoid "trouble with the authorities" and in particular, they want to stay out of jail. They have learned that lying has often helped them to avoid trouble in the past.

Sex offenders are very "street-wise" and know when the officer is operating on "gut instinct" or flimsy information, instead of solid facts. Of course, there are those offenders who have steadfastly denied their offense because of family factors. They have already convinced their parents, wives, and other relatives that they were falsely accused by the complainant, "railroaded" by the court, and imprisoned, in spite of their innocence. These men and women have promised themselves that they must never ever actually admit to their crimes for fear of losing reputation and status with their family members.

Then, there is the offender's personal contention that it really was the victim's fault; for wearing suggestive clothing, for sitting carelessly and allowing views of his or her underwear, or being too friendly, or simply, for not screaming and demanding that the offender stop molesting him or her! And there are those offenders who say very emphatically that they were actually helping the child have a clearer understanding of what sex is all about.

The rationalizations that offenders use to explain how they became "entrapped" in the criminal justice system often makes them appear as victims. They were seduced by the victim, or led by a promiscuous child to commit a sexual act that really wasn't their intent. So, after spending a number of years in prison, offenders are not only resentful and bitter, but also actually angry, almost furious about how they have been treated by the victim and the criminal justice system. Offenders proclaim indignantly that the victims "enjoyed" the encounters, and that they were smiling and happy about what happened to them. How could this possibly be a crime against the child or the woman who was raped? It often takes years of treatment before offenders realize just how wrong they have been, and can admit that *they* were the abuser and that *they* were the cause of both physical and mental injury to a child or another adult.

THE USE OF THE POLYGRAPH IN SEX-OFFENDER TREATMENT

The clinical polygraph examiner is an experienced and skilled technician who uses the polygraph instrument to determine truth or deception, but almost as important, he or she is also an ac-

Sex-Offender Therapy
© 2008 by The Haworth Press, Taylor & Francis Group. All rights reserved.
doi:10.1300/5753_17

complished and effective interrogator. The technical aspect of determining truth or deception is only the first step. The next phase is to get the offender to admit his or her crime and provide the details of what he or she did to the victim. Polygraph has been a part of both treatment and probation programs since 1982. A study was made by the Department of Corrections, Medford, Oregon, and Polygraph Associates of Medford, Oregon, in January of 1991, showing the efficacy of using polygraph testing in sex-offender treatment. In that study statistics were presented showing a pattern of improvement from 1982 to 1991.

Therapists have benefited from the use of polygraph testing before the offender is actually tested. The announcement by the therapist that polygraph testing will be used in the treatment program has prompted offenders to discuss and admit to other victims and sexual behaviors that otherwise would not have been divulged. A number of offenders have already been subjected to polygraph testing by police authorities regarding their sexual crimes, and they have been persuaded about the accuracy of the test when they deliberately lied and were told by the police examiner of their deception.

INFORMATION DERIVED FROM POLYGRAPH TESTING

The clinical polygraph examiner has the responsibility of eliciting information from offenders that will provide the needed data to clinicians and/or probation officers. A number of variables influence and affect the lives of offenders. Some of those variables are stresses from the normal activities of domestic and employment situations. It is helpful for the examiner to collect enough information from the offender in the pretest interview to provide a clear picture of what the offender is facing in his or her private life. See Exercise 17.1 for an example of the information that should be obtained in the pretest interview.

Before the test actually commences, the examiner needs to determine if the offender is a suitable candidate for testing. Ethical practice requires examiners to be satisfied that there are no health issues that could interfere with successful testing. There are a number of health conditions that can prevent accurate results in testing, and could present risk for the offender to go through the testing process.

The testing procedures, although normally not harmful or painful, can cause enough stress to an already fragile physiology to the examinee in jeopardy of stroke or heart attack. It is actually unethical to allow a person to take a polygraph test when such testing could adversely affect his or her health. Where there are indicators of serious health problems, the offender is asked to consult with his doctor, and get a note or letter from the physician to indicate whether testing will be permissible in light of the person's health situation.

The testing usually takes about two hours, sometimes more when there is deception indicated and a lengthy signed statement is taken. It is important that the examiner discuss how the polygraph works and goes over, in advance of the actual testing, the exact questions to be used during the test. There can be no surprise questions!

TYPES OF POLYGRAPH TESTS

An essential part of sex-offender treatment is having the history of sexual offenses and activities of the men and women participating in treatment programs. There are three types of polygraph testing that have been found to be helpful: the full-disclosure test, maintenance testing, and specific-incident testing.

The Full-Disclosure Test

This test is used to determine the offender's sexual contacts during a specified period, depending on the needs of probation officers and therapists. Full-disclosure testing is useful in providing clinicians with the background information necessary to know the entire extent of an offender's list of victims. In this test, the age range is from birth to the date of the testing. Sexual contacts are defined as exposing of the private parts, oral sex, vaginal sex, anal sex, and fondling. A contact can be a male, female, or animal. The detailed information required is written by the offender and includes:

1. Date of first contact (the year, at least).
2. Age of the offender when that contact first took place.
3. First name of the sexual contact (use male, female, or animal if name is not known).
4. Age of the sexual contact.
5. Kind of sexual activity involved (vaginal or anal sex, oral sex, fondling, or exposure of private parts).
6. How many times the offender had sexual contact with that person.

If the examinee (offender) lies during the test, he or she is confronted and urged to fully reveal all of his or her sexual contacts. Once they become aware that the examiner will know if they lie, most examinees will make the necessary admissions. Offenders are told that if they do not reveal all their sexual contacts, they will have to take the test again, and pay the same fee again.

The present sexual habits and inclinations of both men and women are often the result of their sexual experiences from birth to present. It is not enough to know what they have done sexually since they were twelve years old. Very often there are incidents of sexual abuse that have occurred in their infancy and early childhood that have traumatically affected them. Clinicians need to know the details of who touched them sexually, and with whom they were involved in sexual episodes, and whether it was actually sexual touching, nudity, or exhibition episodes.

Many men do not include prostitutes as sexual contacts, as if those kinds of sexual contacts don't count. Men who have been in the military or long-distance tractor-trailer drivers can have extensive histories of using prostitutes. They are very reluctant to admit these kinds of contacts (O'Connell, Leberg, and Donaldson, 1990). This can present a dilemma for the offender in trying to remember dates, ages, and sexual activities involved, particularly where such contacts with prostitutes were extensive and frequent. Sometimes this information has to be approached by asking the offender for an *estimate* of how many prostitutes he has been with in a given year or during a tour of duty.

Prior to a full disclosure polygraph, the offender must fill out a complete sexual inventory list of all partners or victims. Information regarding the year of the incidents, ages, names and types of sexual incident is expected. See Exercise 17.2.

Maintenance Testing

Maintenance testing can be used to help keep the offender on the "straight and narrow path," out of jail, and in compliance with treatment programs. Examiners often hear a probationer say that he has sometimes found himself in tempting situations that make him think twice before reoffending when he thinks about the polygraph test that will be facing him in the near future. Most offenders have a healthy respect for their probation officers and know that none of those officers want to be surprised with information that their probationer has been reoffending or violating probation conditions.

Maintenance testing is most effective when used at six-month intervals. Memory retention for offenders begins to blur if asked to account for their activities for a longer period of time. For offenders with greater potential for reoffense, a three-month interval may be more appropriate. The maintenance test can be tailored to the needs of clinicians and probation officers.

One of the most significant issues is whether the offender has had sexual contact with a minor or anyone under the age of eighteen. In the case of a rapist, the test should probe for any sexual contacts he or she has had in the past six months. Sexual contact is defined as having *any* sexual activity at all with a minor (a person under the age of eighteen), touching, kissing, hugging, exposing of private parts, anal, vaginal, or oral sex. For pedophiles, having a minor (even their favorite grandchild) sitting on their lap is tantamount to sexual contact. Unfortunately, there are many granddaddies that feel they have an inalienable right to bounce their grandchildren on their knees, and they say indignantly that they would never even think of being sexual with their grandchildren. In pre-test interview, the examiner should probe with the following inquiries:

1. In the past six months, have you either touched or had a minor touch you for sexual purposes?
2. In the past six months, have you exposed your private parts to a minor?
3. In the past six months, have you talked to a minor, either in person, by mail, e-mail, or by phone, about sexual matters?
4. In the past six months, have you purposefully brushed against a minor?
5. In the past six months, have you attempted to get the attention of a minor by either staring or making gestures?

The next question that can be used is whether the offender has been alone with a minor in the past six months. Being alone with a minor could be the next progression of activity just prior to reoffense. For the purposes of the testing, "being alone with a minor" means that there is no suitable adult who can hear and see both the child and the offender. "Suitable adult" is one who knows of the offender's sexual history and is free of any felony convictions or sexual-crime record. It is advisable that the offender's probation officer be the person who can designate a "suitable adult." Suggested questions in the pretest interview would include:

1. In the past six months, have you deliberately attempted to be alone with a minor?
2. In the past six months, have you been alone with a minor, even for a moment?
3. In the past six months, have you been alone with a minor in a public bathroom?

The next significant issue pertains to the use of pornography. The use of pornography is a bright red flag of danger. And the offender who is relying on pornography for sexual stimulation cannot distinguish between sexual desire for a minor and sexual desire for an adult. If the offender happens to see or be near a child after he or she has viewed or used pornography, and is still in a state of sexual arousal, he or she would find it difficult to suppress sexual interest, even with the knowledge that sexual contact could lead to later imprisonment. Therefore, the examiner must delve into the details of the pornography situation.

It is important that the offender be aware that using pornography is a violation of his or her treatment rules and is considered a serious transgression! Pornography is defined to the offender as any materials, books, magazines, movies, DVDs, or tapes that contain pictures or writings that depict sexual activities, nude or partially clothed men, women, or children. A clothing catalog can be pornography for sex offenders. Again, a signed statement should be obtained from the offender concerning his or behavior and activities in the previous six months.

The question format for maintenance testing is as follows:

1. In the past six months, have you had any sexual contact with minors that you have not told me about?
2. In the past six months, have you been alone with a minor, even for a moment, that you have not told me about?
3. In the past six months, have you used or possessed any pornographic material that you have not told me about?

The polygraph examiner must be prepared to confront and interrogate the offender who shows deception to these questions. There are reasons why he or she is deceptive, and the examiner should use whatever interrogation technique he or she finds to be most successful for his or her use. A paramount rule for interrogation: do not show anger or raise your voice! Be firm, but patient. Keep your voice controlled. There is absolutely no reason for the examiner to show anger or indignation. And, again, a signed statement should be obtained regarding the offender's behavior and activities, and the offender must read and sign this form! Otherwise, the offender can state that he or she did not tell the examiner certain information, and refuse to admit that he or she actually confessed to misbehavior.

Specific-Incident Testing

This testing is utilized to determine if the offender or suspect is being truthful about a specific event or occurrence, usually about the offense with which he or she has been convicted. For the offender who has somehow convinced his or her family that he or she is entirely innocent, he or she may attempt to maintain his or her denial of being involved in the crime. In the pretest interview the examiner obtains a signed statement from the offender about his or her assertions of what actually happened. That statement is read by the offender, then signed, and told that any variance in telling the complete truth will result in a failed test. If the offender does show deception, he or she is informed and then interrogated to fully reveal the truth. Fifty percent of the time, the offender does provide a complete confession. Another twenty-five percent finally admit to the crime within several months of the testing. The following questions serve as an example of the relevant questions used in this testing format:

1. In the fall of 2003, did you deliberately attempt to have sex with Fran Coulter?
2. Did you ever put your hands on Fran Coulter's vagina?
3. Did you ever put your hands over Fran's breasts?

In this testing format, the accuracy rate is about 96 to 98 percent when conducted by an experienced and skilled examiner. The benefit for probation officers and clinicians to know the details and actual truth of any offender's behavior is of enormous value, not only for treatment, but even more so for community safety. A signed statement should be obtained from the offender.

Polygraph testing assists offenders in becoming accountable for their sexual crimes, and helps to develop the habit of being open and truthful about their past and present activities and feelings. The success of sex-offender treatment very often is dependent upon how *willing* offenders are to talk about their offenses and to be able to verbalize what has happened in their lives to bring them to the point of being a sex offender. Polygraph testing assists probation officers in determining the degree of threat a probationer (offender) presents to the community. The treatment slogan of "NO MORE VICTIMS" is just as critical to the probation officer who is given the responsibility of monitoring and controlling the group of men and women who have the potential of reoffending, and thus, subjecting innocent individuals to the nightmares of sexual assault and molestation.

POLYGRAPH TESTING OF DIFFERENT GROUPS

Adult Males

Adult men have often built up a wall of resentment and have developed various defenses against authority figures (i.e., almost anyone who wears a tie or has any degree of control over the offender). In the first exposure to polygraph testing many offenders present a "tight-lipped," angry demeanor, as if filled with righteous indignation over being subjected to a lie detector test.

Some offenders have "learned" how to use various countermeasures when they are being tested on the polygraph. Experienced "jail-house mentors" have given them advise about clenching their anal sphincter muscle, moving their toes, flexing their biceps, taking deep breaths, or biting their tongues to disrupt the polygraph tracings. There are always offenders who will try some of these so-called countermeasures. The experienced examiner will quickly detect such attempts, and be put on notice that the offender probably has information that he does not want the examiner to know, or the offender would not feel the need to thwart the testing.

At least half of them show up for the test with only a portion of the necessary forms properly completed. Or they say, "Oh, I forgot to bring that form," or "I can't remember who I've been with." This is the kind of testing that they feel is highly intrusive. Almost none of them have ever been asked to account for all the sexual contacts they have experienced.

Another technique that offenders use is the friendly, "I'm a nice guy" approach. The adult offender tries to discuss sports or current events with the examiner, talking about topics that have nothing to do with the aspects of polygraph testing. This offender is trying to convince the examiner that he is a normal, god-fearing, friendly person who does not have the personality or inclination of a child molester. The examiner must quietly but firmly insist that he will discuss only the information needed for the testing, nothing else.

It is important for the examiner to maintain a civil and even disposition with the offender. Although there is no room for friendly discourse, the examiner must be able to maintain a professional rapport with the offender that will carry through the period of polygraph testing (usually the offender will need polygraph monitoring over a span of two or three years).

There is an unpleasant issue that can be of concern to the polygraph examiner. Simply, that, because of his or her efforts to gather information about offender activities, some men can become angry and resentful to the point of retaliation. This examiner has experienced an attempt by an offender to sabotage the examiner's vehicle steering linkage, an act that could have caused a serious accident. There have been instances of vandalism at the examiner's home, and an occasional threatening call left on voice mail. To minimize this kind of retaliation, it is very important to maintain a calm, even temperament with the offenders, with no display of anger, disgust, or condemnation. There are times when the examiner's interrogation requires a firmness of voice and demeanor, but never to the point of raising his or her voice or using insulting language.

Adult Females

Testing adult women in sexual offense matters is somewhat easier than testing adult men. To begin with, they are prone to be less resentful and angry. Most female offenders have admitted their offenses, and have already developed a degree of remorse and shame. This examiner has noticed a decided shift in attitudes of adult females from that of their male counter-parts. Seldom are they rude or confrontational. They present a more respectful, compliant, and cooperative demeanor and are willing to more openly discuss their offenses. There is far less tendency to blame someone else for what they have done, and they seem more able to accept a high degree of personal accountability for what they have done. Female offenders appear more attentive to the requirements in providing a sexual history of their contacts. Seldom do they appear for the testing without having completed the necessary full-disclosure forms.

The testing of female offenders requires that they are under video observation by a member of the office staff. The potential for charges of improper touching of the offender is always present. Offenders should be asked if they mind if the session is observed by camera or taped, and their attention should be directed to the obvious camera. In this examiner's experience no one has ever objected. This provides a strong deterrent against allegations of misconduct by the examiner.

Finally, the potential for retaliation against an examiner is slight. Most female adult offenders who have failed the polygraph test tend to confess their misbehavior, whether it is in a full disclosure or maintenance test.

Adolescent Males

The average adolescent male can be a challenge for the polygraph examiner. First, the examiner must explain in detail how polygraph works, and the procedures involved in taking the test. One of the persistent problems in testing adolescents is in getting them to keep still during the testing. Adolescents, generally between the ages of twelve and eighteen years old, can be flippant, rude, and even arrogant. Some of this is false bravado and can easily be identified by the alert examiner. An adolescent often feels that he must put on a macho front in order to appear fearless and manly.

And there can be an educational level problem. Definitions should be established for descriptions of sexual misbehavior. There are times when those definitions need to be written down and given to the adolescent to study and understand their use. There are many adolescents who have never heard of the word "vagina," requiring the examiner to use the word "pussy" instead. Some don't understand the word "anus," and the description of "butt hole" has to be substituted. Communication with the adolescent must be matter-of-fact and serious. There can be no joking or socializing, and it is important that the examiner does not permit vulgar and profane language from the adolescent. Polygraph testing of minors should involve the use of a release from the parent or legal guardian, authorizing the testing. All testing of minors should include video and/or audio recording.

Adolescent Females

There are relatively few adolescent females involved in sex-offender treatment and fewer yet who end up sitting in a polygraph chair for testing. The transitional period between puberty and adulthood for girls involves both family and peer influences that affect females on a different level than their male counterparts. There is more reluctance to report abuse for fear of not being believed. Although they do use some manipulation and control techniques over their victims, there is less force and aggression involved in their approach and grooming techniques (Mayer, 1992). This factor does allow them to rationalize that they did not really harm the victim.

The adolescent female polygraph examinee is generally far more compliant with the testing protocols than the adolescent male, and tends to be more forthright with the examiner. It is generally more needful to use clinical terms in describing sexual activities. Where the adolescent male has no hesitation to say "pussy" when referring to the vagina, the adolescent female is more apt to use the word "vagina." The adolescent male often refers to the sex act as "fucking." The female counterpart will say "doing it" or "having sex." It should be apparent that no testing should be done without video and audio recording.

Children

The testing of children is fraught with hazards to the examiner. There is an immediate issue of communication. Preadolescent vocabularies are not extensive. This requires careful consideration of age, education, and family background of the child. Most polygraph examiners are leery about such testing, and will refuse to test any child under the age of thirteen unless a full psychological profile is available to them. The lack of emotional maturity can bring immediate issues of being unable to follow directions for the testing. Some children are actually frightened by the thought of a polygraph test, even after the examiner provides a detailed explanation of the procedures. That fear can be disruptive to the point of causing inconclusive charts.

Successful polygraph testing involves the "fight-flight" concept that stirs a defensive mental posture in the examinee. This concept is not as well developed in the preadolescent and may seriously interfere with testing. The child must be able to sense and realize that telling a lie that will be readily recognized by the examiner presents a close and vivid danger to his or her well-being. So, there must be a reasonable expectation by the child that lying during the test will get him or her in serious trouble. The ability of the child to focus on the issue may not be developed enough to create the adrenalin rush of "fear of getting caught."

There is no law against testing children on the polygraph, but there is a consensus among sex-offender treatment professionals that the limited experience, knowledge, and vocabularies of preadolescents create communication difficulties that need careful and studied consideration. A clear caveat in testing children is the potential for introducing information and vocabulary to them that is actually detrimental to their current maturity levels. Some language and explanations required in polygraph testing can be damaging to their concepts of sexuality. Premature introduction of such data to them is risky at best, and damaging at the worst. Few parents want their children to be exposed to sexual terms and words that are inconsistent with their sexual maturity. This makes full-disclosure polygraph testing for children a very questionable enterprise. Even specific-issue testing can require a vocabulary for accurate communication that may create new words and ideas that are not needed or wanted in the child's concepts of the world. The examiner's need to verbalize sexual activities for the child should utilize the child's language for sexual terms, but sometimes the definitions that must be understood by the child can reveal words and situations that ideally should not be a part of his or her current vocabulary.

The polygraph examiner carries a heavy responsibility in making a determination about whether to test the preadolescent, but as a general rule, testing for children under age thirteen is not advisable, and under twelve is borderline. Above all, there must be absolute agreement from parents or legal custodians that such testing is needed, proper, and permissible. The child's legal parents or guardians must know how the polygraph testing is to be administered, the use of certain words and terms, and the possibility that the child will be subjected to terminology and information that he or she may not have been known or experienced before.

SUMMARY

Polygraph testing is essential to the treatment of sexually aggressive adults, adolescents, and children who are at least twelve years of age. Children under twelve years of age are not considered testable. A sex-offender treatment program will rely upon the results of polygraph testing to determine if treatment is merited, and what type of therapy would be most successful with the juvenile offender. In addition, polygraph testing is useful in promoting admission of offenders who deny an offense, and in the monitoring of their behavior while in the program.

EXERCISE 17.1. PRETEST INTERVIEW

1. What is your residence address?

   _____

   _____

2. Do you rent or own the house where are you living? Or, do you live with someone else, like parents or friends? Does anyone else live in the house with you? Any minors? Who are they? What are their ages?

   _____

   _____

3. What is your weight, height, date of birth, and present age?

   _____

   _____

4. What is your Social Security number?

   _____

   _____

5. What are your home and work telephone numbers?

   _____

   _____

6. How far have you gone in school?

   _____

   _____

7. Are you employed, and if so, what is the name of your employer, employer's address, length of employment, and job title?

   _____

   _____

8. What are your criminal convictions, both felonies and misdemeanors?

_____

_____

9. Have you ever had a polygraph test before? Did you pass that test? If no, why not?

_____

_____

10. How is your general health? Do you have any sexually transmitted diseases? Are you taking any medication? If so, what dosage, and for what health problems? Pulse and blood pressure?

_____

_____

11. Have you had any heart problems?

_____

_____

12. Have you had any emotional or nerve problems?

_____

_____

13. Have you had any pills, drugs, marijuana, or alcohol in the past twelve hours?

_____

_____

14. Have you ever been an alcoholic? What is your history of using illegal drugs?

_____

_____

15. Are you experiencing any pain or discomfort now?

_____

_____

EXERCISE 17.2. SEXUAL INVENTORY LIST

PLEASE PRINT

Name: _____   Today's Date: _____

HISTORY OF SEXUAL CONTACTS

#	Date of Contact	Your Age Then	First Name of Contact	Age of Person	Sexual Activity	No. of Times?
1.						
2.						
3.						

(Sexual contact list may include hundreds of partners.)

Chapter 18

Relapse-Prevention Plan

A relapse-prevention plan is an important part of the recovery and treatment received. The plan is a self-control program that enables the patient to learn techniques to combat the risk of relapse. The patient learns how to anticipate potential pitfalls and focus on changing those thoughts, feelings, impulses, and behaviors that created an environment in which offending was acceptable to the patient (Steen, 2001). See Exercise 18.1 for a sample plan.

Relapse prevention was first developed for addictive behaviors, but has been modified to fit a sex-offender treatment program (Flora, 2001). The plan comprises cognitive and behavioral therapies (Flora, 2001). It's important to understand that the sex offender will be in group therapy from one to two hours each week. The rest of the time the patient will be away from the therapist and probation officer. It is important that he or she has a plan to help them understand issues related to individual stresses, emotions, and high-risk situations and most important to avoid relapse (Jenkins-Hall et al., 1989).

It is crucial that the patient take personal responsibility for the plan. Without the personal responsibility from the patient, no plan or treatment will be effective. Once patients buy into the program, the plan becomes less like something that they have to do to be in compliance with program rules and becomes more like a part of their lives. In essence, they follow the plan not because they have to, but because it becomes a part of their focus to do what is needed to avoid having any more victims. Relapse prevention provides a level of confrontation and requires that they accept responsibility and accountability. The relapse-prevention plan also introduces the idea of victim empathy, which is a concept that they may not have focused on before they entered therapy. It is critically important that the patient begin to understand the damage that they have caused their victim(s).

Before going any further, it is important for therapists to understand that the relapse-prevention model is not foolproof. Special considerations as to the intellectual functioning of the offender; the severity of sexual offending, the motivation of the offender, or why some offenders continue to offend after knowing the model should be closely assessed (Birgeden, Owens, and Raymond, 2003).

The relapse-prevention model works best with providing internal and external motivations. The internal components are the ideas, principles, thoughts, feelings, and behaviors that you as the therapist are helping the offender understand to tailor a relapse-prevention plan. The external component of relapse prevention involves supervision in the community to insure that the changes are being followed (Birgeden, Owens, and Raymond, 2003).

Another important aspect of the plan is that the offenders understand their reoffense chain. Such a chain starts off very slowly, developing step-by-step until their version of reality becomes distorted and the unthinkable turns into inappropriate fantasies and becomes a form of grooming and gaining access to their victim. The reoffense chain is a subject that both therapist and patient should become proficient at understanding. The chain clearly illustrates how the patient was able to go from abstinence to relapse.

Sex-Offender Therapy
© 2008 by The Haworth Press, Taylor & Francis Group. All rights reserved.
doi:10.1300/5753_18

Relapse for a sex offender is never an option. Every sex-offender treatment provider should have the philosophy of no more victims. At some point the idea of no more victims should become part of the patients' focus in and out of treatment. As patients become more confident and understand that working a treatment program will keep them from having more victims, they will be able to explore the issues that led to their offense. They should be able to identify the specific areas of the reoffense chain and point out the distorted views that were made each step of the way. Steen (2001) describes each step of the offense chain that the patient passes through in the process.

1. *Abstinence*—At this stage the patient is offense-free and is not having any thoughts or feelings about offending. The word abstinence does not mean that the patient is staying away from healthy and consensual relationships with appropriate adult partners.
2. *Seemingly unimportant decisions (SUD)*—At this step, the patient makes a decision that seems harmless, but actually puts the person at risk for making a decision that will put him or her in a risky situation. As an example of an SUD, an adult male (Dennis) is driving through another state on a business trip and decides to pick up a female hitchhiker (Ann) out of the rain.
3. *Risky situation*—This step is half-way to offending. The patient places him or her self in a risky situation through the distorted views that he or she is starting to develop about the victim(s). At this point, Dennis is alone in the car with Ann and smells his favorite perfume coming from her and notices that she is very attractive.
4. *Lapse*—A behavior that places the patient closer to committing a sexual offense or a fantasy about committing a sexual offense. Dennis finds that he is becoming sexually aroused by Ann and begins to fantasize about touching her breasts and having sexual intercourse with her. He tells himself that no one would ever find out because he's not from the area.
5. *Abstinence violation effect/giving up (AVE)*—At this point the patient is dangerously close to offending. This is the stage that the patient decides that he or she has gone too far and that there is no use in turning back. Dennis reaches over and touches Ann's breast. She becomes panicked and tells him to leave her alone. At this point, Dennis begins to think that he's going to be in trouble anyway, so why not.
6. *Offense*—A crime has taken place. Another victim has been created. The patient has decided to do some type of illegal sexual activity that involves a minor or nonconsenting partner. Dennis pulls the car over and rapes Ann.

PERSONAL SAFETY PLAN

Locating and changing maladaptive cognitions are an important aspect of sex-offender treatment, as most offenders do not understand the difference between appropriate and inappropriate or distorted thought processes. The clinician must provide clients with correct, more affective alternatives. Offenders must learn how their thoughts determine their feelings and ultimately influence the resulting actions. Most adults realize that distorted thoughts learned in childhood change over time or with maturity; however, for some, cognitive distortions block the development of appropriate mature rationale. Offenders are taught to utilize these learned skills, concentrate on how the senses interpret certain situations, and find positive ways in which to steer their actions. Offenders must incorporate a commitment to a lifestyle of sexual abstinence throughout sex-offender treatment, which provides them with an uninterrupted time for self-reflection.

Examining the offense chains provides offenders with the noted triggers, which produce inadequate responses to distorted thoughts and then spirals into reoffending behaviors. Offenders must create an individualized reoffense chain, which provides them with specific details of how their behaviors develop. Having this reference allows offenders the ability to see the antecedents that lead to their offending behaviors and results in encouraging self-exploration. During this exploration, offenders develop another list of alternatives to their distorted thoughts and feelings, which are unique and provide a guideline for future reference.

Knowing what behaviors and situations to avoid in advance will encourage offenders to create ways to escape similar situations, thus putting a block into the cycle of relapsing behaviors. Those seemingly unimportant decisions (SUD) can put offenders into risky positions, which begin their reoffending chains.

Offenders forget to recall the self-talk methods of the escape and avoidance system that was taught in the beginning of treatment. Offenders in treatment are taught that acknowledging ways to escape probable situations can reinforce avoiding sexual reoffending behaviors from happening. Using this self-talk can provide offenders with necessary preventative measures to use in times of relapse. The clinician can utilize specific exercises for the offenders to complete each week, which will strengthen their cognitive abilities to recall their answers during future high-risk times. Using self-talk and changing "stinking thinking" will provide offenders with alternative thought processes to utilize during these risky situations.

A personal safety card should be completed. The patient is to carry this card at all times. A personal safety plan is outlined in Exercise 18.2.

The group member who keeps his or her workbooks and journal will benefit in the future. This manual will provide personalized accounts and self-talk statements to recall when a future high-risk need arises. All reading materials suggested for the client to purchase encourages developing a personal library of worthy resources for a lifelong recovery process.

SUMMARY

The tools used in sex-offender treatment are vital to recovery over a lifetime. The goal of sex-offender treatment is to assist the offender in creating an effective relapse-prevention plan consisting of tools to use throughout his or her recovery. The ultimate responsibility of recovery falls upon the offender; however, providing the necessary treatment tools (used to extinguish possible reoffending behaviors) is the essential job of an effective provider in the recovery process.

Clients create relapse-prevention plans specific to their offense, levels of personal responsibility, needs, thoughts, and feelings. These unique formats diagram precise details of the offenders' old fantasies and behaviors and provide more positive alternatives. The group members also must provide detailed lists of their support system contacts, which become a lifeline in times of risk. The plan ends with the offender stating that he or she is dedicated to having no more victims and commited to implementing this plan for the rest of his or her life.

EXERCISE 18.1. RELAPSE-PREVENTION PLAN

Name: _____

Probation Officer's Name: _____

Therapist's Name: _____

Date: _____

Your relapse-prevention plan is a work in progress. The plan focuses on particular thoughts, feelings, and behaviors that were part of your offense chain and how you can avoid falling back into the same patterns and having the same distorted views before your offense. Spend time working on this plan inside and outside of the group to insure that you have the best opportunity at success in your recovery.

1. Acknowledgment (discuss what you did to your victim): _____

    _____

    _____

    _____

2. Responsibility (discuss your responsibility in your offense and to your victim): _____

    _____

    _____

    _____

3. Triggers are anything (i.e., issues, events, and/or feelings) that cause you to give up and potentially lead to having a victim through sexual offending. Look at your life and identify the biggest triggers that you are dealing with at this time. _____

    _____

    _____

    _____

4. Stressors are the thoughts, feelings, and behaviors that you have allowed, making you more prone to committing your offense. These are not excuses for you, but can be risk factors that add to why you sexually offended another person. Name at least five stressors that you were experiencing at the time of your offense. _____

    _____

    _____

    _____

5. What stressors are you dealing with at this time? Name at least five. _____

    _____

    _____

    _____

6. Grooming behaviors are those behaviors that you used to get you closer to your victim. Oftentimes you befriended the victim and his or her family in some way in order to gain their trust and make it easier to have access to your victim. Briefly discuss what you did to groom your victim. _____

    _____

    _____

    _____

7. Describe the events that led up to your offense._____

    _____

    _____

    _____

8. How long in advance had you planned your offense?_____

_____

_____

_____

9. In what ways did you try to get close to your victim before the offense?_____

_____

_____

_____

10. Explain the specific types of feelings that you had toward your victim before your offense._____

_____

_____

_____

11. What specific types of feelings did you have toward your victim after your offense?

_____

_____

_____

12. Did you know your victim before the offense? _____

_____

_____

_____

13. What was it about your victim that drew you to him or her (physical features, age range, personality type, etc.)? _____

_____

_____

14. What were the reasons that you chose your victim (e.g., easy access)? _____

_____

_____

_____

15. Did you have fantasies about your victim before your offense? _____

_____

_____

_____

16. Did your fantasies about your victim end with masturbation? _____

_____

_____

_____

17. Do you still have fantasies about your victim? Explain your answer. _____

_____

_____

_____

18. What feelings are you currently having about what you have done mentally, emotionally, and spirituality to your victim? _____

_____

_____

_____

19. In what ways are you making amends for the harm that you have caused your victim?

_____

_____

_____

20. If you have the impulse to offend again, what are some positive ways that you can stop these desires (e.g., stop and think before you act)? _____

_____

_____

_____

21. What are some appropriate ways that you can reduce your stress? _____

_____

_____

_____

22. In what ways has your offense changed your relationship with your family and friends?

_____

_____

_____

23. High-risk situations—Just as a recovering alcoholic should not order dinner in a bar, you should not attend places or see people that are likely to cause additional stress and/or be a trigger for you, which will lead to a situation that is considered high risk for you. Being in a high-risk situation does not automatically mean that you will reoffend; however, your risk goes up considerably. It's important that you view your high-risk situations as warning signals that are there to alert you of the danger. It's critical that you remember the risks that surrounded your offense.

a. Where did your offense occur (e.g., at a local department store, playground, or in your home)? _____

_____

_____

b. What was your thought process like at the time of your offense (e.g., fantasies of your victim)?

_____

_____

_____

c. Explain what type of relationship (if any) that you had at the time of your offense (e.g., single, happily married, or you had broken up with your girlfriend or boyfriend).

_____

_____

_____

d. What was your emotional well-being like at the time of your offense (e.g., confident, happy, depresed, feeling sorry for yourself, or angry)? _____

_____

_____

_____

e. What stresses were you dealing with (or not dealing with) at the time of your offense (e.g., financial difficulties, relationship difficulties, or work difficulties)? _____

_____

_____

_____

f. What are your plans to change these thoughts, feelings, and conditions to avoid (as much as possible) high-risk situations in the future? _____

_____

_____

_____

g. How did you convince yourself that what you were doing was OK (e.g., it happened to me or she or he agreed to it)? _____

_____

_____

_____

24. It is important that you have a plan in place for what you will do in the likelihood that you end up in a high-risk situation unintentionally. What are your plans if you find yourself in a situation that is considered high-risk for you? _____

_____

_____

_____

25. Your life has been without a positive direction since you allowed yourself to harm another person. It is important that you have goals for your life. Briefly write three goals that you hope to accomplish in the next year in treatment. These goals can focus on anything in your life that will take you in a positive direction.

Goal # 1: _____

Goal # 2: _____

Goal # 3: _____

26. How will you accomplish these goals?_____

_____

_____

_____

27. How will you know when you have reached your goals?_____

_____

_____

_____

28. Who in your life can you use as a support to help you when you are having difficulties (i.e., friends, church leader, and/or the group)?_____

_____

_____

_____

29. In what ways are you willing and/or motivated to make positive steps to avoid re-offending?_____

_____

_____

_____

30. By the time that you have finished treatment what do you hope will be different about your life?_____

_____

_____

_____

I realize that before this relapse-prevention plan or my recovery can work in my life, I must be willing to be honest with myself and look at all of the unmanageability in my life. I must show personal responsibility, honesty, and strive to live my life without sexual misconduct. I must admit to what I did and express genuine victim empathy and remorse. I understand that there will be consequences if I reoffend. I also realize that if I reoffend, I will create another generation of victims. I pledge that I will have no more victims. I make this promise to the group members, the community that I live in, the victims that I have created, and to myself, one day at a time, for the rest of my life.

Client Signature	*Date Signed*
_____	_____
Therapist Signature	*Date Signed*
_____	_____
Probation or Parole Officer Signature	*Date Signed*
_____	_____

EXERCISE 18.2. PERSONAL SAFETY PLAN

Please carry this card at all times.

1. My triggers are as follows (list as many as needed):

   _____

2. My high-risk situations are (list as many as needed):

   _____

3. My interventions are as follows (list as many as needed):

   _____

4. My support persons are as follows (list as many as needed):

   _____

Chapter 19

The Treatment of Sexually Aggressive Youth

GETTING STARTED

Referrals of children and adolescents who engage in sexually inappropriate behavior typically come from three main sources: social workers, juvenile probation officers, and parents. In most cases, all three parties present with concern and confusion about the etiology of the behavior in such a young person. Frequently asked questions include, "Do you think that's normal?" or "Do you think somebody must have done something to him or her?" Parents are not only puzzled, they're devastated and present with anger, shame, and humiliation. Some parents reject their sexually aggressive child while others rationalize and minimize.

The first session provides the therapist an opportunity to meet the child and his or her caregivers. Initial sessions are also an opportunity for the patient and his or her parents to ask questions and raise concerns. If the patient has contact with potential victims, their safety is addressed. The psychosexual evaluation is useful in organizing all of the patient information. Depending on the age and participation of all parties, the clinical interview will be completed within ninety minutes to two hours. Every effort should be made to interview the family members separately and together. The testing that follows may be scheduled later that day or broken up into intervals. Patients with a short attention span benefit from many short testing sessions rather than making a day of it.

Once the evaluation process is done, the testing results and conclusions are documented. The patient and his or her family should be informed of the findings and recommendations in person since the report itself creates new questions and concerns. If a recommendation is made for treatment, the logical next step is to identify for the patient and his or her caregivers both the diagnosis and the nature of the treatment. Some facilities offer both individual and group treatment while others offer only one or the other.

If family therapy is recommended, a general discussion of the expectations of each family member may require some explanation. Repeat polygraphs may also be part of the treatment protocol (for adolescents) and may require a separate fee. If so, discussing this additional expectation and expenditure early on is highly recommended. If a psychiatric evaluation is warranted, the referral process should be initiated as soon as possible. Because sex-offender treatment tends to be insight-oriented, the mental status of the patient significantly influences outcome. Other general requirements are also addressed, such as attendance and participation. Consequences for treatment noncompliance merit careful discussion with all parties clear on the facility's policies. Ask the patient to sign a written statement of these matters and retain a copy.

Many caregivers shift their attention at this point to treatment efficacy. They ask, "Can you make him or her stop this?" or "How long will it take?" Other questions relate to how far the child has deviated from the norm with questions such as, "Could this just be a stage?" or a remark like, "I didn't know kids could do such things!" A recent study indicates that minors make up approximately 17 percent of arrests in the United States (Righthand and Welch, 2001). The

Sex-Offender Therapy

doi:10.1300/5753_19

137

majority of these perpetrators are from twelve to seventeen years old, yet studies reflect that sexual aggression has been documented by children as young as four (Cavanaugh-Johnson, 1998). Actual numbers of juvenile sex offenders are difficult to estimate given that many offenses are never reported.

SELECTING A TREATMENT MODALITY

Whether or not there is a rise in sexual offending by young people is uncertain. An alternative explanation is that our legal, cultural, and clinical atmosphere may just now be able to acknowledge the phenomenon. In either case, the treatment these young people receive has the potential to alter not only the course of their lives, but the lives of every would-be victim and their families. Uniform Crime Report data showed that arrest rates for murder, forcible rape, robbery, and aggravated assault were higher for older teens than for *any* other age group (Federal Bureau of Investigation, 2000). Consider also that selecting the most effective treatment modality to address not only the act of sexual aggression but any underlying problem is fundamental. Much of the work with sexually aggressive youth focuses on nonsexual diagnoses. The Center for Sex Offender Management identifies numerous areas of comorbid dysfunction in the lives of young sex offenders, including poor impulse control, impaired judgment, learning disabilities, and mental illness (1999). Other studies find familial links to child sexual aggression (Deranek and Gilman, 2003). Researchers have associated sexual misconduct in children with exposure to pornography, substance abuse and family violence (Ryan and Lane, 1997). While the clinician may experience pressure from parents, the courts, and social service agencies to spend every moment of treatment time on sex-offender specific topics, the reality is that sexual functioning does not develop within a vacuum and is not treated in one.

INDIVIDUAL THERAPY

Weekly, one-hour sessions with children and adolescents are generally an effective option. The regular contact aids in building the therapeutic relationship and establishing the significance of the inappropriate behavior. This schedule enables young people to recall work from the previous session while allowing adequate time to complete therapeutic homework assignments. There are several advantages to individual therapy as compared to group or family work. For instance, individual patients do not have to compete for time or attention. They risk no ridicule, teasing, or retaliation. No one is present to support their rationalizations or minimizations. They have no opportunity to learn new ways of offending. The only person with whom to form an alliance is the therapist.

Disadvantages of individual therapy are also apparent, however. One is that children's lives are part of a system. No matter how well patients respond during the sessions, uninvolved parents or other caregivers run the risk of contradicting the therapist or otherwise impeding progress. Caregivers who are not part of the treatment alliance cannot be expected to understand and apply the concepts, even when they have the best of intentions.

GROUP THERAPY

In many adolescent programs, group therapy is often recommended for the treatment of youthful offenders. Advocates of this modality contend that peers effectively confront one another and do not tolerate defense mechanisms. Group members who are more advanced in treatment may also serve as role models for those who struggle. The adolescent notion of invincibility is countered effectively by patients who are eager to point out that they were caught and punished. Certainly, the cost effectiveness of group therapy is obvious for both patients and provider. A single therapist could conceivable treat more than fifty patients in an eight-hour day versus seven or eight individually. The fee for each group member would consequently be considerably less, with potentially positive implications for attendance and completion of the program. The group therapist may manage a much higher number of cases, which means not having to "wait-list" patients who need immediate attention.

Yet, group therapy has its limitations. The opportunity to learn about new ways to groom victims and to offend is arguably the most serious drawback. Therapists who treat sex offenders are well aware of the potential for them to become aroused as they recount details of the misconduct. In group therapy, the young person is inundated with stories members tell of one perverse sex act after another (as part of acknowledging the offending). These detailed accounts have the potential to desensitize the group members and to normalize such behaviors (by the sheer fact that sexual misconduct is typical among these group members who may be admired, respected, and emulated).

The potential negative influence of being in a group of sex offenders is illuminated by considering its impact on a child who has mental health or behavioral concerns that exclude sexual misconduct. Few therapists would advocate exposing a relatively sexually healthy minor to the details of offenders' thoughts, feelings, and behaviors. Opponents of group treatment for sex offenders contend that both offenders and nonoffenders are negatively impacted by repeated exposure to explicit details of others' sexual misconduct. The possibility also exists that the same dynamics that predisposed the offending patient to act out in the first place may also make him or her *more* vulnerable to the exposure during group sessions.

FAMILY THERAPY

Clinicians who utilize family therapy recognize the identified patient as part of a system. The underlying assumption to family work is that changes in one member necessitate changes in everyone else within the system. The concept is similar to Newton's law of physics, which states that for every action there is an equal and opposite reaction (Kanel, 2003). Whether or not family dysfunction precipitated the offending, the impact on family life is significant. Family therapists work with any individual or system which has contributed to the problem or may be a resource for the solution (Franklin and Jordan, 2001). Consequently, family therapists involve family members, the legal system, social services agencies, school personnel, and any other party whose interaction with the identified client may impact his or her treatment outcome. The treatment may include psychoeducation, behavior-management strategies, skills training, and cognitive interventions.

The family systems approach is difficult for some parents in that it focuses on changes that need to be made on a daily basis. The idea that their offending child will be "fixed and returned" is very seductive. Some parents balk at the notion that they share the burden of treatment. Other parents assume *full* responsibility for preventing further offending. Their tendency is to develop a myopic view of family life as revolving around the offender and his or her risk to recidivate. Behavioral disruption of the other children adds stress to the marriage and further contributes to the household's anxiety level. The offending child copes with the overwhelming anxiety by acting out sexually. The patient (and often the family) point to the sexual misconduct as the singular cause of the family's undoing. Yet, from a systems perspective, no one person or event is responsible. The behavior cannot be understood apart from the context in which it occurs (Robbins and Szapocnik, 2000).

When utilizing this sort of scenario with a family, the clinician must emphasize that accountability is not diffused. Each person remains accountable for his or her actions and reactions. The point of family work is to empower each person to make positive changes, *not to saddle anyone with guilt for having unwittingly caused bad behavior in others.* This point is critical and may require a lot of attention.

The advantages of family therapy are many. The entire family benefits from understanding the etiology of the offending and measures for relapse prevention. A strong family supports its members and provides the emotional stability that allows for personal growth and change. The advantages of a strong family system to any child, offender or not, are too numerous to catalog here. The point being made is that offenders who reside with their families cannot sustain significant change without the involvement and support of the family members.

One problem with providing family therapy to child and adolescent sex offenders is that the families have often dissolved long before the referral for treatment is ever made. Many times, social service agencies have been court-ordered to provide guardianship for these young people. The new family system is often a children's home or a string of foster-care placements. Even when family reunification is a goal and families remain essentially in tact, there tends to be a lack of motivation from at least one parent who misses sessions due to work demands, chronic illness, or any number of other reasons.

TREATMENT PITFALLS

Very few elements of sex-offender treatment are formulaic. Adolescent workbooks, relapse-prevention plans, and safety plans are common elements. Yet, the process of completing them varies greatly. Treating juvenile offenders requires constant awareness on the part of the therapist with regard to developmental, educational, and intellectual limitations. Keeping clinical expectations in line with patient potential (which is in a constant state of flux) prevents unnecessary frustration. Furthermore, delineating clinical from nonclinical work may prove difficult. For example, children who greatly dislike reading and writing are not going to cheerfully complete workbook assignments. Their failure to do the assigned worksheets may either relate to treatment resistance or to a sense of incompetence academically. They already have school work they're not completing, what's another workbook page added to the stack? Some of these individuals are free to focus on the content only when the therapist demonstrates some flexibility and reads the information aloud during sessions. The therapist may write the answers for the patient if this is an issue. Therapy is challenging enough without placing undue emphasis on the academics of reading and writing or any other nonclinical area.

Group therapy for sex offenders was started for adults. Although the treatment is effective for an adult population, certain treatment techniques are not found helpful in working with adolescents and children. Youth are not as able to give to one another as compared to adults. They are still in the developmental process. Also, sharing is more difficult for youth in a group setting and recovery is impacted. There have been studies on substance abuse adolescent groups and change is not found in such settings. One is more concerned about being accepted by the peer group than making a constructive change. It takes an ego that is more developed that can tolerate being separate from others and being different. Family therapy, in which the youth can let his or her guard down, is far more effective.

SUMMARY

The treatment of sexually aggressive youth requires a holistic approach to the individual client's clinical needs, the limitations presented by his or her developmental level, and family dynamics. To further complicate matters, legal and educational limitations must also be considered. A real-world approach to treatment planning also takes into consideration the availability of specialized clinicians, treatment facilities, and the client's ability to meet the financial demands of treatment. Geographic location may also create treatment barriers that preclude one type of treatment or another. This chapter has identified various advantages and limitations of treatment choices including individual, family, and group work. The goal is that each young client's treatment plan be developed with great care and with full knowledge of each option so that, at the very least, the treatment process itself will do no harm.

Chapter 20

Sexual Recovery for Children and Adolescents

This chapter explores sexually aggressive children and adolescents and conceptualization of their victims and the strategic use of "victim work" to address offender remorse and accountability. Sexual recovery therapy, a building-block therapy, aims to change cognitive distortions and increase victim empathy. Learning to view victims and potential victims as multidimensional individuals rather than as sex objects requires a paradigm shift that is not easily achieved. Leading the youth through this process requires the therapist to be well aware of the pitfalls and possess a willingness to constantly guard against the offender's faulty, yet highly seductive reasoning.

REMORSE

Importance

Remorse, or a sense of guilt for doing wrong, cannot be demonstrated in treatment by a patient who lacks the four building blocks for this therapeutic work: insight, moral development, willingness to work in treatment, and trust. One underpinning of remorse is true emotional insight—accepting that he or she has done wrong and for reasons that are inherent to his or her psychosexual makeup and by his or her own choice.

If the child client does not acknowledge the behavior or does not acknowledge that the behavior was wrong or that it was by choice, then he or she could not logically feel remorse for that behavior. Therefore, growing in terms of moral development hinges on the patient's attitude toward treatment and willingness to engage with the therapist in a trusting therapeutic alliance (the issue of trust is also discussed in the developmental chapter). Patients who approach others with a sense of mistrust are at a therapeutic disadvantage across the board. They tend to have shallow relationships that impede treatment progress. They easily view their victims as cardboard figures devoid of human traits, in part because their conceptualization of their own value is so skewed.

Treatment and change are difficult and generally are not sought unless the discomfort of the status quo outweighs the discomfort associated with change. An exception is the court-ordered sexually aggressive child or adolescent who enters treatment for a more pragmatic reason—to avoid prison. Youth who participate in treatment because of a genuine sense of remorse are intrinsically motivated for change.

The Therapist's Role

When working with a sexually aggressive child or adolescent who lacks remorse, the therapist must attempt to address the specific deficits as outlined previously (i.e., insight, moral development, willingness to form a therapeutic alliance with the clinician, and capacity for trust). If the clinician observes that the client has a basic lack of trust in others, for example, an immediate goal

Sex-Offender Therapy
© 2008 by The Haworth Press, Taylor & Francis Group. All rights reserved.
doi:10.1300/5753_20

(which will not be immediately achieved) is to form a trusting therapeutic alliance. The most significant barrier is that the offending patient's suspicious behaviors will have to be reported to the authorities (critical to maintaining public safety).

Establishing a trusting relationship with an already untrusting individual under these conditions is daunting. In addition, a therapist who is highly confrontational with this sort of patient risks proving to the patient that his or her assumptions about others are right: "Nobody really cares about me anyway. There's no point in trying." Patients who have a low emotional tolerance for confrontation feel battered in these sorts of groups and subsequently try to avoid attendance and participation.

One avenue for establishing trust is to convey empathy and compassion to the patient. Yet, there is a risk of appearing to empathize with the offending behavior or endorsing the cognitive distortions offered by the offender. For instance, youth and adolescents who were themselves victims of sexual offenses are often keenly aware of the predisposing factor that victimization has on offending. They make the leap to a *causal* relationship and blame their own sexual victimization for their bad behavior. Sexually aggressive individuals who were once sex abuse victims cannot be expected to recognize and process the damage they have done to others if they have not yet recognized and processed the damage done to them. Experiencing their own pain within the confines of a safe therapeutic relationship provides the victimized offender with a reference point for empathizing with his or her victim. A child or adolescent who denies the significance of his or her own pain cannot be expected to endorse the pain of others.

The therapist who offers empathy and encouragement in no way endorses the offending or accepts the offender's tendency to excuse his or her behavior as a natural consequence of the victimization. The point is made repeatedly that many victims of sexual harm never commit sex offenses or any other offenses for that matter.

Remorse-Building Exercises

A letter that is written by an offender to a victim is not necessarily mailed. Sent letters are most appropriate in family reunification work and are not indicated in cases such as stranger sexual assault, stalking, or in other cases that do not necessitate any further contact between the victim and offender. Unsent letters, on the other hand, are free from legal and clinical restrictions and have a great deal of therapeutic value in treatment. Some of the options for letter writing are discussed in the following text along with Exercises 20.1 and 20.2.

The Victim's Voice Letter

This youth's written letter is intended to help the client develop insight and remorse. In this letter, the perpetrator writes a letter to him or her self from the point of view of the victim.

The Letter of Apology

A second type of letter that is useful in treatment is the offender's letter of apology to the victim. Herein, the patient acknowledges the events and apologizes. This type of letter is often not intended to be mailed.

Letters from Victims

Actual letters from victims are provided for clinical use. The perpetrators are instructed to read the victim letters aloud during group sessions and to compare the emotional tone and honesty of their letters to these from actual victims. Discuss how realistically the patients' letters portrayed victims' thoughts and feelings (both during and after the offending).

PROBLEMS VICTIMS WILL ENCOUNTER

As addressed in the beginning of this chapter, victims are a highly heterogeneous group who will react in countless ways. Not every victim will show signs of having been abused while others' lives will appear to revolve around that moment or period in time. After being sexually victimized, an individual may (or may not) exhibit any number of reactions, including but not limited to the following:

- sexual promiscuity/sexual misconduct
- loss of interest in sexual activity
- depressed mood
- sleep disturbance
- flashbacks
- social withdrawal
- difficulty meeting work/social demands
- increase in substance use/abuse
- suicidal and homicidal impulses
- increase in reckless behaviors
- weight loss/weight gain
- marital/relational problems
- inability to achieve emotional intimacy
- dependency in relationships

Ask the patient to identify problems victims will encounter. After recording the list, go back and encourage discussion regarding how the offense contributes to the problem.

Twenty Years Later (Letter from Victim's Viewpoint)

This is another letter written by the sex offender from the point of view of the victim. The time frame for this letter is twenty years past the date of the offending. Having addressed the numerous ways that sexual victimization can impact human life in the previous exercises, the offender has an opportunity in this letter to integrate his or her knowledge with an expression of true emotional insight and remorse.

Legends and Myths of Victims

1. Sexually victimized individuals will become sex offenders.

While sexual victimization is a predisposing factor, it *does not cause* sexual offending. Sex offenders as victims are addressed by Rudy Flora in *How to Work with Sex Offenders: A Handbook for Criminal Justice, Human Service, and Mental Health Professionals* (2001). He postulates that while there is some clinical and empirical evidence to suggest a relationship between sexual offending and prior victimization, the actual numbers are not consistently reported. He notes rates of offenders reporting prior victimization as ranging from 33 percent (Groth, 1990) to 40 percent (Greenberg, Bradford, and Curry, 1993). In either case, the majority of offenders were not identified as having been victimized. Victims of sexual abuse may, for example, become attorneys who specialize in prosecuting sex crimes or nurses who are rape counselors. Victims may become counselors who treat sex abuse victims or even offenders.

2. Victims of sexual assault either consciously or unconsciously brought it on themselves.

A popular cultural and clinical position documented as recently as the 1970s and 1980s holds that sexual victims share blame along with the offenders in the commission of the act (Slovenko, 1971; Sarles, 1975; Lukianowicz, 1972; Virkkunen, 1981). Until recently, the pre-offense cycle of sexual offending was obviously not clearly understood. The seductiveness offenders employed on their victims worked equally well on society at large. While it is true that the victim's appearance, behavior, and demeanor may ignite sexual interest in the offender, *the responsibility of reacting rests soley with the offender.*

3. Decent, intelligent people do not allow themselves or their children to become sexual victims.

The appeal of this myth is that it is comforting. Lumping victims into a category as separate from everyone else provides a false sense of safety and perhaps of superiority. Yet, when reviewing some victims of sexual assault since the beginning of recorded history, one is hard-pressed to identify what constitutes the "right" personality, appearance, faith, or profession. There's a well-known male psychologist, a philosopher, a writer, several actors and entertainers of both sexes and from all walks of life, and even a Miss America who have been victimized.

4. Victims of incest are less troubled than victims of stranger rape because they at least knew the perpetrator.

The logic of this myth is that incest victims get to avoid the element of fear that accompanies stranger sexual assault. The underlying assumption is that the abduction by a stranger is the most terrifying part of it all. The problems with this line of thinking are numerous. First, fear is commonly at the core of incest. There may be brutal violence, sophisticated seduction, or both. Whatever the methods of the offender, the typical victim who is aware that the assault has occurred will respond with fear. Second, when a stranger abducts and rapes, the surviving victim goes home to a safe and loving environment where nobody doubts the legitimacy of the abuse. The victim will likely be offered treatment and support. The incest victim, in contrast, lives at the offense site and often answers to the offender on a daily basis. Nobody acknowledges that anything out of the ordinary has happened. Certainly no treatment is sought. To make matters worse, the incest victim relies on his or her offender for food, clothing, and shelter, not to mention emotional and moral training. This brings up the third major difference in the two types of offenses. With stranger offenses, there are generally no long-term efforts to confuse the victim with regard to what's "right" and "wrong." When the parent, sibling, family friend, or caregiver offends, it is typically over a period of time with a great deal of effort going into convincing the victim that, "It's okay to do this as long as other people don't know about it."

5. Victims of sexual offenses can never really be happy again.

Early on, most victims would probably endorse this position of hopelessness. And it is true that life will never be the same after a sexual assault as it was before. Yet, people do heal and go on to lead happy, healthy lives with meaningful relationships, rewarding jobs, and loving families. More research is needed to bring these individuals into clearer focus.

SUMMARY

Remorse work is extremely important when working with sexually aggressive adults, adolescents, and children. In treating adolescents and children, denial is often found to be less of a problem. This patient group is more willing to admit to their offense when reported. Since developmental stages are still in formation, a therapist will need to be sensitive to the age group receiving treatment. In order to help, the importance of depersonalization and remorse should be explored. The clinician may use certain exercises to enhance victim empathy. Victim letters are often a part of the treatment process. In addition, it is essential that the sexually aggressive adolescent or child understands the physical and psychological harm the victim has experienced. Therapists are encouraged to go slow during this portion of therapy. Many sexually aggressive adolescents and children have been victims of sexual abuse themselves. As a result, work on victims' issues will be merited as well for the patient.

EXERCISE 20.1. THE VICTIM'S VOICE LETTER

Youth's Name: _____

Dear _____ (offender's name here):

Some of the things you said and did to me include: _____

_____

_____

_____

While it was happening, I did and felt the following (include more than anger): _____

_____

_____

_____

The worst part of it was: _____

_____

_____

_____

Because of what you did to me, I have these problems: _____

_____

_____

_____

When I think now of what you did to me, I feel: _____

_____

_____

_____

EXERCISE 20.2. THE LETTER OF APOLOGY

Youth's Name: _____

Dear _____ (victim's name here):

I admit that I (include all pre-offense, offense, and post-offense behaviors): _____

_____

_____

_____

At that time, I imagine you were feeling (include at least three emotions): _____

_____

_____

_____

I feel this way about what I did to you (include at least three emotions): _____

_____

_____

_____

My hope for your life is that you will: _____

_____

_____

_____

My promise to you is that: _____

_____

_____

_____

Chapter 21

Sexually Aggressive Children and Adolescents

TREATING CHILDREN

The number of sexually aggressive children in treatment has increased. Children who display sexual misconduct behaviors as early as three to twelve years of age are being referred for sexual-disordered therapy. Both boys and girls have increased in number with reported sexually aggressive behaviors. (See Appendix III for a case study of a sexually aggressive child.)

Younger youth do not respond to the typical forms of psychotherapy that are used for most other clinical models of therapy. It is important to recognize that most children who exhibit sexual aggression are most likely the victims of sexual trauma themselves. Therefore, the therapist is in a situation in which therapy should include both treatment for sexual acting out as well as victimization issues.

In order for a therapist to be of help to a sexual acting out child, the therapist must complete an extensive clinical psychosocial assessment. Treatment interventions for the sexual-acting child should be modified according to the child's age. As a therapist, you will need to assess yourself for the areas listed in Exercise 21.1.

A clinical diagnosis for the youth will be important. Some clinicians are reluctant to correctly diagnose a sexual-acting child with a disorder that may follow him or her in life. However, an actual clinical diagnosis is important for effective treatment.

Sexual recovery therapy does not always encourage immediate residential care. Damage to the attachment, bonding, and developmental process can occur if the child is removed and placed away from the family. Less-restrictive alternatives do exist. A therapeutic foster care home may permit the child to remain in the community close to the extended-family system. Only seriously dangerous children should be removed from a home or community if no local facilities exist. An inpatient psychiatric facility may be more appropriate. Such facilities are usually many miles from the home. In the event a psychiatric facility cannot be provided, residential care may be considered as an option.

Sexually aggressive children are a confusing patient population group for criminal justice, human services, and mental health professionals. A family systems model is effective in working with sexually aggressive youth. Also, the sexual recovery therapy model should be used. Work with a sexually aggressive child can be slow. It is important for the therapist to follow the extra protocol:

1. Build rapport
2. Use play therapy
3. Develop a behavioral plan
4. Refer a child for a psychiatric evaluation and the use of medications
5. Identify any specific triggers
6. Review high-risk situations

Sex-Offender Therapy
© 2008 by The Haworth Press, Taylor & Francis Group. All rights reserved.
doi:10.1300/5753_21

7. Provide education to the parents for their safety as well as other siblings
8. Use an alarm system at the home
9. The sexual-acting child should be considered for aversion therapies
10. Components of relapse prevention can be used
11. Supportive psychotherapy is helpful
12. Victimization issues will need to be discussed
13. Sessions should be weekly
14. The use of anatomical dolls should be used

In summary, it is expected that more children will be referred for treatment. In the past, many of these children were not asked if they had been sexually abused or their sexual acting out was not reported. The earlier the intervention and ability of the parents to work closely with a therapist, the greater the influence on the prognosis of the child. Research data is still limited about this patient group. Nevertheless, experienced clinicians report many successful outcomes for these children.

TREATING ADOLESCENTS

Sexually aggressive adolescents are much more articulate and verbal than children are. Again it is important to note that there appears to be an increase in both male and female adolescents with sexual misconduct disorders.

It is believed that sexual acting out is being reported more; girls are now receiving almost as much attention as boys. Most likely a lot of this psychopathology was going on in the past, but was being minimized. Regardless of the reasons, in this patient group there is more demand for skilled clinicians to help these impaired adolescents.

A number of excellent residential programs have been established to serve this patient group. Also, the correctional system has become more aware of the need to provide programs for incarcerated adolescents.

Sexual recovery therapy does not advocate the removal of sexually aggressive adolescents unless their risk level is viewed as high for a reoffense. It is always important to first try to treat the sexual-acting youth in the least restrictive setting possible. This does not mean the youth should not be held accountable for his or her crime.

Most sexually aggressive adolescents are found to have been victimized themselves, exposed to severe sexual incidents impacting their development, or are the product of a violent dysfunctional home. Sexual recovery therapy is recommended. Also, elements of cognitive-behavioral therapy, family therapy, relapse-prevention, and supportive psychotherapy is of use. (See Exercise 21.2.)

Longo (2004) reports that it is important to return to basics in the treatment process. Generosity, belonging, mastery, and independence are cited as key elements in helping male and female adolescents stabilize. Giving is not by money or gifts, but by learning to be emotionally intimate with another in a nonsexual way. Adolescents have lost a sense of connection with their family and feel separated and isolated. Being a part of a family or group and truly feeling a sense of belonging is essential. Everyone needs to have a sense of control and mastery in their lives. Independence, as well, is important to the stabilization process. Also, it is not encouraged that adolescent youth be referred to as sex offenders. This form of identification is not appropriate for this patient group.

In helping a sexual-acting adolescent stabilize, a sense of trust is also encouraged. The relationship between the therapist and patient is clinically important. Here in therapy a youth again is permitted to feel safe and grow. There should be an emphasis by the therapist for displaying compassion, genuineness, sincerity, and respect.

Certainly, the surface issues of relapse prevention should be attended to during therapy. As well, fantasy, distorted thinking, high-risk situations, lapse, and reoffending will need to be included in the treatment. Anger and rage may also merit work.

An adolescent is an emotional jungle. A therapist must be willing to tread carefully. Of course, he or she will make mistakes. It is important to admit to an error with an adolescent.

Clinical disorders are an issue. A psychiatric evaluation should be included, as should medications, if needed. Many of the adolescents have experienced problems with anxiety disorders, attention deficit disorder (ADD), attention-deficit hyperactivity disorder (ADHD), learning disorders NOS, impulse control disorders and mood disorders, as well as sexual disorders. Other possible issues include disruptive behavior disorder, conduct disorders, oppositional defiant disorder, and reactive attachment disorder (American Psychiatric Association, 2000).

A therapist will need to work with these issues in the therapeutic process. Also, the actual sexual disorder will need to be a part of treatment. Finally, the adolescent's sexual victimization or other trauma will need to be addressed.

Longo (2004) says enactment exercises are effective in the healing process. One may need to go slow. Flooding was once a type of therapy used to help patients overcome trauma. This can be dangerous if the sexual-acting patient is overwhelmed. Enacting and role-playing are appropriate ways to model behavior and are much less intrusive. This permits the patient to practice over and over again appropriate forms of behavior.

SUMMARY

Sexually aggressive adolescents, both boys and girls, appear to have increased in number. Treatment is important to help such youth not to reoffend. Specialized therapy techniques are recommended for this population group.

EXERCISE 21.1. THERAPIST SELF-ASSESSMENT
REGARDING WORK WITH CHILDREN

1. Do you enjoy working with children?

   Yes _____ No _____

2. What is your knowledge base concerning play therapy?

   Poor_____ Fair _____ Good _____ Excellent _____

3. As a therapist, are you able to help a parent develop a comprehensive plan?

   Yes _____ No _____

4. What is your skill level in family therapy?

   Poor _____ Fair _____ Good _____ Excellent _____

5. How versed are you in aversion therapy?

   Poor _____ Fair _____ Good _____ Excellent _____

6. What is your knowledge base concerning sexual-acting children?

   Poor _____ Fair _____ Good _____ Excellent _____

7. What is your knowledge base concerning victimization?

   Poor _____ Fair _____ Good _____ Excellent _____

EXERCISE 21.2. THERAPIST SELF-ASSESSMENT REGARDING WORK WITH ADOLESCENTS

1. What is your comfort level in working with sexually aggressive adolescents?

   _____

   _____

2. What patient group would you most prefer to treat? Male ___ Female ___

   Why? _____

   _____

3. Adolescents are well known for anger, experimentation, and resistance. How do you see yourself working with this patient group? _____

   _____

4. What is your experience with treating sexually aggressive adolescents? _____

   _____

5. What is your experience with treating adolescents who have been sexually abused?

   _____

   _____

6. What is your experience with working with victims of sexual abuse? _____

   _____

7. Why are you interested in this patient population group? _____

   _____

8. A therapist must be truthful in examining his or her issues in working with this patient group. Do you have a history of sexual abuse? Do you have a history of sexual misconduct?

   _____

   _____

EXERCISE 21.3. TREATING ADOLESCENTS

1. What types of therapy would be of interest to you in working with sexually aggressive adolescents? _____

_____

_____

2. What would you do if an adolescent came up to you as a clinician? _____

_____

_____

3. What areas of treatment are important to stabilizing the youth? _____

_____

_____

4. What development stages are usually found in sexually aggressive adolescents?_____

_____

_____

5. How would you use family therapy and sexual recovery therapy to help the adolescent heal? _____

_____

_____

6. How would you work with an adolescent who denies his or her offense?_____

_____

_____

7. How would you treat an adolescent who is sexually aggressive while in treatment?_____

_____

_____

8. How would you treat an adolescent who shows no remorse or victim empathy?_____

_____

_____

Chapter 22

Defense Behaviors

Defense behaviors are also referred to as defense mechanisms, defense styles, or coping styles. All are found in adults, adolescents, and children. Defense behaviors are the mind's way of limiting the amount of psychological damage or danger, a coping skill to stress. Oftentimes these behaviors operate on the unconscious level and are therefore automatic in their processes (American Psychiatric Association, 2000).

Two schools of thought explain how the mind controls stress (Hutchinson, 1999). One idea considers the ability to cope as a trait of the personality. The other thought sees the defense behavior as a transient state, which is able to change depending upon the situation (Hutchinson, 1999). The therapist should not try to take away one style of coping without replacing it with another defense. Another important aspect of defense behaviors is that they can be adaptive or maladaptive depending upon their seriousness, rigidity, and under what type of circumstance they develop (American Psychiatric Association, 2000). The concept of defense mechanisms originated with Sigmund Freud; however, his daughter, Anna Freud, later developed the definitions and understanding of various defense behaviors in her book, *The Ego and the Mechanism of Defense* (Clark, 1998). As the therapist, you must always be aware of the different defense behaviors that are in place when patients begin treatment. The therapist can be certain to see the styles of protection as denial of their offense and an attempt to rationalize or intellectualize their actions. Others will attempt to minimize the sexual acting out.

DEFENSE MECHANISMS

The following are a series of defense mechanisms, as found in the DSM-IV-TR (2001) and Clark (1998). The list will help you to understand the most common defense behaviors.

Acting Out—The person uses actions (which are generally socially unacceptable) to refrain from dealing with the emotional situation and stresses he or she feels. However, without evidence that the actions have direct correspondence to aforementioned conflict, bad behavior is simply "bad behavior."

Affiliation—The patient's response to stress and/or emotional opposition is to recruit other people to help and support him or her even though these people are sharing the problem with others. This defense mechanism does not mean the person is necessarily denying responsibility for it.

Altruism—The person channels the emotional conflict into service. He or she begins to live for others. In fact, he or she gets a "high" from the response of others.

Anger—This is an emotional state of being that can be caused by internal and external means. These emotions range from frustration to rage. Internally, the patient directs this energy source at him or her self. Externally, the patient directs the energy source at someone else. Positive anger can be used to help a person cope with a difficult situation; negative anger can be an inappropriate reaction causing problem behavior.

Sex-Offender Therapy
© 2008 by The Haworth Press, Taylor & Francis Group. All rights reserved.
doi:10.1300/5753_22

Anticipation—In this mechanism, the patient is planning and thinking ahead of the situation. He or she has experienced the emotional reactions to all possible situations and also rehearsed mentally and/or physically the different responses he or she could have to the consequences of these situations.

Autistic fantasy—The patient's response to stress and/or emotional opposition is to use daydreaming as a substitution for real action.

Avoidance—The patient has a response to stress and or an emotional problem, and the coping skill that has been learned is to avoid difficult situations.

Denial—The patient responds to stress and/or emotional opposition by refusing to acknowledge or accept the reality that is before him or her and acts as if nothing has happened.

Depersonalization—This type of defense behavior allows the person to become emotionally detached from others. It is a common defense behavior found in sexually aggressive patients who use others for their own sexual gratification. Such an individual will treat a person as an object.

Devaluation—When the patient overexaggerates the negative attributes of self or others as a way of rationalizing or understanding the emotional conflict he or she feels.

Displacement—When faced with disappointment or failure by a person or thing, the patient finds another person or thing of similar nature to replace it. This wouldn't be a negative solution in all cases, but displacement can also apply with anger and rage. An individual can look for a substitute to take out negative emotions on.

Dissociation—This involves being able to separate actions and thoughts from the central consciousness. This is an important coping skill, so that one can function normally when faced with stressors in one area of the patient's life. For example, being able to work effectively at his or her job even though the patient is going through a messy divorce in his or her home life. However, dissociation can become extreme to the point that the patient can start to believe that he or she has separate lives or is separate people.

Help, rejecting, complaining—The patient deals with stress and/or emotional conflict through continuously requesting assistance or help only to reject that assistance or help once it is offered. Feelings of hostility or resentment toward others are often motivating factors but are concealed by constant complaining.

Humor—The patient deals with stress and/or emotional conflict by choosing to focus on the lighter side of the situation.

Idealization—The patient deals with stress and/or emotional opposition by convincing him or her self that another person is actually much better than he or she is.

Intellectualization—The patient deals with stress and/or emotional opposition by separating his or her emotions from thought. The patient looks at the utilization of facts and suppresses his or her emotions.

Isolation of affect—The way that the patient deals with stress and/or emotional conflict is to separate the ideas from the original feelings associated with them. The patient is able to shut down the feelings while still being aware of what is going on around him or her.

Minimization—This is a behavior in which the patient deals with stress and emotional conflict to take a view that reduces the significance of what is happening to him or her, or what he or she has done to another person. Often, this behavior is found in sexually aggressive patients.

Omnipotence—The patient deals with stress and/or emotional opposition by believing and/or acting as though he or she has special powers that make him or her superior to the average person.

Passive aggression—In this mechanism, the patient avoids face-to-face conflict by subtly expressing aggressive types of behaviors toward other people. On the surface the patient is compliant; however, this disguises the resistance, hostility, and/or resentment that the patient feels with him or her self.

Projection—The patient deals with stress and/or emotional opposition by convincing him or her self that the unacceptable thoughts, feelings, and/or desires that he or she is having are actually how other people are feeling.

Projective identification—This mechanism works much like projection in that the patient convinces him or her self that the unacceptable thoughts, feelings, and/or desires that he or she is having are actually being felt by others. However, unlike projection, he or she knows that he or she has those thoughts, feelings, and/or desires too. He or she just deems it as a rational response to the other person(s). Sometimes these responses are induced in the other person(s) thus making it difficult to unravel to find where all the conflict began.

Rationalization—This is a way of explaining an act or a behavior that appears to have a negative appearance either to oneself or one's social circle. The patient will give an explanation that is socially acceptable and makes fairly good sense. He or she is not necessarily trying to con or fool anyone. He or she is as much or more misleading to self as he or she is to those around him or her.

Reaction formation—The patient's response to stress and/or emotional opposition is to replace thoughts, feelings, and behaviors that are at odds with his or her unacceptable thoughts, feelings, and behaviors. Repression generally happens alongside this defense mechanism.

Repression—The patient's response to stress and/or emotional opposition is to dismiss the offensive thoughts, feelings, experiences and/or desires from his or her consciousness. The part of feeling may continue to stay in the conscious mind but void of its original intention.

Self-assertion—The patient's response to stress and/or emotional conflict is to appropriately express his or her feelings and behaviors.

Self-observation—The patient's response to stress and/or emotional conflict is to think about his or her feelings, behaviors, attitudes, and ideas and then act properly.

Splitting—The patient's response to stress and/or emotional conflict is to separate feelings into polar opposites, making it impossible for the patient to be able to integrate both good and bad attributes of him or her self or others due to the black and white perspective that he or she carries of these emotions.

Sublimation—The patient's response to stress and/or emotional conflict is to take potentially destructive feelings, behaviors, and/or ideas and positively direct those feelings, behaviors, and/or ideas into actions that are acceptable within society.

Suppression—The patient's response to stress and/or emotional conflict is to purposefully not think about circumstances, feelings or situations that will cause him or her distress.

Undoing—The patient's response to stress and/or emotional conflict is to make symbolic gestures through his or her words or behaviors to offset unacceptable behaviors, feelings, and/or actions.

EXERCISES FOR THE THERAPIST

An important part of the treatment that the therapist provides is to understand the nuances of what patients are saying or not saying. Oftentimes there will be hints of particular defense behaviors that are utilized. It is necessary that the therapist be able to tease these defense mechanisms out of the conversation, as they are often used as a disguise. The more familiar the therapist becomes with defense mechanisms, the more apt he or she will be to identify the specific nature of the defense mechanism and help move the patient and the treatment of the patient forward. Although Exercises 22.1 and 22.2 are for the therapist, the patient needs to have an understanding of his or her own defense mechanisms as well.

SUMMARY

Defense behaviors are present in all patients. Of course, certain defense behaviors are found to be an acceptable and normal way of coping with a difficult situation. In working with sexually aggressive adults, adolescents, and children, such defense mechanisms are used to deny, project, minimize, or blame others. The therapist must be alert to defense features that may occur in a patient during treatment.

EXERCISE 22.1. QUESTIONS FOR THE THERAPIST

1. How often do you find that you deal with patients' defense behaviors in treatment?

   _____

   _____

2. Do you consider defense behaviors as a personality trait, transient state, or a combination of both?_____

   _____

3. Why is it important that you have a firm understanding of defense behaviors?_____

   _____

4. How well do you deal with your own defense behaviors?_____

   _____

5. Have you ever had an occasion that involved one of your defense behaviors slipping into the therapy process?_____

   _____

6. How cognizant are you of your stresses and anxiety? How do you deal with them?

   _____

   _____

7. How do you help your patients deal with their defense behaviors?

   _____

   _____

8. What do you do with a patient that refuses to work with maladaptive defense behaviors?

   _____

   _____

9. What are some of the most likely defense behaviors you will see when working with a sexually aggressive patient?_____

   _____

EXERCISE 22.2. DENIAL, INTELLECTUALIZATION, AND RATIONALIZATION DENIAL

1. What is your definition of denial? _____

   _____

2. On the first day of group therapy, Richard denies his role in the sexual molestation of his six-year-old daughter. The more the group tries to confront him, the more he refuses to admit what he has done. What should the therapist do to encourage the patient to admit his role? _____

   _____

3. Joe reports to the group that his eight-year-old son lied about the sexual molestation that he reportedly did to him. He reports that his son has an underlining reason for lying. He reports that it is quite clear to him that his ex-wife is behind his son's lying about him. Joe reports that he is incapable of committing this offense and is deeply offended that the therapist insists on continuing with this miscarriage of justice. _____

   How should the therapist respond to this patient? _____

   _____

   _____

   How can the therapist encourage the other group members to respond to this patient?

   _____

   _____

4. Confrontation is a necessary step to go through; however, the therapist should also have other techniques that can be used for a person dealing with denial. As the therapist, what other techniques could you utilize? _____

   _____

INTELLECTUALIZATION

1. What is your definition of intellectualization? _____

   _____

2. How will the therapist know when a patient is intellectualizing? _____

   _____

3. Larry talks to the group about his offense of raping his girlfriend. As he discusses the offense, he is very calm and describes the events in detail; however, he keeps a stern look and does not express any emotions. As the group asks questions, he answers them, but without any expression. When one of the members confronts him about this, he simply states, "That's just the way it is." What would be your response to Larry?_____

_____

RATIONALIZATION

1. What is your definition of rationalization?_____

_____

2. How will the therapist know when the patient is using rationalization as a defense behavior?_____

_____

3. Leonard served five years in federal prison for downloading child pornography on his hard drive. While doing his stand-up in group therapy he tells the group that although what he did may not be the right thing in the eyes of society, he feels good that he didn't physically harm any of the children that he downloaded. What would be your response to Leonard's comments about not harming any of his victims?_____

_____

Chapter 23

Dual-Diagnosis Patients

A dual-diagnosis is given to people suffering from a combination of at least two separate, yet prevailing disorders. The combinations for dual-diagnosis are selected from mental illness, mental retardation and/or substance abuse. Also clearly identified as a mental disorder by the *Diagnostic and Statistical Manual of Mental Disorders, Fourth Edition, Text Revision* (DSM-IV-TR) are clinical sexual disorders (American Psychiatric Association, 2000).

Daley and Moss (2002) rightly point out that the word *dual* may falsely identify the diagnosis, since many people dealing with a dual-diagnosis actually have three or more diagnoses at the same time. It should be no surprise that any patient, upon entering treatment for sexual offending, will show resistance and have views that are cognitively distorted; however, treatment for the dually diagnosed must be specifically geared due to their psychiatric impairment. Sex offenders who are dually diagnosed not only have issues pertaining to their sexual offenses, but also must focus on a thought disorder that can limit their response to and understanding of treatment. The therapist who identifies offenders with a thought disorder should consider having a special treatment group that is exclusively for patients with dual-diagnosis. Rapport is essential in order to move the therapy process along. Rapport building is a tool that all therapists must be able to utilize with all members of the group.

The therapist should be aware that the offenders might not always be willing to accept their psychiatric illness. In this event, success with sexual issues will not materialize until the psychiatric symptoms are reduced and the patient has been stabilized. Other issues that the therapist must contend with are the dual-diagnosis patient's refusal to admit that he or she has any issues with either diagnosis and his or her lack of desire for change (Daley and Moss, 2002). Until these issues are shored up, treatment success will be limited. Another issue that the therapist must be aware of is the presense of developmental stressors in the patient with a coexisting psychiatric disorder and clinical sexual disorder.

As the therapist begins to work with the dual-diagnosis patients, he or she must note that this population is a difficult population to treat due to the level of psychological interference that individuals may be subjected to through their recovery. (See also Exercises 23.1 and 23.2.) The following are issues to consider for the dual-diagnosis patient:

- Anxiety
- Difficulty handling stressful situations
- Feelings of inadequacy
- Low self-image
- Difficulty with paranoia, delusions, auditory, and visual hallucinations
- Self-isolating behavior
- Poor concentration
- Parasuicidal gestures
- Suicidal plan
- Poor judgment and insight

Sex-Offender Therapy
© 2008 by The Haworth Press, Taylor & Francis Group. All rights reserved.
doi:10.1300/5753_23

- Self-mutilating behavior (e.g., biting, burning or cutting one's skin)
- Manipulation (may use metal illness as an excuse for not working on issues related to their sexual offense)
- Difficulty taking prescribed medications (in order for treatment to have any effectiveness, the patient must be willing to remain compliant with prescribed psychotropic medications, if they are taking them) (Flora, 2001; Daley and Moss, 2002)

Therapists should be familiar with and understand the following terms when working with a dual-diagnosed sex-offender patient:

1. Dual-diagnosis
2. Thought disorder
3. Personality disorder
4. Mental retardation
5. Borderline intellectual functioning
6. Learning disability
7. Mental illness
8. Attention-deficit disorder
9. Attention-deficit disorder with hyperactivity
10. Mood disorders
11. Impulse control disorders
12. Anxiety disorders

SUMMARY

The dual-diagnosis patient presents unique treatment issues. Insight and judgment are impaired. The ability to connect a stressful event to the offense can be difficult for the patient to realize without in-depth help. However, dual-diagnosis patients can be very receptive to therapy. A supportive psychotherapy model is recommended with relapse-prevention work. Some insight may be required, but the therapist should be careful not to raise the level of stress too high for this patient population group. Dual-diagnosis patients will move at a slower rate and require information to be repeated a number of times. However, many dual-diagnosis patients are found to grasp many concepts of the treatment and will follow through on many changes to their behavior.

EXERCISE 23.1. INSIGHT AWARENESS FOR THE THERAPIST

How well you know your own capabilities will determine how well you will be able to work with difficult populations. Answer the following questions with the same honesty and integrity that you would expect your clients to answer your questions.

1. What type of skills do you feel that you need in order to work with a sex offender with a dual-diagnosis?_____

_____

2. What do you consider your major strengths in working with this population?_____

_____

3. What are your limitations in working with this population?_____

_____

4. What are the difficulties that you have had to face or you foresee facing with this population?_____

_____

5. What countertransference issues might you have with this population?_____

_____

6. How do you feel about working with a sexually aggressive dual-diagnosis patient who is court-ordered to attend therapy but is resistive to the initial stages of the treatment process?

_____

_____

7. Do you feel that it is clinically worthwhile to provide treatment to a sexually aggressive dual-diagnosis patient?_____

_____

8. How far can a therapist take a sexually aggressive dual-diagnosis patient in insight work without causing a clinical relapse to occur?_____

_____

EXERCISE 23.2. SKILLS DEVELOPMENT FOR THE THERAPIST

Personal responsibility is a cornerstone in patients' ability to proceed forward. Despite the limitations they might encounter, they should not be allowed to manipulate the therapist or other group members. The therapist should also understand his or her own professional boundaries. Some clients in the population are very convincing and will try to turn the therapist into a friend. At times the therapist may have to be confrontational. If this is not a strong skill for you then it will be important that you develop it. If this is a strong skill for you then continue to hone this valuable skill; however, remember, confrontation should only be used to produce enough stress to invoke a change in clients that is important for their recovery.

Dual-diagnosis patients should be held responsible for their recovery. Although dually diagnosed, patients are still culpable for their offense. As a part of their recovery they should:

1. Express genuine victim empathy and remorse.
2. Admit to what they did instead of what they were formally charged with in court.
3. Be held accountable/responsible for their offense.

Case Examples

Albert is a twenty-six-year-old black male who molested a five-year-old girl. He served three years in prison. He has been diagnosed with borderline intellectual functioning. He has been in group therapy for six months, but the last three months, he has been missing group meetings on a regular basis. The group is starting to become frustrated with him due to his lack of commitment to the group and, more important, to his therapy. The therapist gingerly confronts him during a group session. Albert reports that he is a "little slow" and doesn't understand what is expected of him in the group, although the rules and group expectations have clearly been defined for Albert.

1. How would you address these issues with Albert?_____

_____

2. What types of interventions would you allow the group to make with Albert?_____

_____

3. Why is it important that the group be allowed to make an intervention with Albert?_____

_____

Jason, a twenty-nine-year-old Hispanic male, had been in prison for fifteen counts of exhibitionism. He was released after two years. After his release, he was an active member of his sex offender treatment group. He was actively engaged in the group conversations and was encouraging to the other group members. What Jason did not tell the group was that he was dealing with some stressful situations. He felt like he could take care of the problems on his own. One Friday evening Jason was out at the grocery store and ran into some old friends. They invited him to have a few drinks and unwind. He thought that the drinks might help him with his stress level; besides, it had been a while since he had been out with anyone. He woke up the next morning in jail. Jason learned later from his attorney that after a few drinks, he had went "cruising" and flashed an undercover police officer.

1. What was Jason's first mistake?_____

_____

2. How should Jason have handled the stressful issues alone?_____

_____

3. How could the group have helped Jason?_____

_____

Johnny is a thirty-two-year-old white male who suffers from Schizophrenia, Paranoid Type, In Remission. He molested a nine-year-old boy. In weekly group sessions, he is unable to keep up with the group discussion. The other members grow impatient with what they feel is his unwillingness to work on his recovery. The group members become more confrontational which confuses him and makes him feel more anxious and paranoid. He becomes even more guarded about revealing information. The members finally decide that they should vote him out of the group. The therapist makes an intervention by posing a question for the group. The therapist asks the group about their responsibility to the weaker members of the group.

1. What are the group's responsibilities to Johnny?_____

_____

2. What are Johnny's clinical expectations to be in the group?_____

_____

3. What are the therapist's clinical responsibilities to Johnny and the group?_____

_____

As the therapist, you have the control over how the members will respond to therapy. Your actions and the way that you respond to each group member will affect the outcome of patients treated in therapy. The dynamics of group therapy is a special energy. There are times that this energy is flowing and other times assistance is merited for a patient. The therapist needs to be very aware of their own biases and prejudices to avoid damaging the patient or the group.

Fred has a dual-diagnosis. He has a Bipolar I Disorder, Mixed Type, Severe, In Remission,Without Psychotic Features. He has attended the treatment group for one year. He has completed his stand-up presentation and has advanced to Phase II in the program. He was involved in the attempted rape of an adult woman, and was sentenced to five years in prison, and was very quiet during the early stages of treatment. Recently, he has been more assertive in the group discussion. Fred has been challenging another member of the group who is in Phase III of the program. Fred feels that this member should be more vocal in group discussions, stop missing group sessions, and act like a senior member and take on more of a leadership role in the group. In addition, Fred has been emerging as a group leader himself and believes he can be of more help to others.

1. As the therapist, you recognize the change in Fred. What would you do as the therapist?

   _____

   _____

2. What could happen if the therapist encourages Fred to take a more active role in being a group leader?_____

   _____

3. What type of clinical damage can be caused if the therapist decides to mute Fred's desire to be a group leader?_____

   _____

4. How will the therapist's decision affect the dynamics of the group?_____

   _____

Chapter 24

Self-Esteem

IMPROVING SELF-IMAGE IN OFFENDERS

When sex offenders first present themselves in treatment, they have been arrested, interrogated, evaluated, and convicted of a sexual offense. Prior to treatment, the sex offender has been dishonest, deceitful, irresponsible, noncaring, and disrespectful to others. The sex offender will often be defensive and will have used many rationalizations to justify the sex-offending behaviors. It is in the beginning part of the treatment process where the sex offender begins to put a stop to the above behaviors. Group norms and rules are explained in detail. Expectations of behaviors are discussed and the sex offender will now be learning a whole new set of behaviors and values. This starts the process of constructing hope for the future and strengthening the positive qualities of each sex offender.

Prior to treatment, sex offenders have very little understanding of the process that led up to their sexual offense. They, like society, often think that the behavior happens because they are essentially hopeless, permanently flawed or evil. This is a point where metaphors can be utilized to show them that the action is the result of thoughts and feelings. The metaphor of the pie can be used at this point in treatment:

After the pie is baked, it is broken up into a certain number of pieces, just like the offenders' personalities. At the moment of their sexual offense, the entire pie was consumed with their negative traits and these pieces became larger than any other piece of their pie. With treatment, they can learn to control their sex-offending behaviors so that these behaviors are only a very small piece of the pie. They will never get rid of these pieces, but with a solid commitment toward their relapse-prevention plan, they can constantly contain their sex-offending thoughts, feelings, and actions. In the future, the sex-offending thoughts, feelings, and actions will only be a very small piece of a very positive, responsible, and committed person. However, sex offenders need to know that these deviant pieces of the pie are always a part of them.

One way for the sex offender to start building the positive pieces of the pie, is to make a list of his or her positive and negative traits. Each group member is asked to make a list of their positive and negative traits. At the beginning of this process, most group members have listed many negatives and very few positives. They then discuss this list with the group to understand how they feel about themselves. They are asked to keep this list with them in each group session. At the end of most sessions, they are asked to bring out their lists and add any "quality" or "positives" to the list that they or the group experienced in the session or they experienced themselves in the past week. This is a very effective way of demonstrating to sex offenders that they are changing and learning new ways of seeing themselves.

ACCOUNTABILITY AND RESPONSIBILITY

The process of strengthening and hope starts in Phase I of treatment. The sex offender learns to be responsible by attending group sessions on a regular basis. If an absence occurs, the sex

Sex-Offender Therapy
© 2008 by The Haworth Press, Taylor & Francis Group. All rights reserved.
doi:10.1300/5753_24

171

offender needs to call the agency and his or her probation officer and bring in a written note from another party explaining the reason for the absence. During the initial phase of treatment, there are often complaints about this process. The offender must be made to understand that this is a means by which he or she is learning to be accountable and responsible. These complaints are actually great opportunities to teach a new set of values and behaviors to group members. At the end of these beginning groups, each member can start adding "responsible" and "accountable" to their positive list.

Sex offenders should contribute for therapy. This is another way of teaching responsibility and accountability. If they don't pay without a legitimate reason then they are sent home and have to notify their probation officers. This teaches them that there are always consequences to their behavior. To let them get away with breaking a rule is to reinforce the sex-offending behavior that we are trying to change. They are told to do all homework assignments and these assignments need to be done to the best of their ability. If not, these instances will be used to teach them how to become responsible and accountable to the group and their own treatment.

At the end of the month, detailed monthly progress reports are written about each group member's progress in the group. This report is given to his or her probation officer and often can be given to the sex offender so that he or she can have a written report of his or her progress in the group. Because he or she begins to get written reports that document how he or she is doing in the treatment process, this is an opportune time to reinforce hope in the sex offender.

The following is an outline of a monthly progress report:

1. Name, address and telephone number of the reporting agency
2. Month and year of the reporting period
3. Name of the client
4. The phase that the client is in, such as Phase I, II, or III
5. Current focus or issues that are being addressed in the group
6. Level of compliance with the treatment goals
7. Whether there is any risk of termination from the treatment program
8. Attitude toward treatment
9. Level of participation in the group
10. Attendance: dates present and absent; excused or nonexcused
11. A narrative from the group leader about the content and process of the group meetings
12. Signature and title of the author of the report

As sex offenders move on from Phase I to Phase II, they begin to take more responsibility for their thoughts, feelings and actions. In the second phase of treatment they will need an equal balance of positive and negative traits. In Phase II, sex offenders will be looking at their sex-offending behavior in great detail. If there is no balance at this time, they could become depressed and give up on treatment or regress to using defense mechanisms such as rationalization, projection, etc. One way of balancing this process is to point out the positive traits that are being demonstrated in the group at the time. They are being honest, taking responsibility for their actions, and dealing with the past in a very courageous way.

The most important ingredient of strengthening the ego and giving hope to sex offenders is teaching them what needs to be learned to be responsible and accountable adults. Sex offenders need to know what is right and not override that feeling. It is helpful to utilize every situation in their lives as an opportunity for teaching what is right. Action methods can be used to teach sex offenders to do what is right. A particular technique borrowed from the method of psychodrama is the use of "surplus reality" (Moreno, Blomkvist, and Rutzel, 2000). Surplus reality is the creation of events that never happened but can be explored further for the purposes of teaching. The following are several examples of how this technique is used in the group:

"Mr. Y's" mother died when he was three years old and as a result of her death, he was passed around to live with several family members. At the age of ten, he lived with his grandparents and his adult uncle. He was very close to this uncle and often slept in his uncle's bed. One night, his uncle undressed him and sexually abused him. In later years, Mr. Y was convicted of doing the same exact behavior to his ten-year-old stepdaughter. After Mr. Y wrote about his own abuse and read it to the group, we looked at the situation using "surplus reality." Mr. Y never told his father of his uncle's abuse because he was positive that his father would not only disbelieve him but would also punish him for telling lies about his uncle.

We looked at this situation differently in the group. What should have happened in this incident? Group members came up with a new reality that Mr. Y would tell his father and his father would have confronted his brother and called the police. We put an empty chair in the room and stated that the ten-year-old Mr. Y was sitting there. Several group members offered different ways of talking to the ten-year-old Mr. Y.

Another example of how "surplus reality" can be used:

"Mr. Why" was convicted of exposing himself to an adult woman. In working on his sexual history, he wrote about an incident that happened when he was seven years old. He was taking a shower and his sister, who was twelve, had her thirteen-year-old friend over at the house. Mr. Why stated that after taking a shower, while he was drying himself off, he called his sister's girlfriend into the bathroom. When she entered the room, he dropped the towel and he was facing her with no clothes on. She quickly left the room and told his father. His father did nothing. As the group asked questions about this experience, Mr. Why told the group that he did what he did "to be noticed by her."

We then looked at this situation from the point of view of "surplus reality." Each group member is now Mr. Why's father. What do you tell your seven-year-old son about this incident? What are other ways of getting the attention of a girl that you like without standing in front of her naked?

As sex offenders progress further into the latter part of treatment, they can learn the beginning steps to emotional intimacy. They can do this by active listening in the group and by giving accurate, empathetic feedback to group members. An example of this is contained in the following illustration:

"Mr. X" was telling the group about an interaction he had on the phone with his ex-wife. He was dictating to her demands that he had in visiting one of his children. He was being unreasonable and getting very frustrated with the interaction on the phone. He shared this incident with the group to get feedback on what he did and what he can do in future interactions with his ex-wife. Several members of the group have unresolved issues with their ex-wives and used this situation to complain about women. Other group members gave him feedback that was problem-solving in nature. I asked the group to listen carefully and put the interaction on the blackboard. Mr. X wanted help from the group and what he got was other group member's issues. By the end of the session, several group members realized that they have problems with their ex-wives that were preventing them from honestly helping Mr. X. They finally gave Mr. X the constructive feedback that he asked for. He was told that he was making too many demands and not understanding his ex-wife's situation. He needed to make her a partner in the problem of arranging visitations with the children. By the end of the group session, Mr. X also realized that he had no other interests in his life except for work and his children. He needed other interests in his life in order to put this problem of visitations in perspective.

We spent the remainder of the session looking at the principles of emotional intimacy.

In the previous illustration, the group process was used to teach group members how to listen to each other and give accurate, empathetic feedback. In all phases of the treatment program, group members are asked to share very intimate sexual details of their lives. They have to do this because of the nature of their crimes. As sex-offender treatment providers, it is essential that we teach them by our own thoughts, feelings, and actions to be firm, fair, caring, and empathetic. The therapist has to be constantly reminded that in order to reach our goals of no more victims, it is imperative that we teach by example how to strengthen the positive qualities in individuals so that they will have the necessary ego strengths to faithfully follow their relapse-prevention plans for the rest of their lives, ensuring that there will be no more victims—including themselves. See Exercise 24.1 for an example of how to increase the awareness of self-esteem.

Another way of increasing self-esteem in the individual is to find qualities in each client that we can respect. Mary Pipher (2000) states the following, "A wise therapist once told me that our first task in any therapeutic encounter is to find something to respect in our clients. Without respect it's impossible to really help anyone" (p. 63). This is sometimes very hard to do with particular clients, so as group leaders we have to work very hard to find qualities that we respect in our clients. There are several ways to accomplish this task. The first priority is to make sure that the group leader has a good sound framework of respect for him or her self. Exercise 24.2 is for the group leader.

If this exercise does not work for you, it means that there is not enough healthy interaction going on in this group. It is time to begin teaching the offenders what their responsibilities are as members of this group. It is time to teach basic feedback and listening skills. It is also time to teach skills that require self-analysis and how to present oneself to the group after working on personal issues. Once this is accomplished, the group leader can go through the exercises again. Exercise 24.3 is aimed at creating a therapeutic environment.

SUMMARY

The growth of self-esteem is an important part of the healing and recovery process for a patient. In order for a patient to regain his or her self-worth, the ego must be restored, in part, opening the door to positive thinking. Many sexually aggressive persons have low-esteem issues long before the misconduct occurs. In order to change, a patient must learn to stop his or her negative thinking. The individual is encouraged to see him or her self as a person who has made a mistake but can again become a productive member of society.

EXERCISE 24.1. AWARENESS OF SELF-ESTEEM

1. Make a list of statements from your childhood that decreased your self-esteem.

_____

_____

_____

_____

_____

_____

_____

2. Take each statement and list what the opposite or remedy is for that statement. This list is your plan for increasing your self-esteem and should be practiced every day.

_____

_____

_____

_____

_____

_____

_____

_____

This exercise can be changed somewhat to assist sex offenders in increasing their self-esteem. A simple exercise that can be implemented in the group is as follows:

1. Put an empty chair in the middle of the room.
2. Have group members imagine that there is a young child sitting in the chair.
3. Have the group members make statements or state actions that will decrease this child's self-esteem. The group leader should be writing each statement on the board for the other members to see.
4. Have the group take each statement and write down what needs to be said or done to reverse the effects of that statement or action.
5. The resulting list becomes the plan for increasing self-esteem in the group.

EXERCISE 24.2. GROUP LEADER AND SELF-RESPECT

1. Make a list of your positive qualities as a therapist:

_____

_____

2. From this list, pick out the qualities that you respect the most about yourself:

_____

_____

3. The qualities that were chosen in step two are those that you should be aware of and emphasize in each group session. Make a separate list that you can look at before each group session to ensure that you are a role model for group members. They are as follows:

_____

_____

Now, repeat the process, focusing on the members of the treatment group.

1. Make a list of all members of your group:

_____

_____

2. By each name write down something positive that you have observed about him or her.

_____

_____

3. If you cannot come up with a positive trait then look at more of the basic traits of the group members. Are they punctual? Do they listen? Do they give feedback to others? Do they make payments on time? Do they answer questions when asked?

_____

_____

4. A last resort is asking group members to give feedback on positive qualities that they observe from individual group members. There might be qualities that others notice that the group member or group leader is not aware of.

_____

_____

EXERCISE 24.3. GROUP LEADER AND THE THERAPEUTIC ENVIRONMENT

1. Imagine a perfect group. What is going on in the group and specifically, how are group members interacting with one another?

_____

_____

_____

_____

_____

2. What is the group leader doing to help create the above environment?

_____

_____

_____

_____

_____

3. What are group members doing to create the above environment?

_____

_____

_____

_____

_____

4. List all the actions from numbers two and three. This is the goal that the group leader is try-ing to achieve in each meeting to enhance the self-esteem of group members.

_____

_____

_____

_____

_____

Chapter 25

Group Therapy

Group therapy is a form of psychotherapy used when two or more individuals meet in a clinical setting with a therapist. Group therapy is encouraged and frequently used in the therapeutic treatment of sex offenders.

Groups for recently convicted sex offenders prepare them for long-term therapy. The primary goal in group therapy is to stop sexually abusive behavior. Patient groups may have between eight to twelve members. Length of group sessions may vary from ninety minutes to three hours. Meeting weekly is recommended to meet treatment goals. The group duration will last a minimum of two to four years depending on the progress made by each patient with his or her treatment issues and goals.

Sex offenders are more positive in a group of their own peers. Putting male, female, and adolescent group members together is not recommended. Rather, each should have their own treatment group.

Group rules are important and give the patient a guideline of what is and is not acceptable in a group setting. Group sessions give the patient a safe, nonthreatening place to work on his or her problems and treatment issues. Honesty and confidentiality are a must. A therapist and co-therapist is recommended for group therapy.

The selection of individuals for a sex-offender treatment group is paramount to the success of the group. Chapter 15 of this book reviews the clinical assessment used prior to placing a patient in a treatment group. Prior to acceptance into a group, the sex offender must have a referral from the community, a face-to-face interview, a thorough psychosexual evaluation, a full-disclosure polygraph, and a penile plethysmograph.

BENEFITS

The benefits of group therapy for sex offenders include:

- The group gives patients a safe, nonthreatening place to work on their problems and treatment issues without time constraints. Confidentiality is critical.
- Open-ended groups allow patients to work at their own capacity and pace.
- Many sex offenders do not have mental health insurance. Fees for group members are lower than for individual treatment.
- Patients in group therapy develop a sense of identity, increased social skills, interpersonal skills, and socialization while becoming a source of support in times of stress for group participants.
- Participants share common characteristics. They can discuss their individual experiences, share events, talk about feelings and thoughts, discuss issues from previous sessions, receive and give feedback, and give support and/or criticism in a nonthreatening manner.
- The group provides an education for offenders as to human sexuality and intimacy. They learn what a healthy relationship is and how to develop such a relationship.

Sex-Offender Therapy
© 2008 by The Haworth Press, Taylor & Francis Group. All rights reserved.
doi:10.1300/5753_25

- Patients in group settings react more like themselves in a group than they would on a one-to-one basis with a therapist. Therefore, patients will increase awareness of maladaptive behavior patterns while increasing their awareness of factors that influence their behaviors.
- The group provides patients with a sense of cohesiveness. It gives them an opportunity for interpersonal learning while instilling hopefulness for those who see themselves filled with despair and hopelessness.
- The group offers direction, education, and support while confronting tough treatment issues such as denial, minimization, and rationalization. Group therapy provides treatment for a larger number of patients. It is found to be more economical and efficient in providing treatment.
- Groups for sex offenders have specific treatment goals. Treatment groups are offered on an inpatient and outpatient basis or in a correctional setting. One goal of group therapy is to provide education for patients as to their particular cognitive distortion, which leads to offending. In group therapy, the goal is to educate patients to report their sex crimes, look at their pattern of sexual interactions, and classify patients as to the types of offenders they are (paraphilia, pedophilia, incest, or rape).

The patient, through the group process, will learn the cycles of sexual offending; acknowledge and accept responsibility for the offense; and learn how his or her crime has affected his or her victim. The offender will be able to verbalize and be sincere in his or her remorse for the crime committed. He or she will identify and accept responsibility for the behavior. The group carefully examines patterns of offending while considering the possibility and consequences of repeat offenses.

The therapist facilitates and reduces the anxiety level in the group. This will help the patient feel more comfortable with self-disclosure. Patients must feel a mutual trust, empathy, support, and respect by the therapist and their peers prior to disclosing their sex crimes.

Research indicates that adult sex offenders do not respond to a confrontive therapy. A talk therapy model that is insight-oriented is found to be more effective. Literature from research indicates that individual, family group, and group therapy is recommended for adults.

Patients not recommended for group therapy are those who are psychotic; those with impairments (significant cognitive impairment); or those with sociopathic traits. The psychotic patient may experience difficulty in a group environment. The patient may have anxiety, depression, loss of touch with reality, hallucinations, paranoia, delusions, or exhibit poor impulse control. These patients may lack the social or coping skills to function well in a group setting.

THERAPEUTIC CHANGE

Irvin S. Yalom is seen as a pioneer in studying how patients respond to and benefit from the group process. He submits that therapeutic change is composed of many elements. Change is a complex process. Yalom (1985, pp. 3-18) identified the following eleven clinical factors that influence sex offenders who are in group therapy:

1. *Instillation of hope*—Sex offenders labeled by society as deviants or monsters often lose sight of the fact they can make positive changes. They enter therapy with a sense of failure. Therefore, the therapist has the role of instilling in patients confidence in the therapist's abilities to help facilitate positive changes and a positive outcome.
2. *Universality*—Sex offenders often feel alone, socially isolated, or socially outcast. Group therapy offers them commonality with others who share similar circumstances.
3. *Imparting of information*—In so, group information and education are provided. Information on sexual deviancy, understanding the cycle of offending behaviors, ways to identify warning signs of reoffending, and developing relapse-prevention strategies.

4. *Altruism*—Sex offenders in a group setting provide support for one another. In turn, this improves their self-esteem, which benefits both patients and their peers.
5. *The corrective recapitulation of the primary family group*—Sex offenders enter group therapy with family history, family dysfunction, and disappointing experiences from their family of origin. Group therapy provides a safe place to revisit their family conflicts and correct their thinking to stop further sexual acting-out.
6. *Development of socializing techniques*—Sex offenders have impaired or limited social skills as well as intimacy inadequacies. Being members of a group, education, guidance, and group interaction provides patients with an opportunity to experience and role-play acceptable behavior.
7. *Imitative behavior*—Therapists role-model or mirror appropriate behaviors for patients. Members are influenced by both therapists and peers. Behavior is imitated when the transference process occurs during treatment.
8. *Interpersonal learning*—Sex offenders change through interpersonal relationships with peers, therapists, and the corrective emotional experience—insight into personal deviancy. Modification in behavior may occur.
9. *Group cohesiveness*—Sex offenders are often suspicious or guarded in group situations. They have the need for a safe environment where they speak freely about fear of rehabilitation. A cohesive group promotes attendance, self-disclosure, and participation. A cohesive group promotes a positive therapeutic outcome.
10. *Catharsis*—Sex offenders may enter into group therapy with resistance or misinformed beliefs and values. Group allows sex offenders to examine their deviant actions. They may experience a strong or life-changing experience that will change their behavior.
11. *Existential factors*—This factor focuses on the basic human ways of life, death, isolation, and freedom. Sex offenders often have childhood problem histories, intimacy issues, poor self-esteem, social isolation, and life without meaning. Sexual aggression is an extreme and inappropriate outlet of unmet developmental needs.

Therapists working in a group with sex offenders are in a unique position. Positive change through group therapy is not only possible, but can be expected to some degree. Exercise 25.1 is a tool for therapists to use in reviewing the dynamics and issues involved in providing group therapy to sex offenders. This exercise is not meant to be an all-inclusive list. There are numerous considerations to be thought out before beginning sex-offender group therapy. Being a therapist or co-therapist treating sex offenders in a group setting can be demanding at times. The exercise is intended to provide insight into the many aspects of treating sex offenders.

SUMMARY

Group therapy is the recommended treatment model to be used for adult sex offenders or persons with sexually aggressive behaviors. Such a therapy style permits patients to feel less isolated and receive support from a group. Many sex-offender groups are viewed by many patients as the only venue in which they can let down their guard and share their experiences and problems. As a group grows, and new patients enter, a therapist may be less directive and encourage senior members to offer information about change. Permitting "the experts" to offer guidance is far more therapeutic for the new patient than listening to the same information being given by the therapist. Also, sex offenders are far more alert to the nuances of a patient who is not working recovery than a clinician. Sex offenders are very quick to manipulate, and another patient who is versed in relapse prevention and is working the treatment program is much more likely to first note the behavior.

EXERCISE 25.1. REVIEW FOR THERAPISTS PROVIDING SEX-OFFENDER GROUP THERAPY

1. What is your previous experience in working with groups, specifically, sex-offender treatment groups? _____

   _____

2. A therapist and co-therapist are recommended when working with sex offenders. What education level, professional qualifications, and personality traits do you expect your co-therapist to have? _____

   _____

3. Do you want your co-therapist to practice in the same profession as you or in a different profession? _____

   _____

4. Have you taken adequate professional precautions? Do you have a valid, current license or certification to treat sex offenders? Yes_____ No_____

   Is your malpractice insurance policy current and sufficient? Yes_____ No_____

5. What professional groups or organizations do you belong to that provide you with education, guidance, or support?_____

   _____

6. As a group leader, will you role model the following attributes while providing group therapy?

   a. Confidence in your group skills and experience as group leader. Yes_____ No_____

   b. Dignity and respect for group members. Yes_____ No_____

   c. Acceptance of group members without judgment. Yes_____ No_____

   d. Ability to set appropriate physical, emotional, and sexual boundaries. Yes_____ No_____

   e. Ability to monitor your speech, tone, demeanor, and verbal and nonverbal behaviors during group sessions. Yes_____ No_____

7. What method will be used to select group members? (Check all that apply.)

   a. Face-to-face interview. Yes_____ No_____

   b. After patient completes a psychosocial evaluation and group therapy is recommended.

   Yes_____ No_____

   c. After a patient takes and passes a polygraph. Yes_____ No_____

EXERCISE 25.1 (continued)

8. Will the group be open-ended or closed to group members? (The authors of this workbook suggest that groups be open-ended due to the referral process)._____

   _____

9. In selecting a physical location, the following considerations are important for patient confidentiality and community safety.

   a. Is your group space located near a school or playground? Yes____ No____ If you answered "yes" please explain how you plan to provide safety for the community.

      _____

      _____

   b. Does your group space provide confidentiality for the patient? Yes____ No____

   c. Is the group area comfortable for the therapist and group members? Yes____ No____

   d. Is the group space well lighted? Yes____ No____

   e. Is there adequate parking for the patients close to the group location? Yes____ No____

   f. Are the patients allowed to stand outside their vehicle to smoke or talk with one another prior to the start of groups? Yes____ No____

   g. Are group members permitted to share rides with one another to group meetings? Yes____ No____

10. Does your group provide safety for you and the group? Yes____ No____

   If "no," what can you do to make group meetings safe? Do you have a security system or "panic button" that alerts other staff or police that there is a problem? Yes____ No____

Chapter 26

Sexual Addiction

ADULTS

Case Study

Hal is a forty-year-old attorney who is regarded as one of the best lawyers in town. He is sought out by many well-to-do clients in the community to provide legal counsel. Hal's practice has evolved from a one man office to four partners, ten associates, and a number of paralegal and related support staff.

He is married to an attorney and is the father of two children. However, five years ago, Hal started to engage in sex with prostitutes. He has spent thousands of dollars each year on high-price call girls. Often, he will fly to Las Vegas for a weekend of sex. In the past year, he has shown a marked increase in his sexual appetite and has started to pick up strange women in bars. He has increased the number of rendezvous from a weekly fling to three or four illicit encounters per week. He now spends time away from his firm many times a week to go see a woman at a hotel.

His partners are worried and have expressed concern about him. He appears irritable and depressed. He has little interest in sports and his favorite hobby of golf. He will often come to work unshaven and dressed in yesterday's suit. Several of his staff members have encouraged him to consider a medical examination. He will attend client depositions with little or no preparation. He has forgotten to file legal briefs on important cases. A number of clients are complaining.

Does this behavior resemble someone who has a sexual addiction problem? The answer is yes for Hal. Hal's sexual acting-out has escalated and he is now out of control. Although his sexual activity has increased, there is a diminished level in actual sexual gratification. In comparison, an alcoholic will increase his or her intake of whiskey, but the pleasure of a euphoric mood becomes less over time.

According to Carnes (2001), sexual addiction is similar to any other type of addictive behavior in which the "mood-altering experience becomes central" to the patient's life. Sexual addiction is a physical and psychological problem for individuals. There is a compulsive action driving the addict to satisfy sexual need. Anxiety and distress will occur if the addictive behaviors are not met.

Research shows that endorphin and serotonin levels of the brain are activated by neurological responses to the addictive activity. Physical exercise that is aerobic can produce the same sense of pleasure without the self destructive features. Many joggers will report a "runner's high."

Sex becomes the driving force in the addict's life. Impaired insight and judgment is found. Rationalization and qualifying behaviors are found. Risk-taking occurs more frequently. An individual will make promises to stop, but is unable to do so.

Sex-Offender Therapy
© 2008 by The Haworth Press, Taylor & Francis Group. All rights reserved.
doi:10.1300/5753_26

Both men and women suffer from sexual addictive problems. Also, sexual addictive behaviors may be found in adolescents and children. Is sexual addiction found in adult sex offenders? The answer again is yes. Addiction is also found in youth who are sexually aggressive.

In most cases, since the sexual acting-out has evolved over a period of time, the individual has become increasingly reckless in sexual activity. Eventually, he or she crosses a boundary and becomes involved with the criminal justice system. Certainly, it is understood that persons with paraphilia behaviors, who have repeated sexual misconduct incidents, are highly sexually addictive, obsessive, and qualify as sex offenders. However, other patient population groups that are less obvious also are found to be addicted to sex and have violated a law in which another person is harmed in a sexual way.

Let's return to Hal—our patient. He continues to have sexual affairs and contact with prostitutes. His behavior has become increasingly reckless. He now sees younger women as well as persons in his own age group. Younger women have opened a new door of sexual interest for Hal. He now enjoys cruising bars or clubs where younger adults hang out. He will select several young females at a nightspot and attempt to engage them in conversation. He has rituals that help him win a specific target. Hal will groom a particular young woman by offering to pay for her drink. He does ask her age to ensure that she is not a minor. His distorted thinking has impaired his judgment to also check identification. As well, he has failed to recognize that many girls will use false IDs to enter a club. On one occasion, he meets a fifteen-year-old girl who says she is twenty-one. He takes the girl to a hotel room and the two have sex. No force is used. However, the girl is a minor by law, and is unable to give consent. Her father learns of the incident and files a charge of rape against Hal. He is arrested and the story is headline news. Now, Hal has crossed the line from having only a sexual addiction to being a sex offender. The patient has broken a law due to his reckless actions and inability to stop.

Carnes (2001) says there are four steps in the sexual addiction process. First is *preoccupation,* in which the addict's mood is dominated with thoughts of sex. Hal experienced a number of fantasy thoughts about sex with other women. As a result, an obsessive search for sexual satisfaction occurs. Second, is *ritualization,* in which certain rituals are used during the hunt for sex. Searching for the escort ads in the telephone yellow pages was one of Hal's first rituals. Hal would become excited. Later, he would become more aroused checking into a hotel room in which he planned later to bring a woman to for sex. Third is *compulsion,* sexual behavior in which the addict is unable to stop his or her sexual acting-out. Hal would make promises that he would stop having sex with other women but failed to do so. Fourth is *despair,* in which the addict displays a feeling of hopelessness. The patient feels powerless to make a change. The addict's life is now unmanageable. Hal became more depressed as he discovered he could not stop his sexually addictive behaviors.

Sexual recovery therapy is a treatment model that endorses the belief that sexual addiction and sexual offending are learned behaviors. Something has occurred in the person that has caused him or her to stray from acceptable behaviors. Rarely do sex offenders or sexual addicts report that they are happy with their affliction and had planned all their life to engage in inappropriate conduct. Research shows that what one experiences in childhood can impact later behavior. Only recently, has the mental health community started to recognize sex offenders as flawed human beings instead of monsters. This does not excuse the sexually addicted or sexual abuse, but gives a different approach in how we are to treat this patient group.

Sexual addicts and offenders are found to possess certain developmental problems that have been repressed. These issues have remained dominant for an extended period of time and then exploded. Please note that many sexual addicts are not arrested. Also, sexual addicts are more receptive to treatment than an offender.

In sexual recovery therapy, patients who are sexual addicts and offenders share the following problems of past childhood incidents, or developmental regression, impacting coping skills.

- A possible history of childhood sexual abuse.
- Usually, a dysfunctional family system that was emotionally, physically, or sexually abusive.
- Childhood trauma at the death of a parent.
- Extreme issues of abandonment, isolation, or trust.
- Difficulty managing rejection, failure, or shame.
- An unrealistic fear over a loss of control.
- Apprehension of change to something new, unknown, or different occurring.

In treating sexual addiction and offending, the clinician cannot remain in "the here and now." This type of therapy only treats the symptoms rather than the core disturbance.

Sexual recovery therapy encourages patients with addiction and offending behaviors to open up the doors that have been closed. Sometimes, revealing sealed wounds can be difficult. Insight is important in recovery work.

The following suggestions may be useful for a clinician:

- Encourage the patient to identify early traumatic events.
- After problem behaviors are identified, a therapist should then help the patient explore his or her feelings of rejection, fear, and shame.
- The clinician will work with the patient on nurturing oneself, in a caring manner, validating what he or she has repressed or denied, and focusing on his or her strengths rather than his or her weaknesses.
- A patient then is encouraged to replace the old negative behaviors with new positive experiences that promote healthy lifestyle changes.
- The therapist helps the patient work on affirmation of a new self-image. Yes, I may have made mistakes, but I am a good person, and I want to make amends.

See Exercise 26.1.

ADOLESCENTS AND CHILDREN

Adolescents may also develop sexually addictive behaviors. Trauma is usually associated with a sexual-outing youth. Sexual aggressive behaviors may be found. Criminal justice, human service, and mental health professionals often experience problems helping, treating, and working with this population group.

Case Study

Marie is a sixteen-year-old girl who lives at home with her parents. Marie's father was an alcoholic. In addition, he is a police officer. In her eighth year, her father started to sexually abuse her. She told her mother, who called her a liar. Later, in an effort to have control in her life, she started to engage in sexual relations with boys at school. She also feels distress if she does not have frequent sex.

Marie found that she enjoyed the power that she had over males by the use of sex. Yet, this behavior appeared to extend beyond her willingness to be sexually active. She found herself having sexual fantasies about particular boys. Also, her thoughts were often preoccupied by sex. She would begin grooming a potential partner by sending him sexually explicit e-mails. Often, she would then follow up with a flirtation encounter at school.

Marie was an attractive, dark-haired girl with green eyes. She was popular in school and maintained a secret lifestyle. However, the sexual acting-out took another form that used high-risk behaviors. She would have sex with boys without condoms. Eventually, she started to take money for sex. In her junior year, she was arrested for prostitution and drug trafficking after she had arranged a wave party for several girls and boys. One of the males turned out to be an undercover police officer. Marie agreed to take money in exchange for sex and was taken into custody by police.

See Exercise 26.2 for questions related to this case study.

Adults, children, and adolescents all are found to have sexual addiction problems. How do therapists recognize sexual addiction, sexual aggression, and offending behavior in patients? Please use the list below as a clinical questionnaire for yourself.

1. The first sexual activity occurred at an early age.
2. Childhood sexual abuse is reported.
3. A history of emotional, physical or sexual abuse.
4. An extensive sexual partner list.
5. Engaging in sex with persons by force, or having relations with minors, or engaging in sexual activity with persons who are mentally incompetent to give consent.
6. An extensive sexual fantasy history.
7. Sexual preoccupation is a problem.
8. Sexual obsession is reported.
9. Sexual rituals are a part of the addictive and offending behaviors.
10. Sexual behavior that impacts social, family, or occupation activities.
11. There is anxiety, distress, frustration, and irritability in behavior, if the patient does not engage in sex within a certain time period.
12. A patient will engage in high-risk behaviors.

Criminal justice, human services, and mental health professionals experience the most difficulty in deciding what service to offer a child who has sexually offended. Many courts are reluctant to have the minor prosecuted. Treatment is the preferred option. However, what type of treatment is sometimes difficult to determine. In many cases, the child is very sexually addictive, sometimes even more so than an adult, for their impulse control system has not matured.

Case Study

Terry is a ten-year-old boy who attempted to force his four-year-old brother to engage in anal sex. Terry was sexually abused since age three by several family relatives. The patient has become sexually aggressive himself. Prior to the incident, he had been found in a school restroom performing oral sex on a younger boy. Last year, Terry was placed in a psychiatric hospital after he used an intimated object and forced it into the rectum of another child. Terry's father is in prison. He lives with his mother. The case has been presented before the county multidisciplinary treatment team for review.

1. Do you believe Terry is sexually aggressive? Do you believe Terry is sexually addicted?

_____

2. What clinical issues are present in this child that merit treatment?

_____

SUMMARY

In summary, sexual addiction, sexual offending, and sexually aggressive behaviors are found in many patients. These behaviors—as sexual addiction—appear related to sexual offending and sexual aggression. Sexual addiction can lead the patient to offending, as the need for new experiences occurs. Sexual recovery therapy encourages clinicians to educate others about treatment and recovery.

EXERCISE 26.1. SEXUAL ADDICTION VERSUS SEXUAL OFFENDING

1. What is the difference between sexual addiction and sexual offending?

_____

_____

2. How are these two behaviors related?

_____

_____

3. Why do you think sexual addiction is seen as less threatening to the lay public? Why do you think that sexual offenders have not received the clinical attention associated with the sexual addiction process?

_____

_____

4. Is Hal a sex offender? Please describe your thoughts on this issue. What are his clinical diagnoses?

_____

_____

5. What do you think caused Hal's sexual addiction? Could the problem behavior have been stopped? Do you think Hal will remain sexually sober?

_____

_____

6. What defense mechanisms existed in Hal during the apex of his sexual addiction?

_____

_____

7. Did Hal display depersonalization features?

_____

_____

EXERCISE 26.2. CASE STUDY QUESTIONS

1. What type of clinical intervention should be offered to Marie?

_____

_____

2. What are Marie's clinical diagnoses?

_____

_____

3. Do you believe that Marie is sexually addictive? Why or why not? Do you believe that Marie is a sexually aggressive adolescent? Why or why not?

_____

_____

4. What clinical issues may occur during Marie's treatment?

_____

_____

5. What developmental stages have been impacted as the result of Marie's sexual abuse and sexual acting out?

_____

_____

6. What diagnoses would you give Marie?

_____

_____

7. Please outline a treatment plan for Marie that would include goals, objectives, and types of interventions.

_____

_____

Chapter 27

Family Reunification

Family reunification is used when an offender is permitted to return to his or her home. Sexual recovery therapy is a recommended treatment model in helping a family to reunite. Once it is decided that an offender may return to the home, this form of treatment should begin.

Sexual recovery therapy may be used in reunification work with adults, adolescents, and children. Reportedly, there has been an incident of sexual abuse. Someone in the home was harmed. Therefore, before any psychotherapy is started, the offender should first be asked to leave the house—or be removed by court order from the residence. Sexual recovery therapy does not endorse any plan to remove a victim, child, or adolescent from their home. An adult is more emotionally equipped to move out. The youthful offender will experience more difficulty in leaving the residence.

In years past, if a child was reported harmed, many agencies used the practice of placing the victim in foster care, or with another family member, while permitting the sex offender to remain in the residence. This approach violates against the youth.

As noted by O'Connell, Leberg, and Donaldson (1990), after a sex offender is identified, he or she should be the one who is separated from the family. Sexually aggressive behavior today is found in adults, adolescents, and children of both genders. Therefore, the lay image of an offender is difficult to ascertain simply by age, appearance, or gender. Fathers abuse daughters, mothers harm sons, and brothers hurt sisters. Other sexual misconduct behaviors involving family members may be reported.

A sexually abusive family system often exhibits a long history of psychopathology. The family may be found to be very enmeshed and overly involved with each member. Another family may be found to be extremely disengaged with little interaction between members. Boundaries may be very loose or extremely rigid.

In some cases, a child who has been sexually abused may require acute care work to begin immediately. As an example, the father is the offender and has been sent to prison. Prior to his incarceration, the daughter attempts suicide and is placed in a psychiatric inpatient hospital for a short stay. The offender should not be permitted contact with the victim. Most courts seek out the opinion of the therapist before contact between an offender and victim is approved. In cases where a mother or sibling is the offender, the same plan may be used. A spouse or parent may elect to visit the offender without the victim. Family therapy should be started without the offender.

If the sibling has harmed another child or adolescent in the home, he or she may be referred to a therapeutic foster home, group home, or residential program, until other members of the family are ready to begin reunification work. Sexual recovery therapy does not advocate that a child or adolescent be removed from the local community, unless all other less-restrictive alternatives have been exhausted. There are many fine residential programs in the United States. However, it is very difficult to help a youthful offender if he or she is placed out of the local area. A key element is to have all family members within driving distance of the outpatient treatment site. Also, placing a youth far from the family can sometimes, no matter how good the program, reinforce

Sex-Offender Therapy
doi:10.1300/5753_27

abandonment, anger, alienation, attachment problems, confusion, depression, mistrust, and psychological trauma, as well as escalate psychiatric disorders. The approach to treating a sexually aggressive child or adolescent is very different from adult treatment. This patient population has many developmental issues that will need to be addressed.

Nearly all sexually aggressive children or adolescents were victimized in the past, or experienced some type of sexual event that was psychologically disruptive. Family violence can also contribute to sexual aggression. Victim issues may need to be a part of the therapy.

A psychosexual evaluation should be completed on an offender. Such an assessment should include a clinical interview, testing, an FDA-approved penile plethysmograph, and a full-disclosure polygraph examination. Such an evaluation may be modified depending upon age and gender. During the testing, the sexually aggressive adult or child should not have any contact with the victim. The victim may need to be seen individually or in family therapy.

Most adult and adolescent offenders are arrested after an offense occurs. Sexually aggressive children usually are referred to sex-offender therapy. Family reunification therapy should not start until other sex-specific treatment services have been completed. However, psychotherapy may continue with other members of the family. If the adult is not jailed, he or she should be referred to group therapy. A youth may need to be seen separate from his or her family for a period of time.

The adult offender or sexually aggressive youth should have no contact with the victim after removal has occurred. No e-mails, letters, or telephone calls should occur. Neither should any type of supervised visitation be arranged. Contact is started with the victim only after the adult offender has nearly finished group therapy.

Eventually, a family may decide to have the offender return to the home. Such a plan should be approved by the court, probation officer, social service worker, and therapist in advance. If all persons support the plan, family reunification may begin.

VICTIM SAFETY

Sexual recovery therapy uses specific safeguards in order to ensure victim safety. They are as follows:

1. Reunification treatment should not occur until the offender, victim, and family have received separate specialized treatment services. It would not work to have an offender begin group therapy and reunification therapy at the same time.
2. The adult sex offender should be in a sex-offender group before reunification treatment is started.
3. If the offender is a minor, he or she should be seen in therapy. If in the community, separate the victim for an extended period.
4. Each member of the family is expected to be a part of the treatment process.
5. Noncompliance is an indication that certain members of the family, or the offender, are not ready for reunification. Sexual recovery therapy should be stopped.
6. Any sexual misconduct by the offender should be reported to the supervising probation officer. Therapy should be stopped.
7. Any anxiety, fear, or reluctance exhibited by the victim should be explored immediately. The therapy should be stopped until the victim is ready to continue.

Several books have been completed on basic rules during the reunification process. It is important that the reunification period occur over a gradual period with no deadline. Safety is an issue. The first home visit should occur during the day with supervision. Short home visits may need to occur with an increase in the stay time over a gradual period. The nonoffending parent will always need to be involved in supervision. However, since this parent was not aware of the sexual abuse, a second family member should be assigned. Both parents may provide supervision if a sexually aggressive child or adolescent is the visitor. No offender should be allowed physical contact of any form with the victim. Also, the offender should be in sight at all times of the supervisor. A security system for bedroom doors and windows should be installed. In the event a computer is in the home, it should be removed. Emergency telephone contact numbers should be kept by the supervisor as well as the offender. Weekly sessions with the therapist, probation officer, and caseworker should be continued.

Madanes, Keim, and Smelser (1995) were the first clinicians to offer specific therapy techniques for use in work with abusive families in reunification. This guide is viewed as a major landmark work in treating sexually abusive families.

SEXUAL RECOVERY THERAPY AND FAMILY REUNIFICATION

Acknowledgment

The offender is to acknowledge to the victim and the family his or her sexual misconduct. Also, he or she must take full responsibility for his or her actions, and exhibit sincere victim remorse. Each family member may offer comments after the offender has completed a summary statement. The victim may choose to talk or withhold his or her feelings until a later session. Rapport-building to join the family is important.

Accounting

In this session, the offender will be expected to account for the harm he or she has cost his or her victim and family. The patient will be expected to bring a financial statement of the monetary cost the offending behavior has cost. During this session, the victim and family may begin to start sharing with the patient the psychological cost of the sexual misconduct. A therapist should be alert to both content and process in all family reunification sessions. (Certain sections may take several sessions to complete.) The therapist may need to be more directive in initial sessions. However, both process and content is always monitored. A therapist may need to be more directive at first in such therapy sessions.

Challenging and Detailing

No more sexual secrets are allowed. The victim and family are permitted to discuss with the patient how he or she abused them. Usually, these sessions can be very intense. The mother is encouraged to talk about the emotional pain she has experienced in learning that she did not protect her daughter. The daughter is permitted to express how fearful she was of her father. Also, she may talk about the details of the actual sexual abuse if merited. This should be monitored closely. A victim does need to heal and recover, but if the information is overwhelming, the session may need to be slowed down, or the details may be postponed, or only a general picture is given. The father is encouraged to apologize for harm that he has caused his daughter. He is also expected to promise that he will never harm her again. Finally, during this session, the offender is expected to get on his knees and apologize to his victim. The mother is as well expected to get on her knees and apologize to her victim. This type of apology is very symbolic. Other forms of such apology may be that each parent stands up in the room, removing their hat or jacket, and offer the victim a formal apology. The victim is not expected to forgive the parents for failing her.

All victims of the father should be revealed as well as other sexual conduct behaviors. The victim may be asked to read a statement to her parents about the pain the sexual abuse has caused her. This homework should be given in a previous session.

Strengthening and Hope

A family should be offered hope. Each member should be encouraged to talk about another person's strengths. Dreams and goals should be discussed. Usually, a sex offender has experienced a number of behavioral problems. A part of this section is to be devoted to how the patient plans on improving his or her behavior. The patient should review his or her relapse plan and emergency support system. The offender is expected to discuss psychological triggers that could lead to a reoffense. Also, the offender should discuss interventions and ways to manage his or her behavior. Family members are encouraged to offer suggestions. In addition, the offender is to explain how he or she could end up in a dangerous or risky situation, although he or she has no attempt to harm someone. He or she will also be expected to provide education about the cycle of offending and what red flags a family member should be alert to, in order to avoid relapse.

Developing Empathy

No parent who cares about their child would harm them in a sexual manner. Something is wrong in a sexually abusive family. It is important for the family at this point in treatment to talk about the offender and empathy. Also, the other parent should discuss how she may have openly or covertly enabled her husband to harm their daughter. In order for remorse to occur, the offender must know the harm that was committed was wrong and how much damage was caused to the family. The abuser depersonalizes in order to harm. The parents will be asked to discuss their relationship and how they set boundaries. Enmeshment and disengagement should be explored by the therapist with the family. What types of boundaries exist in this family? The father should talk with his wife about what cognitive distortions he may have possessed leading to the sexual assault upon the daughter. Some anger may be a part of these sessions as well. Here, the symptoms of the dysfunction have been peeled back, and the family is asked to look into the well and examine their interactions.

Sexual Restructuring

The family is encouraged to find a new way of expression. Sexual acting-out is no longer allowed in this family. Insight will be an important element for the therapist to monitor. In these sessions, the therapist will be less directive or helpful than in past sessions. Family members may experience difficulty at times. A therapist is encouraged to permit anxiety and pauses. It is very important for the therapist at this stage of treatment to permit the family to find the trail out of the forest. Minor directions are helpful, but the burden is placed upon the parents to sexually redefine what is normal for their family. If either parent has been sexually abused, this will be important to talk about in session. Also, how did the parent's abuse impact the current offending? What cognitive distortions did the abuse cause? Sexual education should also be a part of therapy sessions. Some humor may be used by the therapist in helping the family to learn to communicate again. Also, humor is effective in helping sexually abusive families absorb the information and move forward.

Atonement

Atonement is an important element in the healing process. Here the offender promises that he or she will no longer harm anyone. He or she is informed if he or she harms anyone again, he or she will be banished from the family, for he or she cannot be trusted. Also, his or her actions will result in legal consequences. The mother, for example, tells the daughter she will protect her from any harm. Also, the father reports that he again will protect his family from harm. Other family members will be expected to offer their help, protection, and support. Atonement also means repaying for the damage one has caused. An example may be that the father offers to begin a special college fund for the daughter. The atonement task should not be an easy one for the offender.

Termination

The discussion of termination for a sexually abusive family should begin five sessions before the final meeting. Here, the family talks about the goals they have achieved in therapy. The family reviews how they feel and what plans they have for the future. It is important for the therapist to introduce termination in advance. If there is some anxiety and resistance to ending, this may indicate that some issues remain that need to be reviewed. Also, a therapist needs to keep in mind that if a family leaves before they are ready someone can be harmed. No family should be released early or before they have completed the full program.

See Exercise 27.1.

SUMMARY

Family reunification is a specific therapy model that is used in the recovery process. The sexually aggressive patient is expected to meet with the family and offer an apology in a very symbolic manner. Each session is very technique oriented for the patient, and the family should have already completed other components of the treatment program. All family members are encouraged to attend sessions. The patient is permitted to voice the problems he or she has encountered as a result of the misconduct. Other family members are encouraged to talk about the emotional pain they have experienced. Such a therapy may not be appropriate for all patients. Certain patients may be viewed as too dangerous to return to the home, particularly if the victim continues to reside there. In the event that the patient does return home, certain precautions will need to be in place in order to have a safety plan. Family reunification therapy is focused upon helping a family heal (whether the victim is in the home or not) in order for the patient to return to the home. This is the last stage in the treatment process before termination is recommended.

EXERCISE 27.1. THE THERAPIST AND FAMILY REUNIFICATION

1. Please list the most difficult stage of sexual recovery therapy and family reunification for you as a therapist. Why?

_____

_____

2. Do you feel comfortable in offering this type of treatment to a family? Why or why not?

_____

_____

3. What clinician strengths can you offer a sexually abusive family? What are these attributes?

_____

_____

4. How would you manage hearing that a mother was aware of her daughter's abuse by the father, but chose not to intervene? What thoughts do you think they would experience?

_____

_____

5. What other techniques would be applicable in working with a sexually abusive family?

_____

_____

6. Atonement is listed as a way to amend the damage the offender has caused the victim. In addition to text sections, what other methods may be appropriate?

_____

_____

7. Why should family reunification be used? Would it not be easier for the family to reside separate from the offender?

_____

_____

Chapter 28

Risk Assessment

A risk assessment should be included in a psychosexual evaluation of a sex offender. Currently, only adult male risk assessments exist that have been field-tested and standardized. There are no valid adult female risk assessments in place at the present time. Also, there are several risk assessments in use for sexually aggressive adolescents in the field for study.

RAPID RISK ASSESSMENT FOR SEXUAL OFFENSE RECIDIVISM

The first adult male assessment to receive wide support from mental health professionals was developed by Hanson and Phenix (1999). In the past, risk assessments were more subjective. The Rapid Risk Assessment for Sexual Offense Recidivism (RRASOR) is an actuarial risk assessment using a small number of variables as a part of the measurement for sex offense recidivism and has become popular in both the United States and Canada.

Clinical trials have been used to assess the accuracy rate of predication of sex offenders. The test has projection rates for a five-year and a ten-year period. The five-year period is said to be more accurate and reliable. Scoring is based on a 0 to 5 scale. The following guidelines are suggested:

1. *The Index Offense (Sexual Crime):* In scoring the RRASOR, the present index offense is not to be counted for projecting further offenses. A 0 score is listed.
2. *Prior Sex Offenses:* Only sexual offenses in which the patient is actually convicted should be counted. (Refer to the following chart for scoring.)
3. *Age at Release (Current Age):* Persons who are less than twenty-five years of age at their time of release from jail or prison should receive a score of 1.
4. *Victim Gender:* Persons who have committed a sexual offense that involved a male victim should receive a score of 1.
5. *Relationship to Victim:* Sexual misconduct behavior with unrelated estranged victims should receive a score of 1.

Criteria	Score
Previous sexual crimes (the current crime is not counted):	
None	0
1 sentence; 1-2 offenses or charges	1
2 separate sentences or convictions; 3-5 offenses	2
4 or more separate sentences or convictions; 6 or more charges	3

Sex-Offender Therapy
© 2008 by The Haworth Press, Taylor & Francis Group. All rights reserved.
doi:10.1300/5753_28

Patient's current age upon release from jail or prison:

The patient is more than twenty-five years of age	0
The patient is less than twenty-five years of age	1

Male or female victim:

Exclusively female victims	0
Any male victim	1

Relationship to the adult, adolescent or child victim:

Victim is related to the offender	0
Victim is not related to the offender	1

Total =

OTHER RISK FACTORS

The RRASOR also permits additional, but moderate, point scoring for the following categories: a sexual deviant preference that exceeds social norms; early onset of sexual misconduct usually starting as a child or adolescent; paraphilia sex crimes as fondling of a minor; a past criminal life story and history; a patient who has never married and is single; or a patient who has failed to complete a previous sex-offender treatment program. The scoring for this section may be answered in a yes or no format or numerical, and can be added to the previous total.

DYNAMIC PREDICTIONS OF SEX-OFFENDER RECIDIVISM

The RRASOR score may be adjusted "slightly" if the following are noted in the patient: problems of intimacy; negative relationships; an acceptance of sexual assault of another person; problems of impulse control, as in irritable mood eventually leading to a sexual contact; problems of reckless and impulsive actions; poor self-esteem; general lifestyle instability; or a variety of sexual offenses that deal with paraphilia features. The patient is single, and has never married or lived with a companion. The patient failed to complete a previous sex-offender treatment program. The dynamic indicator for a sexual reoffense (the score should be evaluated slightly for the patient) includes: emotional intimacy problems, negative peer influence, tolerance of sexual assault behavior, displaying mood change resulting in sex, and impaired impulse-control problems. Estimated relapse rates are listed for each score. Scoring is based on a 0 to 5 scale. (See also Exercise 28.1.)

Possible Reoffense Rate

Score	Five-Year Period	Ten-Year Period
0	4.4%	6.5%
1	7.6%	11.2%
2	14.2%	21.1%
3	24.8%	36.9%
4	32.7%	48.6%
5	49.8%	73.1%

STATIC-99

The most recent actuarial risk assessment by Phenix and Hanson (2000) is known as the STATIC-99. (See Exercise 28.2.) This assessment is even more specific in the identification of risk, without the use of subjective variables that are available in the RRASOR. A STATIC-99 coding form is provided for a clinician when completing an assessment on a patient. The total scare score is 0 to 12, with a score of 6 considered high. Adult males who have been arrested, charged, convicted, or sentenced of at least one sexual offense involving an adult or child can be evaluated using the STATIC-99. The assessment can be used for first-time sex offenders.

Question	*Risk Factor*	*Criteria*	*Score*
1	Patient is young	Patient is 25 or older	0
		Patient is 18 to 24	1
2	Patient has been married or lived with companion	Patient has lived with companion for two or more years	1
3	An index crime resulting in a sentence, offense was nonsexual		1
4	Previous nonsexual sentences		1
5	Previous sex crime	Arrest	Sentence
	History	None	None
6	Prior conviction before present offense	3 or less	0
		4 or above	1
7	Prior sentences for non-contact sex offenses	0	0
8	Victims not related	0	0
9	Victim is unknown to the offender	0	0
10	Male victim	0	0
	Total =		

STATIC-99 Risk Factor Score with Estimated Reoffense Predication

Score	Risk
0 to 1	Low
2 to 3	Moderate-Low
3 to 4	Moderate-High
6 or above	High

Phenix and Hanson (2000) say the STATIC-99 is a ten-item program to be used to evaluate the potential for sexual relapse. Each section is related to specific sexual relapse and only uses STATIC factors that are not changeable. (See Exercise 28.3 for case study examples using the STATIC-99.)

SUMMARY

The only field-tested risk assessments that exist are for adult male sex offenders. These assessments are actuarial and are not based on subjective interpretation. There are no known risk assessments for sexually aggressive adult females, adolescents, or children that are actuarial, field-studied, and documented by research at the present time. Adolescent subjective risk assessments are available for clinicians, but prediction is based on a subjective review of the patient's history. More research is merited for sexually aggressive females, adolescents, and children for the development of a comprehensive risk evaluation. Risk assessments are important for those professionals who will be working with the patient. Treatment can be adjusted according to risk. Probation and parole supervision can be enhanced. It is very important to know if a patient is at low risk for a reoffense or at a high risk for relapse. As well, such information is important for the court.

EXERCISE 28.1. ASSESSING RISK OF RECIDIVISM—RRASOR

1. Please select a fictional patient and calculate the RRASOR score.

   _____

   _____

2. Please use the fictional score to list a five-year projection rate.

   _____

   _____

3. Please use the fictional patient for a ten-year projection rate.

   _____

   _____

EXERCISE 28.2. ASSESSING RISK OF RECIDIVISM—STATIC-99

1. Please complete a STATIC-99 score for a fictional adult male sex offender.

_____

_____

2. Please write out your scoring list for each question.

_____

_____

3. Please list your score total and assign a level of risk category.

_____

_____

4. Please write out a disclaimer that may be appropriate for use.

_____

_____

EXERCISE 28.3. CASE STUDY EXAMPLES

1. Jackson was convicted of raping an adult female. He was recently released from prison. He has no prior sexual offense history. However, he has an extensive criminal past. He was not related to the victim. He is twenty-four years of age. He has not shared a residence with an adult female companion. Please score this patient, using first the RRASOR, followed by the STATIC-99. _____

_____

_____

_____

_____

2. Mickey is a thirty-eight-year-old male who was recently released from prison. He was incarcerated on a charge of sexually abusing his twelve-year-old daughter. He has a prior arrest for sexual assault of a nine-year-old, nonrelative, neighbor boy. He has lived with his wife for five years, but the two divorced after his second arrest. He has no other criminal history. Mickey is an emotionally detached man who holds down a steady job as a mechanic. He is not involved with family or friends. Please complete a risk assessment on this patient first using the RRASOR, followed by the STATIC-99. Determine the risk level for this patient. _____

_____

_____

_____

_____

Chapter 29

The Internet

SEXUAL PREDATORS

The Internet has enhanced communication on a global scale. Unfortunately, a new form of sexual misconduct behavior has emerged with the Internet.

Sexual predators have emerged by making contact with adults, adolescents, and children. According to Hanson (2005), one in five children is approached sometime during their use of the Internet. In addition, children may be contacted as early as sixty seconds after entering a chat room. Disturbingly, it was also found that as many as 75 percent of parents believe safety software would impair their children's use of the Internet for educational or social purposes.

Salter (2003) says research confirms a growing problem of sexual-disordered persons who make contact with children. She says that one in five adolescents ages ten to seventeen have had contact by persons for sexual misconduct behaviors. Also, it was reported that one in thirty received an aggressive type of solicitation. This would include offline contact by mail, telephone, or in person. A large number of those who make contact with children are antisocial-disordered.

It is important for therapists who work with such offenders to be aware of the clinical characteristics of such patients. The majority of those adults who make contact with children on the Internet carry an Axis I disorder, which usually includes pedophilia, fetishism, exhibitionism, sexual masochism, sexual sadism, transvestism, voyeurism, or sexual disorder NOS. As previously noted, a number of these adults possess an Axis II disorder of antisocial personality disorder. There are other Axis I and Axis II disorders that are found less frequently than those listed here.

The average Internet sexual predator is male and above the age of eighteen. Most are very computer literate and are aware of the online chat rooms that children frequent. In addition, female offenders are now being reported. Also, adolescents as young as thirteen are an emerging group.

In treating online offenders, it is often surprising to therapists to find the level of depersonalization that is found in this patient group. Many view the child and adolescent victims only in the abstract form created for their sexual pleasure, and do not see them as actual persons. Online contact is emerging as the cocaine of the sex-offender patient group. Internet use and the abuse of youth appears to be highly addictive with only one experience leading to a patient's need to secure the euphoric effect.

Case Study

Jake, a twenty-nine-year-old white, married male with two children, is employed as an accountant. He was arrested for downloading and trafficking child pornography. He reported in the clinical interview that he also was involved in numerous chat lines with preadolescent females. Jake says he developed what he describes as an obsession to viewing child pornography. He says he had first started viewing adult porn sites, but one day happened to find a teenage Web

Sex-Offender Therapy
© 2008 by The Haworth Press, Taylor & Francis Group. All rights reserved.
doi:10.1300/5753_29

page. This lead to an interest in younger children in a variety of sexual acts. He says he knew what he was doing was wrong, but really never saw the children as victims.

See Exercise 29.1 for review questions.

Blogging

Blogging has become popular among children, teenagers, and young adults. Personal histories are available on the Internet. Sexual offenders scan these on a regular basis, selecting possible victims.

TYPES OF PREDATORS

Adult Males

A nonclinical term references Internet child predators as polymorphous and will prey upon anyone. Four basic nonclinical groups are identified. The sexual-disordered patient is not listed with the NCMEC (National Center for Missing and Exploited Children, 2007) but has emerged as a separate group. Most of this group are male offenders. They are as follows:

1. *Collectors*—Such persons are considered to be at an entry level and have no prior criminal history. Collecting starts with child photographs taken from the Internet. As the interest continues, behavior increases with more time spent seeking graphic images. Chat rooms are used by such offenders depending upon victim target group and physical appearance.
2. *Travelers*—This type of Internet offender will engage in online chat rooms with minors. The interest is sexual, and such persons will attempt to manipulate or coerce a child into a meeting place. Travelers also collect child porn. Relationships online with a child usually are developed between two to four sessions. Grooming of victims is a part of the process, in an effort to develop trust and a relationship with a child.
3. *The sexual-disordered patient*—These offenders seek out victims for sexual purposes. They may use blogging Web sites for reference. The goal is to have sex with the victim. Such persons can be dangerous. In males there are persons who exhibit features of sexual sadism and other bizarre fetish behaviors. Many meet the criteria for pedophilia.
4. *Manufacturers*—This type of offender makes and distributes child porn photographs, tapes, and CD-ROMs. All manufacturers are collectors. To purchase products, this type of offender will have a PayPal system. Many manufacturers will take in runaways, are likely to have criminal histories, and will frequent places where children gather.
5. *Chatters*—This type of individual tends to be a mentor to children online. Child porn does not interest most chatters. The chatters also will encourage the use of the telephone to enhance the relationship. They will attempt to reach children and quickly elevate their interaction to sex. Chatters rarely attempt to meet children in person.

Adult Females

Cybersex addiction is not limited to men. Carnes (2001) reports that approximately 40 percent of cybersex addicts are female. Cognitive distortion and impaired insight and judgement are found to be clinical features of many of these women. The anonymity of being able to test a relationship from their home is an attraction. However, like men, women as well become addicted to cybersex use.

One group of women who possess a cybersex addiction prey upon children and adolescents. Young males are often a target population for these women. Research is limited about this growing population. Several cases involving cybersex, adult women and adolescent males, have been reported in the national media. The adult female may be a school teacher, neighbor, relative, family friend, or stranger. All occupational groups are found among this group of adult females who offend. Also, both married and single women are reported to abuse. Female cybersex offenders will use this form of interaction to secure emotional intimacy. In many cases a youth is elevated to a partner-level status by the woman. In addition, she may use many adolescent expressions in order to gain trust. Some female cybersex offenders limit their interaction to e-mail and chat rooms. Others use the Internet to lead to a meeting with a potential victim.

Eventually, the female cybersex offender turns the conversation to sex. As a result, within a period of time, a meeting is arranged. However, the grooming process continues, and sex often does not occur at the first meeting. Several secret "dates" may occur before the adult female engages in sexual relations with the adolescent. A relationship may be long-term with a single victim by an adult female offender. The relationship is a key element for the female offender. She will report that the victim is the only one that she can talk to openly. The cybersex offender will increase contact with the youth as the relationship grows. Sex becomes more frequent as the relationship grows.

There are three types of adult female offenders. These are as follows:

1. *Chatters.* This type of offender limits contact with a victim to online e-mail or chats. A period of grooming will occur and shared interests are expressed. However, the adult female offender eventually turns the conversation to sex. This type of offender does not engage in contact with the victim in other forms. Emotional intimacy is important for this offender. Clinical disorders often found in such patients include anxiety disorder, avoidant personality disorder, borderline personality disorder, dependent personality disorder, panic disorder, social phobia, and a history of sexual abuse.
2. *The teacher/lover.* Such an adult female offender is in search of an emotional relationship. Adult relationships have not met her needs. As a result, this type of cybersex offender will engage in e-mail and chatroom relationships with the youth. Sexual themes are used after the victim is groomed. In some cases, this type of female cybersex offender will arrange a meeting with the victim. Sexual relations may occur. This offender will maintain long-term relationships with the victim. Emotional intimacy is a key element in the relationship. Clinical disorders found in this type of offender include anxiety disorder, borderline personality disorder, dependent personality disorder, and a history of sexual abuse.
3. *The sexual-disordered offender.* These cybersex offenders are extremely manipulative and plan out an assault. Their intent is to engage in sexual relations with an adolescent. Such female offenders will search chat rooms and Web sites. A meeting will be arranged for the purpose of sexual relations. Emotional intimacy is not important. This type of female offender is usually found to have an antisocial personality disorder or is a pedophile. A history of sexual abuse is often found in these patients. This type of female offender is rare.

Adolescents

Cybersex offenders also include adolescents. Many youth now have access to the Internet without parental supervision. Such youth will prey upon younger children or same-age level groups. Some adolescent cybersex offenders only use e-mail or online chat. Others encourage face-to-face meetings. Certain adolescent groups use trading and downloading as a part of their sexual offending. The trading and downloading of pornography is a federal crime. In certain cases, the trading and related trafficking involves child pornography.

The adolescent cybersex offender is usually male. Offenders may be found to be between thirteen and seventeen years of age. Their developmental growth has been impaired, in many cases, by the use of the Internet. It is not unusual to find adolescents who are sexually addicted to extreme forms of inappropriate materials or Web sites. Experimentation of sexual Web sites impacts the adolescent development. Young persons are not emotionally equipped to manage seeing inappropriate sexual misconduct. As a result, certain adolescents become fixated or sexually addicted to cybersex.

Adolescent sex offenders (nonclinical) include the following groups:

1. *Chatters.* This type of patient is involved in pornography and online chat rooms that include sexual discussions. Fantasy is a part of this patient's addiction. Sex is included in online chats.
2. *Collectors.* This group of adolescents is found to be involved in pornography and online sexual Web sites. Pornography is gathered by the youth.
3. *Traders.* This group is involved in child and adult pornography. Selling, trading, and downloading are common features in this patient group. Offenders will often engage in online activities that include adults as well as children. Sexual themes are discussed. Certain patients will groom adults as well as adolescents. Pre-adolescents may also be a target. Clinical disorders may include pedophilia, frotteurism, exhibitionism, paraphilia NOS, and sexual disorder NOS. Many patients are victims of child sexual abuse.
4. *Sexual-disordered adolescents.* This group's intent is to make online contact with a potential victim in order to groom him or her. A meeting will be arranged in order to engage in sex.

SUMMARY

A new type of sexual abuse has developed by the use of the Internet. Sexually aggressive adults and adolescents, both male and female, are using the Internet to contact potential victims. The grooming or seduction of the intended victim is by the use of e-mail and chat rooms. Several different nonclinical types of offenders are found to exist by mental health and law enforcement professionals. The age range of these sexually aggressive patients may begin as early as thirteen years of age. However, most of those offenders now being arrested are adults. Some patients only use sexual language with a victim during conversation in a chat room, while others will make personal contact with the intended prey for sexual purposes. Usually, the victims are children, adolescents, and adult women.

EXERCISE 29.1. CASE STUDY QUESTIONS

There are no right or wrong answers in this exercise.

1. What treatment problems should be listed for Jake? Use the sexual recovery therapy model. _____

    _____

2. What treatment objectives should be established for Jake? Use the sexual recovery therapy model. _____

    _____

3. Complete a clinical diagnosis for Jake. _____

    _____

4. What restrictions would be agreed upon if you decided to see Jake for therapy? _____

    _____

5. What clinical issues will be important in treatment? _____

    _____

6. How would you, as a clinician, help Jake with his lack of remorse, or help him see the children he viewed as victims? Also, how would you as a therapist address the patient's depersonalization issues? _____

    _____

7. What clinical limits should be recommended for the patient? _____

    _____

8. What stressors or triggers could cause the patient to relapse? _____

    _____

EXERCISE 29.2. IMPORTANT TERMS AND BEHAVIORS

Therapists will need to know the following terms or behaviors:

1. Describe a chatter and the features of such a person.

   _____

   _____

2. What type of offender is most likely interested in meeting a child in person?

   _____

   _____

3. Describe manipulation and coercion as it relates to online offenders.

   _____

   _____

4. What group of online offenders is most likely to engage in coercion, force, use of runaways, child prostitution, and other forms of human trafficking?

   _____

   _____

5. What age groups are found to use the Internet to contact victims?

   Adults _____   Adolescents _____   Children _____

6. Which gender is more likely to use the Internet to contact a victim?

   Male _____   Female _____

7. What group is most likely to arrange a meeting with a potential victim for sexual contact?

   _____

   _____

8. What group is the least likely to make physical contact with a potential victim for sexual
   contact? _____

   _____

Chapter 30

The Therapist's Role in Teaching Protection Methods to Children and Adults

The number of estimated sexual assaults in the United States is chilling. The Rape, Abuse, and Incest National Network (RAINN, 2006), a national sexual assault Web site and hotline, reported a new sexual assault every three minutes between 2003 to 2004. This included a staggering total of 205,000 sexual assault incidents; half of the rape victims were under age eighteen. Salholtz and colleagues (1990) report that the United States has a rape rate nearly four times higher than Germany, thirteen times higher than Great Britain, and more than twenty times higher than Japan. Only 16 percent of sexual assault victims report the incident to police (Greenfeld, 1997). In addition, it is estimated that an adult woman is raped every six minutes, and every hour approximately sixteen female victims confront a rapist. Three out of ten children who were rape victims had not reached their eleventh birthday.

According to RAINN (2006) known sexual assaults have dropped in the last decade by 64 percent and almost 25 percent since 2000. However, the number of reported sexual assaults has increased by 50 percent in the last five years.

The Center for Sex Offender Management (CSOM, 2007) is a Web site and resource center utilized by professional counselors, probation officers, and other professionals working with the sex-offender population. This group reports that over the last ten years, a survey revealed 76 percent of adult women were raped by someone that they were intimately related to, including husbands, partners, or dating companions.

As clinicians, a goal is to educate patients on how to protect their children and themselves against the possibility of a sexual assault or rape. It is important to teach patients a holistic approach to protect the mind, body, and spirit, as these three aspects involve physical, mental, and emotional safety beginning at home and during the patient's everyday life.

To a therapist, the parents are the most valuable resource in prevention methods to combat possible sexual assault incidents. Also, encouraging parents to talk to their children is a key to a their safety. For a child, being aware that his or her words do not fall on deaf ears is reassuring. Such a parent and child interaction permits both persons to voice questions and concerns. Parents must be open to discussions about sex and prevention issues. It is important for a parent to permit a child's questions about life, smoking, alcohol and drugs, dating and friends, grades and school, and his or her body and sex. Answers and questions should be based upon the child's age, and limited to areas that merit attention, without frightening or overwhelming the child.

For adults, it is imperative that the therapist teaches family and friends to listen to an adult victim, as being sexually assaulted is just as traumatic as it is to a young child. The number of rape crisis centers and support groups have increased in recent years, offering solace, assistance, and refuge to those faced with discussing the horror of sexual assault. Nonetheless, adults can be as reluctant to report their sexual assaults as children for the fear of embarrassment, humiliation, guilt, shame, harassment (by an offender), and a secondary experience of violation. A therapist can model how adults can discuss such issues with spouses, partners, family, friends, and co-

Sex-Offender Therapy
© 2008 by The Haworth Press, Taylor & Francis Group. All rights reserved.
doi:10.1300/5753_30

workers. This freedom of expression allows individuals to diminish some anxiety and stress over how to voice their fears, pain, and worry, as the process of healing and recovery occurs.

TREATMENT RESOURCES

A multitude of reference material is available to therapists and patients at the present time. No longer is sexual abuse kept a secret.

From Darkness to Light

One nonprofit organization, From Darkness to Light (2007), encourages professionals and other adults to teach prevention methods, offer education, be aware of the signs of abuse, react appropriately, and notify law enforcement immediately of any abuse committed. Many police departments are now very versed in the interview and investigative process of victims of sexual abuse.

The organization offers a wide array of information about sexual abuse. From Darkness to Light (2000), recommends educating parents and communities about sexual abuse, and using this information to help others. The group's data states:

- one in four girls, and one in six boys are sexually abused prior to their eighteenth birthday;
- one-fifth of children using the Internet are solicited by a sexual predator for sex;
- approximately 70 percent of all assaults happen to children under seventeen years of age;
- the average age of sexual abuse is nine years of age;
- nearly one fifth of victims are under age eight;
- half of child victims of forcible sodomy, sexual assault with an object, and/or forced touching are under age twelve;
- most children, about 90 percent, know their attacker;
- approximately one-third of all children are victimized by a member of their family; and,
- sexually aggressive adolescents represent approximately 40 percent of all child sexual abuse.

The National Center for Missing and Exploited Children

The National Center for Missing and Exploited Children lists on their Web site valuable information on how to protect children and adolescents from sexual predators.

Stop It Now!

This center provides parents and professionals important information in regard to child safety and sex offenders.

PARENT TIPS FOR PROTECTION

The National Center for Missing and Exploited Children (2007) offers the following guidelines in protecting youth:

1. Always be aware of the location of your child or adolescent, both day and night.
2. Do not leave a child or adolescent in a vehicle alone or with the engine running.

3. Do not permit your child or adolescent to believe hitchhiking is safe. Even the most hard-core sex offenders do not hitchhike in fear of being harmed.
4. Take an active involvement in your child's or adolescent's activities at church, school, sports events, or other activities outside the home.
5. Use active listening skills.
6. Take notice when a child or adolescent expresses concern about an adult who interacts with him or her, inside or outside of the home.
7. Be alert to adults or older adolescents who take an unusual interest in your child, offer special attention interest, or do favors, or give gifts.
8. Review the word, "NO," and what is appropriate and inappropriate touch.
9. Be alert to changes in your child or adolescent that are different from typical behaviors.
10. Always screen any person who will be providing baby-sitting activity, child care, and transportation.
11. Review with your child how to use the restroom alone or with a friend.
12. Review with your child how to use a telephone to call for help.

Stop It Now! (2007) has the following recommendations regarding clinical and nonclinical signs of possible sexual abuse of a youth:

1. An expressed fear of certain persons
2. Problems sleeping, nightmares, night terrors, a change in sleeping habits, requests for a nightlight, new fears about monsters at nighttime
3. Play that is sexualized and sexual drawings
4. Mood changes, changes in impulse control, quick to anger without reason
5. Anxiety, depression, sadness, or worry
6. Crying spells, panic attacks, trembling, or distress
7. Provocative dress or dressing in an unattractive fashion
8. A change in eating habits, stomach aches
9. Offers overt or covert "clues" that would lead a parent to talk about sexual concerns
10. School refusal, separation anxiety
11. New words for private areas of the body
12. Displays a change in bathing or a lack of good hygiene
13. Displays a change in toilet use
14. Reports a new special friend or refuses to talk about a new special friend
15. Possesses money or toys that were not given by a parent
16. Engages in self-injurious behavior
17. Displays a negative self-image

THERAPIST AND RISK ASSESSMENT

Risk assessment is important. Any place a child or adolescent is while not being supervised by a parent will present a risk for harm to a youth. Clinicians have the obligation to instruct parents on how to minimize risk by knowing the facts. Salter (2003) recommends that low-risk and high-risk levels be used to ascertain safety. This may be determined by how much unsupervised time away from a parent a child will inccur. An example of this is dropping off a child for a soccer game and not remaining, and not knowing the coach is very high risk, as compared to attending the practice, knowing the person in charge of the event, and staying until the practice is completed.

Low-risk situations are places that a parent wants his or her child to be at a particular time with an approved supervisor and any supervision provided by the mother or father lessens the danger even more. High-risk situations are places that the minor is without parental supervision. The location may be questionable, and the qualification of the person providing supervision of the child may be debatable.

It is recommended that parents evaluate how much to tell a minor in order to keep him or her safe while limiting anxiety. Age may be used as a determining factor. A child may need to know what appropriate and inappropriate touch by another would include, while an adolescent may merit more specific information. For example, an adolescent who plans on going to the mall with friends may benefit from much more detailed facts about how to protect him or herself from danger, such as staying close to his or her friends and not being lured away by a stranger, or even an adult known to the youth.

Sex offenders tend to be found in situations in which they have an opportunity to be alone with a child or adolescent. Isolation is a part of the offending process. Grooming is the first stage. In order for a sex offender to harm a child or adolescent, he or she first must have an opportunity to provide the target victim some type of attention, befriending him or her and winning the trust of the child or adolescent.

There are several different types of sex offenders, as noted in earlier chapters. However, the random sex offender who roams in areas where children and adolescents can be found will be the most immediate risk when parental supervision is not present.

This type of offender is likely seeking victims who are without supervision. It is often easy to offer an adolescent who has been separated from friends or parents a ride home. Other offers of help may be rendered. The goal is to harm the victim and escape without being caught.

Some sex offenders also groom parents in order to have contact alone with a child. Certain offenders even seek out single parents who are feeling overwhelmed and merit help. Offers to carry in the groceries, mow the yard, or provide child care are techniques to have increased access to the target victim, the child. Dating a single parent, or even marrying a father or mother in order to sexually abuse the child, is reported.

One needs to be alert to the man or woman who does not have children and appears unusually eager to provide child care, supervise an event, or other activities. Persons who have children of their own are more likely to volunteer for an activity since one of their children is involved in the event.

Recent media exposure has shown that certain sex offenders may be found in child care, priesthood, teaching, and other similar occupations, where the child or adolescent is easily accessible. However, these reports can be somewhat misleading, since sex offenders are actually found in all occupations, from factory workers to judges. Indeed, most lay persons and professionals have no interest in harming a child and would intervene if they saw a youth in danger. The public has become more alert to the nuances of sex offenders, thus increasing the monitoring. There is no known clinical study that has found an increase in sexual abuse as compared to fifty years ago. What is known is that sexual abuse is being reported more than in the past.

However, the Internet can be directly cited as a new way for sex offenders to harm children, adolescents, and adult women. The Internet has presented the sex offender with a new format in how to prey upon others. Children, adolescents, and adult women are at increased risk by using this technology. Sexual predators will use blogs, chat rooms, e-mail sites, or other Web sites that children, adolescents, and adult women frequent.

Parents should never permit a child to have unsupervised use of a computer. Also, parental guards and filters should be used. Web cams should not be used. Parents should be versed in computer jargon that children and youth use. If a parent elects to permit use of the Internet, random checks should be made by a computer expert.

Salter (2003) reports the Internet is one easy way for a sex offender to contact a potential victim. She reports that research has found one in five children and adolescents, ages ten to seventeen years of age, were contacted by a sex offender; one in thirty youth received a very aggressive pitch for sexual contact (such an approach was termed, "aggressive," in form and was defined by the sex offender making an "offline" proposal, by way of the mail, telephone or even in person); youth between eight to eighteen, most often used a chat room for approximately thirty-one minutes per day; the largest number are between eight and thirteen years of age, spending about one hour each day using a computer. During that sixty-minute period, this group was involved in Internet chat rooms for about eleven minutes. Misspelled e-mails are a typical way to first contact a potential victim.

ADULT FEMALE VICTIMS

Salter (2003) also lists low- and high-risk situations for adult women. An adult woman who has known a dating partner for an extended period is far less likely to be raped than a female who dates a male she has only known for a short period of time.

Sex offenders look for adult female victims by using Internet chat rooms, singles bars, and college parties. Dating services and online ads can be high-risk situations for an adult woman. Blogging is a new Internet format that includes pictures and personal information about a potential victim. Such activity is very risky. RAINN (2007) reports one-sixth of all women in the United States have been subjected to an attempted rape or were raped.

Hazelwood (1995) reports that adult women may find themselves in low-risk situations, moderate-risk areas, or very high-risk environments. He reports low-risk victims are persons who have occupational, social, and family lifestyles that do not place them in areas of danger on most occasions. Moderate-risk victims are those same persons who elevate in risk by working late at night, visiting an area where criminal activity is known to occur, or changing their lifestyle in some more radical format. For example, meeting a dating partner without a significant history background check, using personal ads over the Internet, or taking chances that they normally do not experience, such as going to a singles bar and walking home alone. High-risk victims are women who regularly expose themselves to dangerous situations, lifestyles, and environments in which the risk of a rape is significant. Such persons may be associated with people involved in criminal activity, such as those using or selling drugs, may be involved in sexual service groups, such as prostitution and escort services, or may lead a sexually addictive lifestyle.

According to the U.S. Department of Justice (2005), 93,934 forcible rapes occurred in 2005, which were reported to the criminal justice system. The National Center for Injury Prevention and Control maintains a Web site for adult women. According to the NCIPC (2000), during 1992 and 1993 approximately 172,400 adult females were sexually harmed within a twelve-month period. Another Web page available for adult females is UCSC Rape Prevention Education (1999). This group found one woman in three has been physically harmed and or has been forced, manipulated, threatened, or coerced into sexual activity worldwide. An estimated 91 percent of reporting persons were female, 9 percent were male, and 99 percent of the offenders were male.

One of many sources of rape prevention in the United States is local police departments. Listed on the Web page of the Hendersonville Police Department in North Carolina (2007) are the following recommendations for adult women:

To Prepare Oneself for a Possible Sexual Attack

1. Be aware that a woman is a possible rape target and dismiss distorted thoughts that a sexual assault only happens to others.
2. Educate oneself on rape-prevention information and ways to avoid assault.
3. Learn where rape-prevention centers are located in your local community.
4. Become more alert as to places or situations in which a sexual assault could occur and then avoid or limit your exposure to these situations or use special precautions in order to not be harmed.
5. Rape is considered the fastest growing offense in the United States involving adult women.

Use Special Safety Techniques at Home

1. Change all locks on a residence when rented or purchased.
2. Keep doors locked at all times, day and night.
3. Do not immediately open a door when someone knocks. First, check the name and identity of the person. Service personnel should show their identity. However, if one remains uncomfortable, refuse admission.
4. Do not admit to being alone in a residence.
5. Do not list your name on a mailbox. It is best that a post office box be used.
6. Keep all outside entry ways well lighted.
7. Leave lights on in the house when away.
8. Use caller ID and block unlisted callers.
9. Keep a cellular telephone in the bedroom.

Safety Tips While on the Street

1. Never walk alone.
2. Stay in well lighted areas duing the night.
3. Never enter a deserted area.
4. Always walk near a curb, avoid unlit doorways or heavy shrubbery, or other areas that someone could hide in to avoid detection.
5. Do not hitchhike.
6. If asked for help from a stranger who is in a vehicle, do not get close to the car.
7. Scream, shout, yell if a vehicle approaches and one senses danger.
8. If followed, drive to the nearest open store, fire department, or emergency squad or police office.
9. Carry a cell phone in your purse and keep a carry bag close to your body.
10. Have a key ready for entry to a vehicle or residence.

Driving Suggestions

1. Do not pick up strangers.
2. Vehicle doors should be locked while driving.
3. Always check the rear area of a vehicle before entry.
4. In approaching a parked vehicle, check nearby areas where a person could be hidden, before entry.
5. Drive on well lit streets when possible.
6. Always keep an adequate amount of gas in the fuel tank.
7. Do not leave your vehicle if followed or bumped.

8. If your car is being repaired, always leave the key only with the repair shop owner or department service manager.
9. If a vehicle breaks down and help is offered, only lower the window slightly for conversation. Request them to call for a family member, repair shop or police if a cell phone is not in the car.
10. Walk to a parked car with a known escort.

Reaction to a Sexual Assault Attempt

1. Do not panic.
2. Use common sense.
3. Remember to look for escape options.
4. If people are close, attempt escape by running, yell.
5. Try to remember a description of the person for police.
6. If a weapon is used, again use common sense.

Passive Resistance

1. Talk in a calm manner.
2. Report a pregnancy, sexually transmitted disease, or AIDS. Vomit and state illness.
3. Attempt to discourage. Faint, cry, act mentally unstable.
4. In one's residence, inform the offender a friend, spouse, or family member is coming.

Active Resistance

1. Use common sense, for no one can assess the situation as well as the potential victim.
2. There is no right thing to do in a dangerous situation.
3. If resistance is used, yell, fight, and struggle.
4. Attempt to hit areas of the body that are sensitive such as eyes, groin, instep, and throat.
5. Martial arts training is helpful in dangerous situations.
6. Some potential victims carry weapons, but training should be used and weapons should be used in compliance with the law. Some offenders will attempt to disarm a potential victim.

Acceptance

1. In situations in which additional harm may occur, acceptance of the sexual assault may be merited.
2. During this stage do not fight.
3. If trapped with no escape, remaining alive is the most important action; if sexually harmed be prepared to recall details of the offender.
4. Do not feel guilty. It is the offender who has committed the violation.
5. Do not fight, yell, or struggle if possible.
6. Again, remember remaining alive is the most important goal.

After Being Raped

1. Contact the police right away.
2. Never shower, use a douche, change clothing, or freshen makeup.
3. Complete a medical examination.
4. Provide details of the assault to a rape crisis counselor and police.
5. Do not feel guilty.

Other Suggestions

1. Seek out clinical treatment with a skilled therapist familiar with sexual assault. Remember, a victim does not cause a rape and one should not feel guilty.
2. Contact friends and family for support.
3. Do not stay alone, ask for help, and accept assistance.
4. Take off time from work or don't take off time from work. Some people need time to recover, others use activity to heal.
5. Let your mind, spirit, and body recover. Exercise.
6. Victims can be harmed again. Use the precautions listed above. Buy a dog. Use a security system.

DeBecker (1997) recommends that anxiety and worry is not to be confused with the signals for real fear. He reports that some persons will experience unnecessary anxiety that manifests itself into fear that is not real.

Some clients will use one experience and then enhance it with distorted thoughts, confusing actual fear with situations that will not occur. Therefore, it is important to use caution, but not rely on distress or worry which may impair a person's judgment.

DeBecker (1997) notes in spousal abuse and murder situations that there are pre-incident warnings that are not noted by a victim. These warning signals, although not written in particular for adult women who are sexually abused, may be applicable. The following are several important signals:

1. The adult female has a feeling that she is at risk.
2. During the initial courtship period, the male increased the pace of the relationship, taking such action as sharing an apartment.
3. The male often uses bullying, intimidation, and violence to solve a relationship problem.
4. The male is verbally abusive.
5. The male uses behaviors that are abusive and controlling.
6. The male will attempt to limit outside support, embarrass the partner in front of others, threaten suicide, and resist freedom.
7. He has used battering behavior and violence in previous relationships.
8. The partner will abuse alcohol and drugs.
9. There is a criminal history of violent behavior.
10. There is jealous behavior.
11. The partner displays mood swings.
12. The partner possesses weapons.
13. The partner controls the money.
14. He will minimize his inappropriate behavior.

Many sex offenders who are married or involved in a relationship will display the previously listed features. Often female partners will attempt to help the male rather than terminate the relationship. Such male partners will be demanding about sex. If the female is unavailable or unwilling to engage in sex, the male will become violent. Many of these pre-incident signals are found in marital or partner rape and related stalking incidents.

SEX OFFENDERS AND POLICY

There is no excuse for sexual abuse. However, in order to help examine this growing clinical problem, it is important to know most sex offenders were once victims. Adams (2003) reports 70 percent of sex offenders have been sexually abused themselves. Others were emotionally or physically abused. As a result, their sexual development has become impaired. Most victims of sexual abuse do not become offenders, but instead present trauma that is acted out in a similar manner. Therefore, this clinical data is important in working with sexually aggressive adults, adolescents, and children. In addition, such information is significant in work with parents, victims, and youth.

The sexually addictive cycle is a part of the clinical picture. Over and over again, it is repeated, generation to generation, offender to victim. This is not to indicate family to family incest, but that distorted sexual behavior passes from each era to another generation, by allowing sexual abuse to occur without accountability. In the past, sexual abuse was denied, minimized, or not reported. Increased media attention and victim advocacy groups have brought this problem to the public's attention.

In times past, when the male adult was seen as the only individual capable of committing sexual acts of harm, it was easier for the lay public to react in a harsh manner. However, as new information arrived and now a shift in the patient population has occurred, it appears this new group has complicated attempts to offer a simplistic solution to a very complex problem.

Now the adult female offender has become a part of the patient population group. Also, children and adolescents have entered the clinical picture. These groups are now being seen in therapy for sexually aggressive behaviors in addition to adult males. In the past, adult females, adolescents, and children were only viewed by professionals and the public as victims.

Today's clinician is faced with many ethical problems. Imagine, as a therapist, interviewing a ten-year-old girl who has sexually abused multiple victims and has a history of sexual abuse herself; a fourteen-year-old boy who is both a victim and offender; an adult woman who has sexually abused a neighborhood youth and was raped as a girl; an adult man who was repeatedly molested by extended family most of his life, and eventually became an offender himself; a serial rapist with no history of prior sexual abuse; or an aggressive male adolescent who enjoys inflicting pain upon victims. Which persons merit therapy? Who requires therapy and a reprimand? Are some individuals not treatable?

What about a patient who is in recovery? What about the patient who works a recovery program and does not reoffend? What about sexually aggressive children, adolescents, and female offenders? How do we make social policy more clinically helpful, less fear oriented and more realistic to this patient group?

Due to the current image of the adult sex offender, fear based public and professional reaction, inappropriate treatment, no treatment, and the belief that all sex offenders are dangerous people is a defense mechanism. How does society view car thieves and embezzlers if they are held accountable for their actions and remain offense free? Does society continue to see these persons in the same context as forever being dangerous? There are three levels of risk assessment for sex offenders (see Risk Assessment section) which are low, moderate, and high for the potential to reoffend.

Social policy is defined by what we believe to be right and wrong. Sexual addiction or sexual disorders are almost dismissed at the present time. And now, with a new patient group of child and adolescent sexually aggressive youth and female offenders, is our global view of offenders correct or misplaced as a result of fear or reaction to the nature of the crime.

SUMMARY

There are no easy answers. However, it is time that cultural values be examined and bias be deleted. This is not to infer that a sexual crime is alright. People do need to be held responsible for sexual misconduct. However, there is a vast difference clinically between a child who is acting out sexually and an adult with hundreds of victims.

Sexual addiction is also an issue. Social policy does not recognize sexual obsession, sexual compulsion and/or sexual addiction. Many adults can be treated effectively by medication and psychotherapy after being held accountable for a sexual offense. In fact, a part of sexual recovery therapy requires that an individual take responsibility for his or her actions. If he or she reoffends, another victim is harmed.

A renowned international expert of sex offenders was asked if a certain new procedure would work. His answer is said to be, "No." Yet, social policy experts could not imagine how he could be so wrong and they could be so right. As a result, millions of dollars were invested in this program over the course of years. Still, there is no research yet indicating that the use of this technique has changed any sexual misconduct behavior. It is suspected that the selected treatment technique was used as a result of fear-based behavior regarding sex offenders in general. Thus, the expert's advice was dismissed because it did not meet the need to further advance fear-oriented prevention methods instead of focusing on what really works in limiting sexual aggression. Law makers and social policy experts appear reluctant to listen to the clinicians who work with sex offenders. This problem impacts community safety and possible future victims.

Sexually aggressive adults, adolescents, and children have not been seen as treatable people as a patient population and are given a poor prognosis for recovery by many clinicians inexperienced with sexual disorders. As illustrated previoulsy in this book, research has found a large majority of these patients are very treatable. Therefore, the more emphasis placed on treatment, the fewer people expected to be victimized, but not all patients do respond to therapy and remain dangerous to the community. Community safety is always a priority. Yes, certain persons are not treatable.

In changes to social policy to protect adult women, adolescents, and children from sexual harm, the following concepts may be considered:

1. Social policy needs to become more proactive than reactive for treating sexually aggressive adults, adolescents, and children.
2. Due to the fact that a sexual disorder is viewed with some disdain, a weakness akin to treatment of substance abuse in the 1970s, social policy experts have been slow to make change, although the victim population continues to increase.
3. Social policy has not fully acknowledged that a large majority of adult males possessing a sexual disorder are treatable.
4. Social policy has failed to recognize that the three most likely groups to be harmed are adult women, male and female adolescents, and children. This failure, in part, is related to gender and age bias and this patient group is viewed as lacking political power. If the reverse were occurring, and adult males were the primary victim group, social changes would have occurred long ago.
5. Recognize that sexual disorders are an impairment.
6. Women and child advocacy groups have advanced the protection of victims more than any other single group.
7. Media involvement has become increasingly alert to problems of victims but sometimes still sensationalizes clinical problems.

8. More emphasis on treatment and funding. All treatment should be court-ordered. Most states mandate only a limited amount of monies for treatment for adult sex offenders, which does limit success and increases the likelihood of future victims.

9. Mandatory treatment for all persons convicted of a sexual offense. Therapists are more likely to recognize possible offending behavior, which then can be shared with the criminal justice system.

10. Indefinite probation for certain felony crimes involving sexual abuse.

11. No sexually aggressive patient should be referred to a generic therapist who is without training and experience in working with offenders.

12. An increase in child protection service workers, foster care workers, police officers, and probation and parole officers. These groups are on the front line and are often under-staffed and overworked. Salaries do not always reflect the importance of the work of these professionals.

13. More funding for research of sexually aggressive adults, adolescents, and children at both the state and federal level. Right now, research funding is very difficult to obtain for this patient group.

14. Additional treatment money is merited. Many offenders come out of prison and do not have funds to enter therapy. Yet, therapy is needed. In some states, if the offender does not comply he or she is returned to prison. In other states, he or she is simply permitted to be released from therapy. Thus, the potential for reoffense increases for the offender. How much do we estimate the cost of one victim—a child or adult woman that could be protected by having an offender in therapy?

15. Mandatory federal guidelines for all states. Currently, each state is allowed to determine their own guidelines for sex offenders. Such inconsistent policy creates confusion, which impacts intervention, treatment, and supervision of sex offenders.

16. The single most dangerous sex offenders, in general, are not those who have been arrested, but those who have not been discovered. Many such sex offenders have hundreds of victims.

17. Stronger support by advocacy groups. Right now, most are dependent upon charitable donations to protect children and adult victims.

18. Fear based tactics, such as marking the home where a sex offender resides, or listing the individual's name on the internet, have no current research to validate such techniques.

19. Megan's Law has prompted more effective community notification standards.

20. Amber Alerts are very useful.

Chapter 31

Conclusion

Sexually aggressive adults, adolescents, and children are a growing patient population group. Every day there are 234,000 adult sex offenders in care by the criminal justice system. The sex-offender prison population has increased by 330 percent since 1990—second only to drug trafficking. About 60 percent of these offenders are monitored in the community. Adolescent sex offenders account for 16 to 17 percent of all sex crimes (Righthand and Welch, 2001). The number of sexually aggressive children is unknown, but referrals continue to increase. Adult female offenders are now being prosecuted, but the exact percentage of such patients remains unknown, although many male victims report abuse by girls and women. Sexually addicted patients continue to be reported. The national media has helped the public become aware of all these patient population groups.

Local, state, and federal law makers remain unsure as to what to do about this rising patient group. Research shows that the mild to moderate offenders are impacted by treatment. Recidivism rates are low for those patients who complete treatment programs. Even certain moderate high offenders are being managed today in the community.

Seriously disordered pedophiles who cannot control their behavior and sexual sadists often are too dangerous to be considered for outpatient treatment. Many states have started to use civil commitment law to provide a structured environment for such persons if released from prison.

Yet, over and over again, many states are failing to offer services that have been proven to be effective to the treatment of sexually aggressive patients. Funding is an issue. Also, there appears to be a lack of information by some policymakers. Some states report that the whereabouts of only one half of their registered sex offenders is known. Other states fail to offer extended probation and parole periods for released sex offenders. In some areas, treatment is not a condition of parole, nor is it an expectation of the court. Court-ordered medication is not used by the judicial system with high-risk offenders in a number of localities.

The community has become more verbal. As the result, the national media has started to advocate for change. Unfortunately, these lay groups are often unable to distinguish a very dangerous offender from someone who is very treatable. Law makers have expressed fear, and sometimes only offer more prisons. Nevertheless, a sexually aggressive patient will be discharged. Anxiety is understandable. There is no excuse for sexual harm. However, research has shown that many sexual addicts and offenders can lead offense-free lifestyles with help.

Sex-offender providers, probation and parole officers, human service workers, and other professional groups find themselves in a situation in which they may serve as the voice for their patients, while protecting public safety. It is known that many patients who are committed to recovery are still harassed and have numerous obstacles to overcome. A number of employers will not hire sex offenders, and finding housing can be difficult. If a sexually aggressive patient fails, not by reoffending, but by a violation of parole, he or she is viewed as proof that all clinical and criminal justice efforts do not work. One should note that it is a condition of many parole boards that an offender hold full-time work and find suitable housing. Also, even basic medical and

Sex-Offender Therapy
© 2008 by The Haworth Press, Taylor & Francis Group. All rights reserved.
doi:10.1300/5753_31

mental health services are denied to a certain number of patients as the result of a lack of knowledge and information.

Sex-offender treatment has advanced a great deal in the past twenty-five years. More victims are now reporting offenses. Courts are more active in holding offenders accountable. Human Services is quicker to respond to a sexual abuse complaint. Clinical treatment is available and research has demonstrated that it is effective as compared to patients who receive no psychotherapy. The media is more active in advocating for change. Victim groups have become more vocal. Registration has been started since the implementation of Megan's Law. A national monitoring system may be merited. There have been no field studies as to whether it is effective to place the photographs and names of sex offenders on the Internet.

Medication is now bringing help to addiction and offending patient groups. No longer do many patients need to struggle with such psychiatric problems without medical assistance. More research is still needed to advance public safety. The physical and psychological harm to a victim is long-term. The cost of recovery for victims is very high, emotionally and financially. Funding for treatment of sexually aggressive patients who respond to therapy is very cost-effective. It also sets into place another professional to monitor behavior. Yes, it is important that offenders be held accountable and pay for a portion of their treatment costs. In reality, many hold low-income wage positions, if employed, cannot afford therapy, and have no health insurance; it is far more cost-effective in these situations for states to offer increased treatment funding as compared to incarceration. It only costs several thousand dollars per year per patient for treatment and probation supervision. In contrast, prison stays average $20,000 and up per year. There is very little research money available now in the clinical community for study of the sexually aggressive patient. This is a concern because additional research is vital to increasing the level of public safety.

The Federal Food and Drug Administration PPG must be a requirement of all sexually offending patients. Also, the polygraph should be viewed as a helpful clinical tool for assessment and monitoring of sex offenders. GPS and electronic monitoring is effective. Also, more funds are needed for probation and parole officers who monitor offenders. Additional positions are needed. Many probation officers carry very high caseloads. Law enforcement is in need of more police officers to work sex crimes. Court-ordered medication is important per individual. Advocacy, education, treatment, prosecution, protection, and prevention will limit future victims.

Certain states are proactive regarding sexually aggressive patients. These include Minnesota, Utah, Vermont, Virginia, and Washington. Other states are increasing attention on sexually aggressive patients. Many federal districts are increasing their attention on sex offenders as well. Many positive changes are occurring. There is much hope for the future.

Appendix I

The Psychosexual Evaluation

The psychosexual evaluation is the single most important report that is completed on a sex offender. This assessment can have a serious impact on a patient. In addition, the victim, family (offender and survivor), and local community are affected by the information.

The intent of the work is to determine if a patient is appropriate for treatment. Therefore, the evaluator should not determine guilt or innocence of a patient in a report. The use of the word *alleged* is recommended if a report is ordered by a court prior to an adjudication hearing. In the event the patient is found guilty of an offense and a clinical psychosexual evaluation is requested, the use of alleged is not required. Other reports may be requested by a probation officer or a human service agency. Such persons may have already been adjudicated and have been placed on probation supervision by a court.

It is recommended that a psychosexual evaluation be performed on each patient who is referred to a sex-offender program. Evaluators should inform patients that they are not serving as their therapist, and what is said may be reflected in the work. Persons who have admitted guilt may be freer to talk of the incident, but the warning is still applicable. More victims may be discovered during the interview and testing process.

Certain patients may be found to be inappropriate for outpatient therapy and are recommended for a more structured setting. Other persons may be receptive to psychotherapy, but display a number of high risk factors to a community, if released. Finally, there are offenders who present a low, mild, or moderate risk for a reoffense and may be suitable for treatment.

A clinician that agrees to do an evaluation should be very skilled in working with sex offenders. This is not a clinical report that should be undertaken by a novice. Also, it is not recommended that a seasoned professional accept a referral for this type of evaluation without training and experience with offenders. Many sex offenders are manipulative and can exploit a worker. Several states require a certification, in addition to a license, in order to work with sex offenders.

Simply put, some men and women are dangerous and have no intention of making a change in their behavior. Others may believe that they can manage their actions, but exhibit impulse-control problems that could lead to a reoffense. Therefore, a skilled sex-offender therapist is recommended.

Ethically, a sex-offender provider is expected to evaluate the ability of a patient to manage his or her behavior in the community without harming others. It is important that the polygraph and penile plethysmograph be used as a part of the clinical evaluation.

The sexual recovery therapy model is recommended for use by evaluators. This type of evaluation is formatted in a building-block form in order to paint a clinical picture of a patient. The work should be used as much as possible.

Factory-type reports are highly discouraged. Although they are time-efficient, such works limit patient information and often repeat basic information in other reports unrelated to the patient in question. Also, a clinical diagnosis should be given, if appropriate, using the current manual by the American Psychiatric Association (2001). No use of unauthorized diagnoses should be employed.

In certain states or federal jurisdictions, HIPAA law mandates that a copy of the report be released to the patient if requested. However, if an evaluation may cause psychological harm to the patient, it is best to seek out counsel or ask the judge for direction. In the event that the document is to be released to the patient, a mental health professional should review the evaluation with the individual prior to release. A psychosexual report may be written by one author with other treatment members contributing to the work.

Sex-Offender Therapy
© 2008 by The Haworth Press, Taylor & Francis Group. All rights reserved.
doi:10.1300/5753_32

A sample of the report is as follows:

The Sex-Offender Treatment Center
757 Sunset Drive
Telephone: (540) 595-7423
South Bay City, Virginia 22232
PSYCHOSEXUAL EVALUATION

Identifying Information:	**Report Date:** 07/07/07
Patient Name: James Smith	**Address:** 554 West Bay City, VA 22232
Patient No: 012345	**Telephone:** (540) 595-9797
DOB: 06/15/81	**Next of Kin:** Sally Smith, Wife
Age: 26	**Marital Status:** Married
SSN: 222-222-222	**Race:** Caucasian

The material contained in this report is of a sensitive nature, and is intended exclusively for the use of professionals involved in this case, including the court, commonwealth attorney, probation and parole, social services, and all attorneys and mental health professionals. Further release of this report is not authorized and may constitute a violation of state code. It may not be discussed or released to the patient without the availability of a mental health professional. Any exceptions should be approved in advance by the court. The conclusions and recommendations made in the report are based upon data available at the time of the evaluation.

Sources of Information

1. Clinical interview with James Smith, patient, on 05/30/07. Mike Grey, Licensed Clinical Social Worker, Certified Sex-Offender Treatment Provider.
2. Clinical testing on 05/30/07 by Summer Redford, PhD, Clinical Psychologist, CSOTP, Certified PPG Clinician.
3. Review of court order date 04/10/07 by the Honorable Samuel Jones, South Bay County Circuit Court.
4. Reviewed Commonwealth of Virginia attorney information on Mr. Smith, including criminal complaint, warrant of arrest, South Bay County Sheriff's Report, past criminal history, and victim statement on 05/31/07, by Mike Grey, LCSW, CSOTP.
5. Interview with Sally Smith, wife, 05/31/07, by Mike Grey, LCSW, CSOTP.
6. PPG completed on patient 06/01/07 by Andrew Howard, Certified PPG Technician.
7. Full-disclosure polygraph examination completed on 06/01/07 by Bill Jackson, Licensed Polygraph Examiner. Reviewed South Bay Psychiatric Hospital report dated 11/12/06 by Paul Evans, MD, Psychiatrist.
8. Reviewed South Bay Psychiatric Hospital report dated 11/12/06 by Paul Evans, MD, Psychiatrist.
9. Reviewed South Bay Psychiatric Hospital report dated 11/12/06 by Rita Mark, PhD, Clinical Psychologist.
10. Reviewed presentence report dated 03/30/07 by Mick Brown, Probation and Parole Officer.
11. Review of South Bay County School incident report of 11/02/06.

Reason for Referral

James Smith was referred for a psychosexual evaluation by the Honorable Samuel Jones, South Bay County Circuit Court. The patient is scheduled for a sentencing hearing on 08/28/07. Mr. Smith is now on bond pending the hearing. He was charged with one count of indecent liberties of a child. He was found guilty of this offense by the court on 04/10/07. The patient entered a plea of guilty to the offense. The victim is a sixteen-year-old girl.

Childhood History

Mr. Smith was born on 06/15/80 at the South Bay City Hospital in Bay City, Virginia. No complications were reported at birth. "I am the eldest of four kids," said Mr. Smith. "My mother and father are retired and live in Florida. My two brothers are both employed here in South Bay City at the South Bay College. One brother teaches science . . . and the other is a professor in the history department . . . my sister lives in Florida near our parents and works as a nurse."

"My father drank heavy when we were growing up," Mr. Smith said. "I don't blame him . . . he had a lot of stress on him . . . he worked in sales for a heavy equipment outfit. Mom stayed home and took care of the kids and house. She always worked hard, but she had time to listen when one of us needed to talk. Dad would just come home and start drinking, eat supper, and then would resume drinking as he watched television . . . he was a mellow alcoholic."

The patient says he was sexually abused as a child by a neighbor. "He lived on our street and was always involved in community activities. He coached Little League. During one practice, he asked me to stay over to work on my batting. We went down to his office to get a ball bat. It was then that he started to touch me. I just froze. I didn't know what to do. He asked me to touch his penis and to stroke him. He came . . . and then I ran off . . . but I never told Mom or Dad . . . I was so ashamed. I should have told them. I love both of them and visit Florida when I can."

Marital History

Mr. Smith is married to Sally Wynn Smith, age twenty-five. The couple was married in 2003. The couple has one son, Toby, age one. Mr. Smith describes his marriage as follows: "I met Sally in college. We were studying education and wanted to work with special-needs children. She has been a great wife and is a good mother to Toby. I love her a great deal."

However, Mr. Smith admits he has been unfaithful to his wife. He says he has had three affairs since the marriage and was involved with other women during the time they dated. He says his wife is unaware of his affairs. "Sally is a good person. She is also very attractive. I think she wants more children . . . and that scares me . . . I can see myself ending up like my parents . . . living from paycheck to paycheck . . . and I don't want to live like that now."

In a separate interview with Mrs. Smith, she said, "I was shocked of the charge that they filed against Jim. I have had a hard time even believing he could do something to a child. It makes me sick. I have thought about divorce. I do love Jim, but I have suspected that he has not always been truthful with me. We dated in college . . . and he was always flirting with other girls . . . and even after we married . . . he continues to look at other women at restaurants or other places when he is with me . . . and it hurts. I am not sure if the marriage will survive. I wish this awful thing would never have happened . . . and I feel so sorry for that girl and her parents. I can't even imagine what they are going through right now."

Mrs. Smith is employed as a special education teacher for the South Bay County School System. She says her spouse attempted suicide in 2006. "Jim was depressed last year. I asked him what was wrong. He said he was just having a tough time with some of the kids in his class, and it was nothing to worry about. However, I noticed he was not sleeping or eating well. I was worried about him. The call from the hospital was so frightening . . . that Jim wanted to kill himself, and now this happening to us."

Medical History

Mr. Smith reports no history of head injury. He says he is in good health. Also, he reports no allergy problems.

Military History

No military history reported.

Religion

The patient says he attends the United Methodist South Bay City Church with his wife.

Education

The patient reports no special education history. He is a college graduate. He says he attended South Bay College and majored in education.

Substance Abuse History

Mr. Smith reports no alcohol problems or use of illegal drugs. He admits to social drinking behaviors. "I like to drink a beer now and then with a pizza." According to the presentence probation and parole report, the patient has no known alcohol or drug abuse problems. He used pain medication to overdose, which he kept following a prior knee injury.

Criminal History

None. All records were checked by probation and parole for the presentence report. No criminal behavior was found.

Psychiatric History

James Smith was admitted to the South Bay Psychiatric Hospital on 10/20/06. He was discharged from the inpatient facility on 11/12/06. According to hospital records, the patient had experienced depression and had attempted suicide by overdose using some pain medications. This was his first psychiatric inpatient admission.

The patient's discharge diagnoses were as follows:

Axis I: Major depression, recurrent, moderate, without psychotic features. (Improved.)
Axis II: Deferred.
Axis III: No health problems.
Axis IV: Psychosocial stressors (upon admission): an affair ended, was experiencing anxiety, sleep problems, and stress, attempted suicide.
Axis V: Current GAF: 70

Paul Evans, MD, Psychiatrist, noted in his discharge report that Mr. Smith had engaged in a number of sexual affairs before and during his marriage. "The patient became distressed in September of 2006 after he learned that a woman he was seeing was involved with another man. Mr. Smith reported a history of depression that has a recurrent basis. It appears the end of the affair impacted the patient's coping skills. He attempted to kill himself by overdose, using some painkillers that he kept following a prior knee surgery. The patient was severely depressed upon admission. Psychiatric, psychological, and therapy services have been used in combination with a medication protocol. The patient's status has improved and discharge is recommended with follow-up treatment."

A report by Rita Mark, PhD, Clinical Psychologist, was completed on Mr. Smith. "Mr. Smith has been involved in a number of sexual relationships. He reports that he does not become emotionally intimate with the women he sees and views the relationship in a rather depersonalized way. He tends to see women as objects rather than people other than his wife, mother, and sister, who he places in a Madonna-like role. Also, he rationalizes his sexual misconduct as a way to cope with stress. It appears his affairs often occur during a depressive episode. He was sexually abused as a child. There appears to be some connection between his abuse and his current lifestyle."

A report by Greg Black, LCSW, Clinical Social Worker, was completed on the patient. "Mr. and Mrs. Smith met for family counseling on three occasions. The patient refused to tell his wife of his dual lifestyle. Mrs. Smith was very concerned about her husband during therapy. She described his recurring depressive episodes as 'those dark periods.' The Smith's did agree that James would continue on medication and they accepted a referral for outpatient therapy. James also agreed to contract not to harm himself, voiced no current plans of suicide, and was willing to seek out his wife or others if in danger of harming himself. Mrs. Smith expressed fear that somehow she had failed her husband. Mr. Smith reassured his wife that his depression was not her fault. Both agreed to additional treatment on an outpatient basis."

Mr. Smith says he did not follow through on the recommendation for outpatient therapy, for fear that his wife would learn of his affairs. He says he was able to convince his wife that he was all right as long as he remained on his antidepressant.

Mental Status Examination

James Smith came to the clinical interview on time. He was dressed in a suit and tie. The patient was found to be cooperative in the session.

Mr. Smith was alert and oriented to time, person, place, and situation. His mood was dysphoric and his affect was blunted. His eye contact was good. "I know I am in trouble," he said, "this is a difficult time for me and my family."

The patient reported periods of anxiety, crying spells, depression, hopelessness, and sadness. Also, he said he experienced problems in sleeping and had periods of low energy with no interest in eating.

"Things seem really piled up for me right now. I have problems keeping my attention on television, or even reading the newspaper. I suppose it is the worry, but even my concentration to do chores around the house seems off-balanced . . . I really have to focus."

The patient reported his recent memory was impaired, but his remote recall was good. His insight and judgment was found to be within normal limits. "I feel forgetful these days . . . I guess I have too much time to think . . . but I am always losing my keys . . . and forgetting where the television remote was last placed."

No thought disorder was found. The patient reported no history of auditory or visual hallucinations. He voiced no delusions.

"I do feel depressed," he said. "No, I don't plan on harming myself. I have found out that children who have parents who commit suicide are more likely to harm themselves . . . and I don't want to leave that legacy for Toby." The patient reported no suicidal ideation or current plans to harm himself or others.

He reported that he became depressed after learning the woman he was seeing had discontinued the relationship. "I really don't know why I got so upset," Mr. Smith said. "I didn't love her. The only woman I love is my wife. She does not know about my affairs. I have tried to stop myself. I feel ashamed of my behavior. Also, I am very sorry that I hurt the girl. This was the first time I have ever been involved with a minor. She was mature physically for her age. I simply forgot what I was doing."

Mr. Smith says he has experienced recurrent depressed moods most of his life. "I really can't ever recall a year that I would not experience a problem with depression. It seems like it would come . . . but never leave." The patient said the antidepressant was of help.

Mr. Smith said he enjoyed his work as a special education teacher. Also, he said that his hobbies included reading, jogging, and golf.

"I believe I am a good person," he said. "However, what I have been doing to Sally is wrong. Also, I have gotten myself in some serious trouble. And I hurt a young girl. Sometimes, I feel hopeful that things will all work out."

Sexual History

James Smith was charged with one count of indecent liberties of a child. The victim was a sixteen-year-old girl who attended a special education class led by the patient. According to probation and parole reports, the patient asked the girl to stay after class one day and then placed his arm around her waist and kissed her. Also, reports indicate the patient then fondled the youth's breasts. The girl is then said to have slapped Mr. Smith and fled the room.

Mr. Smith admits to the offense. He was found guilty of the crime by the court. He is scheduled for a sentencing hearing. The patient has no prior sex crime history.

The patient admits to a history of adultery. He says that he has been unfaithful in his marriage. "I have seen three other women. Also, I cheated on her while we were dating."

Mr. Smith says he was sexually abused himself as a child. He says that he did not report the incident. The patient says he has visited prostitutes approximately ten times during his lifetime. Also, he says he has engaged in sexual relations with married women before he met his wife. "I got a thrill out of having sex with married women . . . I knew it was dangerous . . . that was more fun than the sex itself."

The patient denies indecent exposure incidents or any exhibitionist acts. Also, he denies any pepping behaviors or acts of voyeurism. In addition, he says he has not been involved in cross-dressing or transvestism behaviors. He does report he has encouraged his wife and other women he sees to wear garter belts and black hose during sex.

In addition, he says he has engaged in incidents of bumping or rubbing against women in crowds and other frotteurism incidents. "Yes . . . I have been doing this for years . . . I never harmed anyone . . . I would place myself in a crowd and appear to accidentally bump into a woman."

The patient denies use of pornography. Also, he denies the use of Internet sexual Web sites.

The patient says he has also engaged in sex with more than one partner in one day. In addition, he says during a college party, he was involved in multiple-partner sex with two girls. "We had all been drinking," he said.

The patient denies any sadism, in which another partner is harmed during sex. Also, he reports no incidents in masochistic behavior in which he was harmed by a partner during sexual activity.

Test Information

The following psychological interpretations are hypotheses and should not be used by the reader of this report in isolation from other sources of information in this matter. Personality inventory results present characteristics of individuals who have provided test response patterns similar to the examinee. Although test results are presented in an affirmative manner, they remain probabilistic in nature. The reader should interpret these findings cautiously because it is impossible to tell from tests alone if the patterns and defects described below existed prior to the events in question or are the result of the events.

(Due to a trademark, no particular test is used, and a fictional result has been used for the purpose of the report. Fictional representation is used in place of all tests.)

James Smith completed the Howard-Jones Examination, the Elton Sex Test, and the Randal Intellectual Examination. These tests were administered by Summer Redford, PhD, CSOTP, Clinical PPG Clinician and Technician.

Clinical testing found that Mr. Smith possessed problems of attention span, concentration, and comprehension. He presented himself for clinical testing as an individual who has made life-event mistakes. There was a finding that demonstrated a lack of self-confidence and his self-esteem was also found to be impaired. He did not reveal any history of animal cruelty or fire-setting behavior.

In addition, clinical testing revealed there is some denial in the patient. He tends to rationalize the harm that he causes others or the emotional pain that a loved one may experience as the result of his actions. He was an individual who tended to justify his actions due to a need to seek relief from depression and stress. The patient did show significant findings in depression that revealed a long-term problem with this disorder.

Also, clinical findings showed that the patient found women in general to occupy a less important role than males, a position that is subservient for females. He also displayed irresponsibility by life incidents. He was found at times to see things in an immature manner or a reflection or irresponsibility. Test results found his full scale I.Q. to be at 115. He is an articulate, educated man. He was found to enjoy social interaction, and recreational sports, but was uncomfortable being alone for periods of time. Test results show he does fear abandonment, and has a reluctance to trust easily, even those closest to him. No significant thought disorder was revealed in testing. Nor was there an indication of any specific personality disorder revealed in testing.

The patient is concerned about his sexual performance and masculinity. Testing also found he does have several deviance problems and feels distress if he is unable to act out. No suppression of results was found.

A full-disclosure polygraph was completed with Mr. James. The examination was administered by Bill Jackson, Licensed Polygraph Examiner. The patient was found to be truthful in testing. He admitted to offending the victim that lead to his current charge. No other minor victims were reported. However, his sexual partner inventory was more extensive. Mr. James was found to have been involved with more than 200 partners since age twelve. This does not include the incident in which he was sexually abused. Test results found that approximately seventy-five of the women were prostitutes. Also, it was found that he has had more than three affairs since his marriage. According to a written statement before the polygraph, the patient revealed a total of twenty sexual partners, separate from his wife. In addition, all the sexual partners were married. He did not engage in relations with any single women after marriage.

In addition, he revealed he has engaged in accidental touching with more than 500 unknown victims. No homosexual activity involving men was reported. No incidents involving pornography use or Internet sexual Web sites was reported.

The PPG was completed on Mr. James. This examination was administered by Andrew Howard, Certified PPG Technician. Results of this test were evaluated by Summer Redford, PhD.

Mr. James displayed clinically significant arousal to the following: (1) Female Adult Persuasive; (2) Female Adult Coercive; (3) Female Adult Violent; (4) Female Teen Persuasive; (5) Female Teen Coercive; (6) Female Teen Violent; (7) Preadolescent Female Coercive; (8) Preadolescent Female Persuasive; (9) Prepubescent Female Persuasive; (10) Infant Female Coercive.

Diagnoses

      Axis I: 302.2 Pedophilia
                302.9 Sexual Disorder, Not Otherwise Specified
                296.33 Major Depression; Recurrent, Severe, Without Psychotic Features
                302.89 Frotteurism
                302.81 Fetishism
                V61.21 Sexual Abuse of a Child (Offender)
                V61.21 Sexual Abuse of a Child (Victim)
      Axis II: None
      Axis III: In Good Health
      Axis IV: Psychosocial Stressors: Charged with a sex crime, pending court hearing, victim of child
         sexual abuse, wife considering divorce, job loss possible.
      Current GAF: 60

The patient was found to show sexual attraction to minors, which was revealed by the current offense and related clinical testing. He also meets the criteria for pedophilia due to his contact and interest in minors. Sexual disorder NOS occurs when persons have multiple partners as the result of fear about their sexual performance or masculinity. A mood disorder was found in this patient. He suffers from recurrent bouts of depression. On one occasion, he attempted suicide and was hospitalized.

Also, the patient was found with frotteurism disorder. This occurs when a person bumps or rubs unsuspecting victims in a crowd for sexual purposes. He also has a fetishism disorder and is attracted to inanimate objects. Also, as the result of his own sexual abuse, he meets the criteria for sexual abuse of a child. The same disorder is also used for his sexual offending of a minor.

Risk Assessment

(A trademark name is not used. A fictional risk assessment was used on Mr. Smith.)

A risk assessment was completed to determine the potential to reoffend for this patient. **However, such an evaluation does not necessarily indicate the potential for a patient to reoffend, or not offend, but is used only as an instrument for measuring risk to the community.**

James Smith is charged with one sex offense of a minor. He has no prior sexual offense history. Also, the victim was female and was known to him. Mr. Smith has no other criminal history. The potential for a reoffense is divided into three major groups, which are low, moderate and high. In each group, a subgroup is further specified with low, moderate and high levels for a potential reoffense. Mr. Smith was found to score a low-moderate range for reoffending.

Summary and Conclusions

James Smith is a twenty-six-year-old, Caucasian, married male from South Bay City, Virginia. He has been found guilty of one count of indecent liberties of a minor. The victim was a sixteen-year-old student.

Mr. Smith has no prior sexual offense history. He was employed to the offense as a teacher for the local school system.

According to clinical reports, the patient has been involved in numerous sexual relationships through the years. He was sexually abused as a child. It appears he continues to act out this sexual abuse which has led him to come in contact with the criminal justice system. His sexual misconduct has also led him to living a rather dual lifestyle and he has been unfaithful to his wife. Mrs. Smith is not aware of her husband's adultery. He has engaged in a number of high-risk behaviors with prostitutes and married women. He is reported to have had at least twenty affairs during the marriage. Also, he has intentionally bumped or rubbed against more than 500 unsuspecting victims for sexual purposes.

The patient has expressed remorse for his actions. He does show victim empathy for his actions. However, the patient is also found to rationalize his behavior. He appears to be an individual who has been elevating in his risk taking behavior by displaying more and more reckless actions.

Mr. Smith has experienced a long history of recurrent and severe periods of depression. This has caused him, he believes, to engage in sexual acting-out. In part, this is true, but this impaired thinking has placed him at-risk with minors. Testing shows he is sexually attracted to infants, children, and adolescents.

In the event that the patient is not incarcerated, he is an appropriate candidate for sex-offender treatment. Also, couples therapy is recommended for Mr. and Mrs. Smith if they are interested in maintaining their relationship. Mr. Smith should have no unsupervised contact with minor children. He should reside in another residence outside of the home at the present time. All visits with his son should be supervised by the wife and/or another designated adult. In addition, the patient should have no access to day care centers, playgrounds, parks, schools, or other places that children gather. Active probation should be considered if a jail or prison sentence is not court-ordered. The patient may be considered as a candidate for GPS monitoring. All court services should be limited to the main service only. He should not be permitted to possess any type of pornography or have access to a computer, e-mail, or the Internet. If he continues to work at the Bay South County School System, he should not be permitted to hold a position in which he has contact with children.

Active probation is recommended if the patient is not jailed. Also, if not jailed, he should have no contact with minors, including his son, without supervision. He should not be permitted to live in his home with a minor child until he and his wife, if they elect to continue their relationship, complete family reunification therapy.

Mike Grey, LCSW, CSOTP
Licensed Clinical Social Worker,
Certified Sex-Offender Treatment Provider

Appendix II

Juvenile Psychosexual Evaluation

The juvenile evaluation form that follows is intended as a worksheet for organizing all of this historical and collateral information along with the clinical impressions formed during the assessment interview. Spaces are provided for documentation of details and clinically significant remarks of the patient, the patient's family, and the victim.

Identifying Information

Date of Intake: _____

Patient Name: _____   Identification No.: _____

Date of Birth: _____   Age: _____

Social Security No.: _____   Race: _____

Gender: _____   Current Address: _____

Telephone: _____

Reason for Referral

Referral Source Statement:

_____

Developmental History

Location of Birth: _____ , _____ , _____
              Town/City   State   Hospital

Birth Mother's Name: _____   Birth Father's Name: _____

Prenatal Care Received: _____   Gestational Age: _____   Birth weight: _____

Complications of Gestation/Delivery; Prenatal/Postnatal Substance Use or Abuse by Biological Mother:

_____

Birth Order: _____ of _____ children. Siblings (Names, Ages, Genders):

_____

Progress Toward Developmental Milestones (e.g., WNL, periods of regression, delays):

_____

Wetting/Soiling Accidents After Age Three; Specify Parental Response:

_____

2008 by The Haworth Press, Taylor & Francis Group. All rights reserved.
doi:10.1300/5753_33

Sex-Offender Therapy
© 2008 by The Haworth Press, Taylor & Francis Group. All rights reserved.
doi:10.1300/5753_33

Domestic Violence Between Parents:

_____

Sleeping Arrangements for Household Members:

_____

Parental Abandonment Issues (e.g., absentee parent, death, incarceration):

_____

Discipline Methods Utilized/Persons Administering Discipline/Efficacy of Each Method:

_____

Attachment Concerns:

_____

Sexual Mores Within the Home (e.g., attitudes about nudity, toileting in privacy, pornography in the home, easily overheard sexual activity, age to begin dating, parental cohabitation or overnight dates, provocative clothing, children being bathed together):

_____

Current Relationship with Parent(s) and Sibling(s):

_____

Parental Response to the Patient's Sexual Offending:

_____

Out-of-Home Placements (e.g., foster care, hospitalizations, and residential facilities):

_____

Specify Other Significant Behavioral Concerns (circle all that apply): fire-starting, property damage, harming animals, self-mutilation, thrill-seeking, risk-taking, suicidal gestures, running away, stealing, homicidal gestures, fighting, lying, parented a child, abortion(s), other.

Details: _____

Substance Abuse History

Circle all that apply: Alcohol, amphetamines, cannabis/hashish, hallucinogens, inhalants, nicotine, sedative, hypnotics, anxiolytics, cocaine/crack, opiates. Details: _____

_____

Education

Current School: _____

Current GPA: _____ Current Grade/Highest Grade Completed: _____

Grades Repeated: _____ Dramatic Changes in GPA: _____

Previously Attended Schools: _____

_____

Details: _____

Note Any Educational Testing or Intellectual Testing: Details: _____

_____

Religion

Religious Affiliation: _____

Medical History

Name of Physician. Does Patient Have Allergy History? _____

_____

Medical Diagnoses: _____

Deficits/Limitations *(Circle all that apply):* speech, hearing, physical mobility, vision, other.

_____

Accidents/Injuries/Illnesses *(Circle all that apply):* motor vehicle accidents, fall(s), head injuries, burns, fractures, childhood illnesses, high fevers, seizures, total number of ER visits, total number of hospitalizations, other. _____

Criminal History

Probation Officer: _____

Record of Sexual and Nonsexual Offenses (beginning with most recent, including sentences):

_____

Specify Criminal Activity for Which No Charges Were Filed:

_____

Indicate Patient's/Family's Attitude Toward the Legal System:

_____

Criminality of Family Members:

_____

Patient's Reasons for Offenses (e.g., thrill-seeking, for money, for peer acceptance):

_____

Current Culpability for the Offense(s) (e.g., blames others, feels justified, verbalizes remorse, presents as apathetic):

_____

Psychiatric History

Current Psychoactive Medications (include dosing details and purpose of each medication): _____

_____

Prescribing/Current Physician: _____

Psychiatric/Sex-Offender Treatment: _____

_____

Family History of Psychiatric Illness (including treated and untreated symptoms):_____

_____

Details: _____

Risk of Harm to Self or Others: _____

_____

Details: _____

Mood *(circle all that apply):* depressed mood, feelings of worthlessness, anhedonia, difficulty concentrating, significant weight loss or gain, recurrent thoughts of death, insomnia or hypersomnia, fatigue, psychomotor agitation or retardation, inflated self-esteem/grandiosity, decreased need for sleep, poor self-esteem, flight of ideas/racing thoughts, psychotic features, distractibility, mood swings, increased goal-directed activity, rapid cycling, excessive pleasure-seeking, hypomania, hopelessness, irritability.

Details: _____

Anxiety *(circle all that apply):* Symptoms of the following: panic, agoraphobia, obsessive-compulsive disorder, post-traumatic stress disorder, acute stress disorder, generalized anxiety disorder, social phobia, specific phobia.

Details: _____

Intellectual Functioning. Details: _____

Attention-Deficit and Disruptive Behavior Disorders *(circle all that apply):* attention-deficit disorder, oppositional-defiant disorder, hyperactivity disorder, adjustment disorder with conduct disturbance, conduct disorder, child or adolescent antisocial behavior.

Details: _____

Mental Status Examination

General Appearance *(circle all that apply):* distinguishing features, abnormalities, health, posture, appears stated age, body build, older/younger than age, disheveled, neatly dressed, eye contact, in seasonally appropriate clothing, other.

Behavior and Psychomotor Activity *(circle all that apply):* hyperactivity, slumped, agitation, psychomotor retardation, hand-wringing, rigidity, abnormal movements.

Attitude Toward the Examiner *(circle all that apply)*: cooperative, guarded, seductive, apathetic/bored, defensive, evasive, hostile, other.

Mood *(circle all that apply):* pervasive, sustained emotion, depressed, hopeless, euphoric, irritable, labile, expansive, other.

Affect *(Emotional Responsiveness) (circle all that apply):* mood congruent, blunted, mood incongruent, flat, constricted, other.

Speech *(circle all that apply):* hesitant, good verbal self-expression, normally responsive to cues, poor verbal self-expression, stuttering, volume, slurring, poverty of speech, long pauses before answering, other.

Perceptual Disturbance *(hallucinations) (circle all that apply):* visual, auditory, tactile, olfactory, gustatory, command, somatic, illusions, depersonalization, derealization, other.

Thought Processes *(circle all that apply):* loose, tangential, circumstantial, relevant, goal-directed, slow, rambling, perseverative, punning, blocking, other.

Thought Content *(circle all that apply):* persecutory, grandiose, somatic, nihilistic, erotic, guilty.

Sensorium and Cognition *(circle all that apply):* fully alert, somnolent, clouded consciousness, lethargic, other.

Orientation *(circle all that apply):* oriented to person, oriented to time, oriented to place, oriented to situation.

Memory *(circle all that apply):* fully intact memory, rapid decline reported, short-term memory impairment, confabulation, long-term memory impairment.

Concentration *(circle one):* below average, average, above average.

Abstract Thinking *(circle one):* below average, average, above average.

Impulse Control *(circle all that apply):* aware of socially appropriate behavior, unaware of socially appropriate behavior, able to evaluate potential danger, unable to evaluate potential danger, information impacts behavior, information does not impact behavior.

Details: _____

Judgment and Insight:

Judgment *(circle one):* poor, good, above average.

Reliability *(circle all that apply):* truthfulness, memory, intellect, developmental level.

Sexual History

Sexual Orientation: _____

Frequency of Masturbation: _____

Sexual Fantasies (including content and frequency): _____

_____

Complete the following information for each allegation of sexual offending and sexual misconduct, beginning with the most recent. (Reproduce pages as needed.)

Allegations of Sexual Misconduct (including source of allegation, legal charges and sentences):

_____

_____

Parental Response/Care-Giver Response: _____

Evaluate the Patient's Response (e.g., truly remorseful, boastful, complete denial):

_____

Evaluate Parental Response (e.g., minimizing, blaming others, actively seeking help):

Victim Name: _____ Relationship to Patient: _____

Age of Patient at the Time of the Offense: _____

Age of Victim at the Time of the Offense: _____

Offending Began/Ended on These Dates: _____

Nature of Offending *(circle all that apply):* digital penetration: anal, vaginal; object penetration: anal, vaginal; penile penetration: anal, vaginal; oral sex: fellatio, cunnilingus; voyeurism, exhibitionism, sexual sadism, sexual masochism, frotteurism, other.

Location of Offending: _____

In the Commission of the Offense, the Patient Utilized *(circle all that apply):* grooming, force/violence/threats, weapon(s), coercion, alcohol or other drugs, other.

Victim Impact (including biological, psychological, social and sexual): _____

_____

List Mental Health and Medical Care Provided for the Victim: _____

_____

Victim Statement (if available): _____

_____

Current Contact With the Victim: _____

Other Sexual Concerns *(circle all that apply):* scatologia, zoophilia, partialism, necrophilia, urophilia, coprophilia, pedophilia, transvestic fetishism, fetishism, gender-identity confusion, other.

Patient's History of Sexual Victimization (Complete the following information for each allegation of sexual victimization):

Patient Age: _____ Perpetrator's Age: _____

Perpetrator (name and relationship to patient): _____

Offending Began/Ended on These Dates: _____

Nature of Offending *(circle all that apply):* digital penetration: anal, vaginal; object penetration: anal, vaginal; penile penetration: anal, vaginal; oral sex: fellatio, cunnilingus; exhibitionism, frotteurism, sexual sadism, sexual masochism, other.

Reason Offending Ended: _____

Location of Offending: _____

In the Commission of the Offense, the Perpetrator Utilized *(circle all that apply):* grooming, force/violence/threats, weapons, coercion, alcohol or drugs, other.

Patient's Statement Regarding the Risk of Reoffending: _____

_____

Diagnostic Impression

Axis I: _____

Axis II: _____

Axis III: _____

Axis IV: _____

Axis V: Current GAF: _____ Past GAF: _____

Risk Assessment

(Disclaimer: No empirically validated actuarial tool for the risk assessment of sexually aggressive children and adolescents is currently available. Risk assessment is therefore based on clinical judgment. While some risk factors are more significant than others, none should be considered in isolation from the complete evaluation. Commonly accepted factors that have been associated with recidivism follow.)

Patient History Is Positive for the Following Risk Factors *(circle all that apply):* familial factors: criminality of family member(s), substance abuse by family member(s), family values consistent with violence, child abuse or neglect, attachment difficulties, parent-child separation, spousal abuse, lax sexual mores within the home, sexually charged home environment (e.g., provocatively dressed mother, parents easily heard having sex, pornography easily accessible).

Individual Factors *(circle all that apply):* complication of gestation or delivery, ADD or ADHD, head trauma, mood/anxiety disorders, antisocial traits, substance abuse, cognitive distortions, limited intellectual functioning, anger-management problems, poor social skills, association with delinquent peers, values consistent with violence, engages in thrill-seeking behaviors, cognitive distortions, absence of values, belief system or goals, early physical maturation.

Offense-Specific Factors *(circle all that apply):* early onset of sexual offending (prepuberty), deviant sexual fantasies, blames others/the victim, offense(s) involved planning, grooming, force, weapons, coercion, more than one victim, more than one type of offense (e.g., exhibitionism and frotteurism), imbibing victim with alcohol or other drugs, poor victim empathy.

Based upon the available information, the patient's risk to reoffend is as follows:

_____

Summary and Conclusions

Synopsis of Mental Health, Substance Abuse, and Developmental History:

_____

_____

_____

_____

Brief Review of Sexual Orientation, History of Victimization and Offending, and Risk Assessment:

_____

_____

_____

_____

Recommendations for the patient. Some options include:

1. No unsupervised contact with minors.

2. Psychiatric care to treat mental health symptoms.

3. Medical care to address medical problems.

4. Sex-offender treatment to examine issues of historical victimization and offending and to manage the risk of recidivism.

5. Placement (e.g., with the family of origin, foster home, children's home).

Clinician Signature and Credentials

_____

_____

Appendix III

Case Study of a Sexually Aggressive Child

Identifying Information

Evaluation Date: 01-10-07
Name: Hallie Jean Baxter
Social Security Number: 227-99-2207
Gender: Female
Current Address: TriCities Children's Home
40012 Oakmont Avenue
Allentown, VA 24231

Telephone: 276-555-6788

Identification No: 02213
DOB: 7-21-1998
Age: 8
Race: Caucasian
Guardian: Joe Jarney, Social Worker
Jackson County DSS
1414 Holcourt Drive
Allentown, VA 24231
Telephone: 276-555-2131

Reason for Referral

Hallie was referred for a psychosexual assessment by her social worker, Mr. Joe Jarney, with Jackson County Department of Social Services in Allentown, Virginia. Mr. Jarney related that numerous allegations of sexual misconduct have been made against Hallie since her placement at TriCities Children's Home on 11-9-06. She has been observed by staff to masturbate in common areas of the home while other children are present. She has also touched the genitals of several peer-age children, both male and female (through clothing). The most serious allegation is that she has targeted a six-year-old developmentally delayed male resident, Dominic, and has forcibly kissed and fondled him repeatedly. She was observed to have unzipped his pants on one occasion and appeared to be about to perform fellatio on him when staff walked in.

Developmental History

Hallie was born at Carter Memorial Hospital on July 21, 1998, in Marion, Tennessee, and is the only child of Talessa Moorer Baxter and James Brice Baxter, Jr. Her parents reportedly separated within months of her birth and divorced soon afterward. Their relationship was marked by numerous domestic violence complaints and subsequent brief incarcerations for Mr. Baxter. He has not been involved in Hallie's life and does not provide child support. Until January of 2005, Hallie was living with Ms. Baxter and her live-in boyfriend, Justin Holmes. Ms. Baxter works part-time in fast food restaurants. Mr. Holmes draws disability for a back injury.

Ms. Baxter stated that she had "picked another winner" in Mr. Holmes and said that he was physically and verbally abusive toward her, "almost from the beginning." She denied that Mr. Holmes ever abused Hallie, but later said that he, "flew off the handle in front of Hallie all the time." Ms. Baxter estimated that Hallie has witnessed domestic violence at least once per month since infancy.

During her pregnancy with Hallie, Ms. Baxter states that she stopped using alcohol "the day I found out I was pregnant, at about eight weeks." She went on to say that she "threatened miscarriage all the time" and explained that the abuse she suffered from Mr. Baxter escalated during pregnancy. She alleged that her husband punched her about the face and abdomen. She had ambivalent feelings about the un-

Sex-Offender Therapy
© 2008 by The Haworth Press, Taylor & Francis Group. All rights reserved.
doi:10.1300/5753_34

planned pregnancy, but says she never intentionally provoked him. In her words, "I started thinking that this baby might be the only good thing I'd ever get out of him, and I was right."

She recalls that she drove herself to the hospital and delivered 5 lb. 7 oz. Hallie without complication (and without Mr. Baxter being present). The only problem Ms. Baxter recalls is that Hallie had some difficulty feeding in the beginning. The issue was successfully resolved with Hallie growing and reaching developmental milestones within normal limits. Yet, Hallie's temperament in infancy is described in rather negative terms by her mother, who says Hallie was "always difficult" and "easily upset." However, she identified no remarkable behavioral problems with Hallie and denied that Hallie has ever displayed any sexually inappropriate behaviors.

Discipline was handled exclusively by Ms. Baxter and involved spankings. Hallie reported that her mother also yelled and called her names such as "stupid" and "dumb ass." Hallie attempted to justify her mother's behavior and repeatedly offered explanations to absolve her mother from any responsibility. She denied that she has ever been struck with any objects or that her spankings ever left any marks or broke the skin. She denied that her mother's boyfriend, Justin, had ever spanked her and added, "I don't want to talk about him." She was consistently unwilling to speak about Mr. Holmes.

According to Ms. Baxter, her boyfriend didn't acknowledge Hallie's existence except to tell her to go to her room or to be quiet. He reportedly did not usually interact with her directly, but sometimes became enraged at her behavior and "took it out on me," claimed Ms. Baxter. When she was working, she had "no alternative" but to leave Hallie in Justin's care. Hallie often had tantrums when her mother left the home and appeared quite fearful of Justin. Yet, Ms. Baxter reasons, "Somebody had to earn some money if we wanted to eat." She stated that she thought Hallie was just trying to manipulate her into staying home.

Hallie's family relocated often and reportedly had lived in a total of twelve different homes when she was taken into the custody of Jackson County DSS (Department of Social Services).

They lived for approximately one year in a motor home and traveled the east coast. Finally settling in Virginia in June 2006, they lived in an abandoned trailer on some property that belonged to Ms. Baxter's elderly uncle.

The DSS investigation began on 09-01-06 and was prompted when the Bridle Grove School System reported that Hallie was not attending school regularly. When she did, she was dirty and often wore the same clothing for several consecutive days. Her hair was matted. The investigation revealed that the trailer did not have indoor plumbing. On the day of the DSS home visit, both Ms. Baxter and her boyfriend were obviously intoxicated although they both denied any recent substance abuse.

Hallie was placed in a couple of temporary foster-care settings before space was available at the TriCities Children's Home. In these temporary settings, she was observed to be chronically angry and to kick and slap the family pets. She refused to bathe and became sullen and irritable when the foster fathers were in the homes. She did not interact with the other foster children and remarked to one foster mother that she wished she could be "invisible."

Marital Status

This patient is a child and has never married.

Substance-Abuse History

Reluctantly, Hallie endorsed a history of experimentation with alcohol, marijuana, and nicotine cigarettes. She is unsure of the age when she first used each substance, saying, "I can't remember back that far. I've just always done it." The parties held in her home routinely took place for multiple days with substances left on tables around the house. Yet, she stated that there was really "no place to go to get away" and explained how she often discovered her bedroom to be inhabited by Justin's friends who were "drunk and high."

Education

This second grader is currently earning As, Bs, and Cs in private school at TriCities Children's Home. She repeated first grade due to frequent moves and difficulty learning to read. She previously attended

Bridle Grove School where her frequent absenteeism and unkempt appearance led to her being removed from her mother's home. At Bridle Grove, she was failing every subject except math.

Religion

Ms. Baxter stated that she comes from a "good Christian family" and added that her maternal uncle was a Baptist minister.

Medical History

By her mother's report, Hallie was exposed to alcohol in utero during the first two months of gestation. No prenatal care was received in spite of spotting and physical abuse of the mother on a regular basis.

Hallie did not receive regular well-baby checks and immunizations. However, her shots were caught up before she entered kindergarten. She first received dental care two weeks ago, with one cavity scheduled to be filled. Medical care is being provided by Dr. Mandy who serves all the children at TriCities Children's Home. He identified no medical concerns at this time and prescribed no medications.

Criminal History

Hallie has never been charged with a criminal offense. No charges are pending.

Psychiatric History

Hallie has never received inpatient or outpatient psychiatric care or been prescribed psychoactive medications. She further reports that Hallie's biological father had "wild mood swings" and abused multiple substances on a long-term basis.

Mental Status Exam

Hallie presented for the evaluation in seasonally appropriate clothing. She was well groomed and appeared her stated age. Rather thin, she sat quietly and rigidly during the initial part of the session, later relaxing. She displayed no psychomotor agitation or retardation. Her attitude toward the examiner was inconsistent, at times guarded, at other times cooperative. Her mood was depressed with irritability and blunted affect noted. Speech was of normal rate and rhythm with good verbal self-expression noted. No perceptual disturbance was reported or evidenced. Thought processes were goal-directed with thought content devoid of delusional ideation. She was fully alert and oriented to person, place, time, and situation. Hallie was able to perform intellectual tasks such as simple arithmetic with ease. Deficits were noted with her general fund of knowledge.

No memory deficit was noted with concentration rated as average. Abstract thinking was consistent with her age and developmental level. She did not display significant frustration or emotionality when answering or failing to answer questions. Impulse control was observed to be good during the session. Her verbalizations and behavioral history indicate that she is aware of socially appropriate behavior and most often chooses behaviors based on this information.

Judgment, as evidenced by her answers to four hypothetical questions, is good. She is capable of discerning right from wrong and explains logical reasons for her answers. Insight is characterized by complete denial of sexual offending with her repeated claim that allegations are lies. Her position is that nothing is wrong with her and that everyone one else has a problem.

In spite of her poor insight and denial of her acts of sexual aggression, other aspects of her history have been confirmed either by her mother or by her social worker, Mr. Joe Jarney. She does not lie for sport and clearly understands the difference between fact and fiction. In general, she is regarded as a moderately reliable reporter. She is clearly secret-keeping.

Hallie denied any suicidal or homicidal ideation but acknowledged that she has wished she were dead approximately ten times over the past year. She refused to elaborate and said that she was "a lot happier now." She denied that she ever formulated a plan or that she would act on the thoughts. She also endorsed a history of homicidal ideation and said she thought of ways her mother's boyfriend could die "almost every day." She stated that she knew killing him would be wrong, but said she would have if she could have. She refused to elaborate on her intense feelings toward Mr. Holmes, saying that she planned never to see him again. She regretted that her mother was "stuck with him" and looked suddenly relieved when she considered that, "Maybe Mommy will kill him." She then stated that she was just kidding.

Sexual History

Hallie denied that she has ever had sexual contact with anyone or that she masturbates. She further denied that she has ever had a sexual fantasy or that she is attracted to males or females. Staff documentation reflects that public masturbation was a problem beginning on November 10th with her having been placed in the home the day prior. She was also observed to spend lengthy periods in the restroom and was suspected to be masturbating during those times.

Victim Name	Victim Age	Victim Gender	Nature of Offense(s)	Date of Offense
Serena	8	F	clothed genital fondling	11/15/06
Jason	7	M	clothed genital fondling	11/21/06
Serena	8	F	clothed genital fondling	12/23/06
Mario	9	M	clothed genital fondling	12/23/06
Jessi	6	F	clothed genital fondling	01/05/07
Dominic	6	M	clothed genital fondling and kissing his mouth	01/06/07
Dominic	6	M	unzipped pants and was in position to perform fellatio	01/08/07

Questions about her own potential sexual victimization were met with strong objections. She disclosed no history of exposure to nudity in the home and denied that pornographic materials were ever viewed by her. She stated that she never saw the party crowd engaging in sexual activity or nudity and added that she did not see or hear her mother engaging in sexual intercourse with Mr. Holmes or anyone else. She further denied that Mr. Holmes, her mother, or anyone else had made sexual advances toward her. She stated that she has "just always known about sex" and could not offer specifics about when she was introduced to the subject. A court hearing is scheduled for February 1, 2007.

Tests Administered

Hallie was referred for psychological testing to Ralph Speary, PhD. Testing was completed by Dr. Speary on December 1, 2006.

Test Results

Dr. Speary's report indicates that Hallie is a clinically depressed child with significant symptoms of anxiety. She has low self-esteem and approaches her future with a sense of hopelessness and impotence. Social functioning is also impaired with a sense of isolation noted. Few items related to suicidality and homicidality were endorsed by Hallie, indicating that she poses a low to moderate risk of harm to herself and others. Dr. Speary recommends treatment to address this risk as well as her mood, anxiety, and social skills deficits. Dr. Speary made reference to recent intellectual testing completed by the school system and indicated that Hallie's presentation was consistent with her score within the high-average range of intellectual functioning. Her history of academic difficulties is discussed as secondary to extreme emotional disturbance. Current success in private school is related to the high teacher-to-pupil ratio and the experience of her current teachers in working with disturbed children. There was indication in testing that the child may have experienced severe trauma.

Diagnostic Impression

Axis I: 296.22 Major Depressive Disorder, Single Episode, Moderate
             302.9 Paraphilia Not Otherwise Specified
             V61.21 Sexual Abuse of Child (Aggressor)
             V61.21 Rule Out Sexual Abuse of Child (Victim)
             309.81 Post-traumatic Stress Disorder
Axis II: No Diagnosis
Axis III: Slightly underweight, cavity to be filled next week
Axis IV: Psychosocial stressors: lack of parental involvement and support (father), educational problems, placement outside the home, inadequate finances within the home, exposure to substance abuse within the home, history of frequent relocation, and subsequent social isolation, possible sexual victimization
Axis V: Current GAF: 50 (serious symptoms resulting in serious functional impairment)

The diagnosis of major depression relates to her symptoms of depressed mood, anhedonia, decreased appetite, and disturbance of sleep onset and sleep maintenance. Her poor self-esteem and recurrent thoughts of death were also considered. These symptoms were reported to have been present for the past year.

The paraphilia NOS diagnosis was made because she has recently exhibited both exhibitionism (exposure of one's genitals) and frotteurism (sexually touching a nonconsenting person). She does not meet criteria at this time for a more specific paraphilic diagnosis. These behaviors are also not typical of an adjustment disorder and merit a separate diagnosis.

The sexual abuse of child diagnosis indicates that she has sexually targeted children. There will also be substantial clinical attention on the possibility that she was also sexually victimized. While preschool-age children may disrobe, masturbate, or fondle other children without raising much clinical concern, these behaviors are not developmentally appropriate for an eight-year-old. Her apparent intent to perform fellatio on another resident would be a concern at any age.

The post-traumatic stress disorder diagnosis follows her history of witnessing her mother being beaten on a regular basis and the subsequent fear and sense of helpless she experienced. Her disturbed sleep is noted to involve nightmares. She also asks repeatedly whether or not Justin can get to her at the children's home. She looks for his vehicle while playing inside and becomes highly agitated when she thinks she has spotted it. She was also described by her current caregivers as irritable and hypervigilant with an exaggerated startle response (particularly when caregivers awaken her in the morning).

Axis II is no diagnosis because she is of average intelligence. Her pediatrician's notation that she is slightly underweight is recorded on Axis III along with her dentist's diagnosis of a cavity. There are no other known medical problems or concerns at this time. Axis IV spells out her psychosocial and environmental stressors which have already been addressed in this evaluation. The global assessment of functioning (GAF) is rated fifty because of her serious symptomatology and functional impairment. This rating takes into account her suicidal and homicidal ideation, depression, and sexual misconduct as well as her social and academic impairments.

Risk Assessment

(Disclaimer: No empirically validated actuarial tool for the risk assessment of sexually aggressive children and adolescents is currently available. Risk assessment is therefore based on less-reliable clinical judgment. While some risk factors are more significant than others, none should be considered in isolation from the complete evaluation. Commonly accepted factors that have been associated with recidivism follow.)

Hallie's familial risk factors include substance abuse of family members, parent-child separation, and spousal abuse. She has been neglected as well. Individual factors include complications of gestation, her substance abuse, and poor social skills. Also noted were her mood disturbance, angry outbursts, and an absence of values and life goals.

Her offense-specific factors which have been associated with recidivism, are numerous. They include the early onset of her offending (prepuberty), having more than one victim, and having both male and female victims. In addition, she has committed different types of sexual offenses (e.g., touching and exposing) and takes no responsibility for the harm she has done. The rapid escalation of offending is also noted with her having more than one incident in a single day and incidents on consecutive days. She selected a developmentally delayed victim for her most intrusive offense (fellatio) and engaged in planning to get him alone in advance. This evidence of preoffense planning is indicative of willfulness and indicates that she has engaged in deviant sexual fantasies, regardless of her denial.

This child is considered at high risk of sexual reoffending.

Summary and Conclusion

Hallie is an eight-year-old female who is in the custody of Jackson County DSS due to neglect. She resides at TriCities Children's Home in Allentown, Virginia, and has been caught in numerous acts of sexual misconduct with other children living in the home. She denies the behaviors and states that she has never been the victim or perpetrator of any sort of sexual acts.

A socially isolated child, she presents with major depression and chronic difficulties with adjustment. Disturbance of conduct is noted. Symptoms of post-traumatic stress disorder are chronic. Her risk factors for further sexual offending are numerous. There are concerns that this child has been sexually abused.

Recommendations for Hallie include:

1. Immediate removal from TriCities Children's Home to prevent further harm to children there. She merits placement in a therapeutic foster home that has no other children. Her foster parents will need education and training in dealing with her sexual behaviors.
2. Because of the risk she poses within the school environment, she must either be shadowed by a trained adult throughout the day or be home schooled. If she attends school, teachers and principals must be informed of her history. A written safety plan would be a minimal requirement for school attendance.
3. Psychiatric services.
4. Psychosexual therapy on an outpatient basis is suggested to begin immediately.
5. Continued DSS supervision of family contact is warranted (if/when the mother participates).
6. There should be no unsupervised contact with minors. All supervising adults must be educated about her history and appropriate child behavior-management techniques. Written safety plans are required for any frequently visited location such as parks, the babysitter's, or church. Caregivers must be involved in the safety planning and must have a copy of this evaluation.
7. If family reunification were to be considered, Ms. Baxter and her boyfriend would need to consistently display major lifestyle changes. Ms. Baxter would benefit from counseling to address her history of depression, sexual victimization, and spousal abuse. She is recommended to complete substance-abuse counseling and complete a parenting course as well. If her relationship with her boyfriend continues, he would also need to complete drug rehabilitation and demonstrate that he is able to live a drug-free lifestyle.

Signature, Credentials

References

Abel, G.G. (1989). Paraphilias. In H.I. Kaplan and B.J. Sadock (Eds.), *Comprehensive Textbook of Psychiatry* (pp. 1069-1085). Baltimore, MD: Williams and Wilkins.

Adams, M. J. (2003). Victim issues key to effective sex offender treatment. The Trowbridge Foundation. http://www.Trowbridgefoundation.org/docs/victim_sex_offender_treatment.htm.

Alexander, M.A. (1998). Sexual offender treatment efficacy revisited. *Sexual Abuse: A Journal of Research and Treatment, 11*(2): 101-117.

American Psychiatric Association (1994). *Diagnostic and Statistical Manual of Mental Disorders* (fourth edition) (2001). Washington, DC: American Psychiatric Association.

American Psychiatric Association (2000). *Diagnostic and Statistical Manual of Mental Disorders* (fourth edition, text revision). Washington, DC: American Psychiatric Association.

American Psychiatric Association (2001). *Diagnostic and Statistical Manual of Mental Disorders* (fourth edition, text revision). Washington, DC: American Psychiatric Association.

Barbaree H., Hudson, S., and Seto, M. (1993). Sex assault in society: The role of juvenile offenders. In H. Borbaree, W. Marshall, and S. Hudson (Eds.), *The Juvenile Sex Offender:* 10-11.

Barbaree, H.E. and Marshall, W.L. (1991). The role of male sexual arousal in rape: Six models. *Journal of Consulting Clinical Psychology, 59:* 621-630.

Bays, L. and Freeman-Longo, R. (1989; Eighth Printing 1998). *Why Did I Do It Again? Understand My Cycle of Problem Behaviors.* Brandon, VT: The Safer Society Press.

Beck, Aaron T. (1975) *Cognitive Therapy and the Emotional Disorders.* International University Press, Inc.

Berger, P., Berner, W., Bolerausu, J., Gutierres, K., and Berger, K. (1999). Sadistic personality disorder in sex offenders: Relationship to antisocial personality disorder and sexual sadism. *Journal of Personality Disorders, 13*(2): Summary, 175-186.

Birgeden, A., Owen, K., and Raymond, D. (2003). Enhancing relapse prevention through the effective management of sex offenders in the community. In T. Ward, R. Laws, and S. Hudson (Eds.), *Sexual Deviance: Issues and Controversies* (pp. 317-334). Thousands Oaks, CA: Sage Publications, Inc.

Boeree, G.C. (1998). Personality theory: Abraham Maslow. Retrieved October 25, 2005, from http://www.ship.edu/~cgboeree/maslow.html.

Bureau of Justice Statistics, Criminal Offenders Statistics—Women Offenders 12199 NCJ175688 http://www.ojp.usdoj.gov/bjs/cimoff.htm.

Bush, J. W. (1996). *Cognitive Behavioral Therapy, The Basics.* New York Institute of Cognitive and Behavioral Therapies. Quarterly Review, pp. 23, 45-47.

Byrne, P. (1998). *Monarch 21 PPG Level II Clinician Training and Report Samples in Level I & II MONARCH 21 PPG Training Manual,* (pp. 6, 15). Salt Lake City, UT: Behavioral Technology, Inc.

Byrne, P. (August, 2005). *Training on Use of PPG.* Salt Lake City, UT: Behavioral Technology, Inc.

Card, R. (2000). Client preparation for conditioning therapy. In *Modifying Deviant Sexual Arousal in Sexual Offenders, A Clinical Guidebook* (p. 3). Salt Lake City, UT: Behavioral Technology, Inc.

Carich, M. and Mussack, S. (Ed.) (2001). Sexual abuse evaluation. In *Handbook for Sexual Abuser Assessment and Treatment* (pp. 13-14). Brandon, VT: Safer Society.

Carnes, P. (2001). *Out of the Shadows: Understanding Sexual Addiction* (third edition). Center City, MN: Hazelden.

Cavanaugh-Johnson, T. (1998). Child perpetrators: Children who molest children. *Child Abuse and Neglect: The International Journal, 12*(2): 219-229.

Center for Sex Offender Management (1999). *Understanding juvenile sexual offending behavior.* Silver Spring, MD: Author.

Center for Sex Offender Management (2007). www.scom.org.

Child Development Institute (2005). Stages of social-emotional development in children and teenagers. Erikson's eight stages of development. Retrieved March 4, 2006, from http://www.childhooddevelopmentinfo.com/development/erikson.shtml.

Clark, A.J. (1998). *Defense mechanisms in the counseling process.* Thousand Oaks, CA: Sage Publications, Inc.

Sex-Offender Therapy
© 2008 by The Haworth Press, Taylor & Francis Group. All rights reserved.
doi:10.1300/5753_35

Collins, B. (2001). Expect Miracles. *Psychotherapy Networker,* September/October.

Daley, D.C. and Moss, H.B. (2002). *Dual Disorders: Counseling Clients with Chemical Dependency and Mental Illness* (third edition). Center City, MN: Hazelden.

DeBecker, G. (1997). *The Gift of Fear and Other Signals That Protect Us from Violence.* New York, NY: Dell Publishing.

Deranek, T. and Gilman, D. (2003). Children as sex offenders, why? *ERIC Reports-Research/Technical, 16:* 4-5.

Federal Bureau of Investigation (2001). Uniform crime report. Washington, DC: U.S. Government Printing Office.

Flora, R. (2001). *How to Work with Sex Offenders: A Handbook for Criminal Justice, Human Service, and Mental Health Professionals.* Binghamton, NY: The Haworth Press.

Franklin, C. and Jordan, C. (2001). Guidelines for conducting family therapy. In A. Roberts and G. Greene (Eds.), *Social Worker's Desk Reference.* Oxford University Press.

From Darkness to Light (2007). Statistics. www.darkness2light.org.

Greenberg, D.M., Bradford, J.W., and Curry, S. (1993). A comparison of sexual victimization in the childhoods of pedophiles and hebephiles. *Journal of Forensic Science, 23*(2): 432-436.

Greenfeld, L. (1997). *Sex Offenses and Offenders: An Analysis of Data on Rape and Sexual Assault.* Washington, DC: U.S. Department of Justice, Bureau of Justice Statistics.

Groth, A.N. (1990). *Men Who Rape: The Psychology of the Offender.* New York: Plenum Press.

Hall, G.C.N. (1995). Sex offenders recidivism revisited: A meta-analysis of recent treatment studies. *Journal of Consulting and Clinical Psychology, 63:* 802-809.

Hanson, C. (2005). Dangers children face online: *Dateline* hidden camera investigation turns spotlight on internet predators. November 3. New York: *Dateline,* National Broadcasting Company.

Hanson, R. and Bussiere, M. (1998). Predicting relapse: A meta-analysis of sexual offender recidivism studies. *Journal of Consulting and Clinical Psychology, 66:* 348-364.

Hanson, R. and Phenix, A. (2001). Coding for Scoring the STATIC-99. Ottawa, Canada. The Solicitor General Canada.

Hazelwood, R. R. (1995). Analyzing the rape and profiling the offender. In R. R. Hazelwood and A. W. Burgess (Eds.), *Practical Aspects of Rape Investigation: A multidisciplinary approach, Second edition* (pp. 155-181). Boca Raton, FL: CRC Press.

Hazelwood, R.R. and Burgess, A.W. (Eds.) (2001). *Practical Aspects of Rape Investigation: A Multidisciplinary Approach* (third edition). Boca Raton, FL: CRC Press.

Heffner, C.L. (2001). Personality development: Freud's structural and topographical models of personality. Retrieved March 4, 2006, from http://allpsych.com/psychology101/ego.html.

Hendersonville Police Department (2007). Rape Prevention. North Carolina, Hendersonville. http://www.hendersonvillepd.org/PreventionTips/RapePreventionTips.html.

Hislop, J. (2001). *Female Sex Offenders: What Therapist, Law Enforcement and Child Protective Services Need to Know.* Ravensdale, WA: Issues Press.

Hutchison, E.D. (1999). *Dimensions of Human Behavior: Persons and Environment.* Thousand Oaks, CA: Pine Forge Press.

Jenkins-Hall, K., Osborn, C., Anderson, C., Anderson, K., and Shockley-Smith, C. (1989). The Center for Prevention of Child Molestation. In R. Laws (Ed.), *Relapse Prevention with Sex Offenders.* New York, NY: Guilford.

Kahn, T. (2001). *Pathways: A Guided Workbook for Youth Beginning Treatment* (third edition). Safe Society Press.

Kanel, K. (2003). *A Guide to Crisis Intervention* (second edition). Pacific Grove, CA: Brooks/Cole.

Knopp, F.H. (1984). *Retraining Adult Sex Offenders: Methods and Models.* Syracuse, NY: The Safer Society Press.

Lane, S. (1991). Special offender population. In G. Ryan and Shane (Eds.), *Juvenile Sexual Offending: Causes, Consequences, Correction* (pp. 299-332). Lexington, MA: Lexington Books.

Law and Psychiatric Institute (LPL) of the Hath Shore Long Island Jewish Health System (2000). 516-719-3150. 13 Kee, Johnson, and Hunt (2002). Burnout and social support in rural mental health counselor. Gramm, Stone, and Pittman (2003). NIMH and Mental health and mental disorder: A rural challenge. http://www.northshorelig.com/body.cfm?id=739>.

Laws, R. (Ed.). (1989). Direct monitoring by penile plethysmography. In Law, R. (Ed.), *Relapse Prevention with Sex Offenders* (pp. 106-113). New York, NY: Guilford.

Lieb, R., Quincy, V., and Berlinger, L. (1998). Sexual predators and social policy. In M. Tony (Ed.), *Crime and Justice* (pp. 43-114). University of Chicago.

Longo, R. (2004). Identifying and treating youth who sexually offend. In R. Geffner, K.C. Franey, T.G. Arnold, and R. Falconer (Eds.), *Identifying and treating youth who sexually offend* (pp. 193-213). Binghamton, NY: The Haworth Press.

Lukianowicz, N. (1972). Incest I: Paternal incest. *British Journal of Psychiatry, 120:* 301-313.

Madanes, C., with Keim, J.P. and Smelser, D. (1995). *The Violence of Men. New Techniques for Working with Abusive Families: A Therapy of Social Action.* San Francisco, CA: Jossey-Bass, Inc.

Matthews, J.K. (1998). An 11-year perspective of working with female sex offenders. In W.L. Marshall, Y.M. Fernandez, S.M. Hudson, and T. Ward (Eds.), *Source book of treatment programs for sexual offenders* (pp. 259-272). New York: Plenum Press.

Mayer, A. (1992). *Women Sex Offenders.* Holmes Beach, FL: Learning Publications, Inc.

Minuchin, S. and Fishman, C.H. (1981). *Family Therapy Techniques.* Cambridge, MA: Harvard University Press.

Moreno, Z., Blomkvist, L.D., and Rutzel, T. (2000). *Psychodrama, Surplus Reality and the Art of Healing.* London: Routledge.

National Center for Injury Prevention and Control (2000). Rape fact sheet. Georgia, Atlanta. http://www.medhelp .org/NIHib/GF617.html.

National Center for Missing and Exploited Children (2007). Internet child sexual predators. Retrieved May 12, 2007. http://www.crisisconnectioninc.org/sexualsexualassault/internet_ child_sexual_predators.htm.

National Center for Missing and Exploited Children (2007). Know the rules. General tips for parents and guardians to keeping children safer. http://www.missingkids/servlet/resourceservlet?languagecountry=enus.

O'Connell, M.A., Leberg, E., and Donaldson, C.R. (1990). *Working with Sex Offenders: Guidelines for Therapist Selection.* Newbury Park, CA: Sage Publications.

Phenix, A. and Hanson, K. (2000). Coding rules for the STATIC-99. *Coding Rules for the STATIC-99 Connections Research.* Ottawa, Canada: Department for the Solicitor General of Canada.

Pipher, M. (2000). My most spectacular failure. *Family Therapy Networker,* November/December, p. 63.

Pithers, W. D. and Gray, A. S. (1996). Utility of relapse prevention in treatment of sexual abusers. *Sexual Abuse: A Journal of Research and Treatment,* 8(3): 223-230.

The Rape, Abuse, and Incest National Network (2006). Statistics. Washington, DC www.rainn.org.

Righthand, S. and Welch, C. (2001). *Juveniles Who Sexually Offend: A Review of Professional Literature.* Washington, DC: Office of Juvenile Justice.

Robbins, M. and Szapocnik, J. (2000). *Brief Strategic Family Therapy.* U.S. Department of Justice, Office of Justice Programs, Office of Juvenile Justice and Delinquency Prevention.

Roberts and Greene, G. (Eds.). *Social Workers Desk Reference.* Oxford University Press.

Ryan, G. and Lane (1997). *Juvenile Sexual Offending: Cause, Consequences, and Correction.* San Francisco: Jossey-Bass.

Salholtz, E., Clift, E., Springen, K., and Johnson (1990). Women under assault: Sex crimes finally get the media's attention. *Newsweek, 22* (July 16): 22-24.

Salter, A.C. (1988). *Treating Child Sex Offenders and Victims.* Newbury Park, CA: Sage.

Salter, A. (2003). *Predators, Pedophiles, Rapists, and Other Sex Offenders: Who They Are, How They Operate, and How We Can Protect Ourselves and Our Children.* New York, NY: Basic Books.

Sarles, R.M. (1975). Incest. *Pediatric Clinics of North America,* 22(3): 633-642.

Schwartz, B.K. and Canfield, G. (1996). *Facing the Shadow: A Guided Workbook for Understanding and Controlling Sexual Deviance.* Kingston, NJ: Civic Research.

Sex Offender Treatment (1991). Department of Corrections, Medford, OR. Polygraph Associates, Medford, OR.

Sickmund, M., Snyder, H., and Poe-Yamagats, E. (1997). *Juvenile Offenders and Victims: 1997 Update on Violence.* Washington, DC: Office of Juvenile Justice and Delinquency Prevention.

Slovenko, R. (1971). Satutory rape. *Medical Aspects of Human Sexuality, 5:* 155-167.

Steen, C. (2001). *The Adult Relapse Prevention Workbook.* Brandon, VT: Safer Society Press.

Stop It Now! (2007). Warning signs about child sexual abuse. http://www.stopitnow.com/warnings.html.

U.S. Department of Justice (2005). Forcible rape. Washington, DC. http://www.fbi.gov/ucr/o5cus/offenses/ violent_crime/forcible_rape.html.

Virkkunen, M. (1981). The child as participating victim. In M. Cook and K. Howells (Eds.), *Adult sexual interest in children* (pp. 121-134). New York: Academic Press.

Yalom, I.D. (1985). *The Theory and Practice of Group Psychotherapy* (third edition). New York: Basic Books.

Index

Abstinence, offense chain, 124
Abstinence violation effect/giving up (AVE), offense chain, 124
Accountability/responsibility, offenders, 171-174
Accounting, sexual recovery model, 13
and family reunification, 195
Acknowledgment, sexual recovery model, 13
and family reunification, 195
Acting out, defense mechanism, 157
Acting-out phase, 38, 39
Adams, M.J., 221
Adolescents
   case study, 243-248
   and cybersex, 209-210
   and sexual addiction, 187-188
   sexual predators, types of, 209-210
   sexually aggressive, 152-153
Adult female patients
   cruising, 79
   and cybersex, 208-210
   and domination, 78-79
   exercise, 80-81
   fantasies, 78-79
   grooming, 79
   male-coerced/male accompanied, 74
   mentally ill, 75-78
   predisposed sex offenders, 75
   role-modeling, 76-77
   sexual predators, types of, 208-209
   teacher/lover, 74
   treatment, 79
   underreporting of offenses, 73
   versus male patients, 78
Adult male patients
   characteristics of, 65-67
   cruising, 69
   and cybersex, 208
   exercise, 71
   fantasies, 68-69
   grooming, 70
   rituals, sexual, 67-68
   sexual predators, types of, 208
   thinking distortions, 66
The Adult Relapse Prevention Workbook, 21
Adult sex offenders, 56
   females. *See* Adult female patients
   males. *See* Adult male patients
   sexual addiction and, 185-187

Affiliation, defense mechanism, 157
Aftercare and maintenance phase, 47
Alexander, M.A., 1
All or nothing, negative thinking, 21
"Alleged," avoid use of, 95
Altruism
   change and, 181
   defense mechanism, 157
Anatomy versus Shame (Will), 11
Anger, defense mechanism, 157
Anger management, 34
Angry offenders, 49-51
Anticipation, defense mechanism, 158
Antisocial personality disordered (APD), 83-84
Apology and atonement, sexual recovery model, 14
Assent, thinking distortion, 67
Assessing Risk of Recidivism—RRASOR, exercise, 203
Assessing Risk of Recidivism—STATIC-99, exercise, 204
Awareness of Self-Esteem, exercise, 175
Atonement, and family reunification, 197
Autistic fantasy, defense mechanism, 158
Aversion conditioning therapy, 103-104
Avoidance, defense mechanism, 158

Barbaree, H.E., 67
Basic Trust versus Basic Mistrust (Hope), 11
Behavioral Technology, Inc., (BTI), 101
Berger, P., 84
Blogging, sexual predators and, 208
Boundary-setting, therapist, 4
Build-up phase, 38, 39
Burgess, A.W., 68-69
Bussiere, M., 1
Byrne, P., 101, 103

Card, Robert, 104
Carich, M., 102
Carnes, P., 185, 186, 208
Case examples
   angry offender, 49-50
   antisocial personality disordered, 84
   cruising, 69
   cycle of offending, 38-39
   Internet, 207-208, 211

Sickmund , M., 1-2
Snyder, H., 1-2
Social policy, sexual harm and, 221-223
Specific-incident testing, polygraph, 115
Splitting, defense mechanism, 159
STATIC-99, 201
Steen, C., 21, 66, 124
"Stinking thinking," 125
Stop It Now!, 214, 215
Strengthening and hope, sexual recovery model, 13
    and family reunification, 196
Stress, therapist, 4
Structural family therapy, 16
Sublimation, defense mechanism, 159
Superego, 10
Suppression, defense mechanism, 159
Surplus reality, 172-173

Tape-recording, sexual recovery technique, 19-20
Teacher/lover, female sex offender, 74, 209
Telephone scatologia, 32
Termination, sexual recovery model, 15
    and family reunification, 196
Therapist
    boundary-setting, 4
    countertransference, 4
    and defense mechanism, client's, 159
    grounding, 57-58
    Insight Awareness for the Therapist, exercise, 167
    office space, trouble finding, 3
    patient resistance, 4
    personal inventory, 4-5
    in remorse, 143-144
    Review for Therapists Providing Sex-Offender
        Group Therapy, exercise, 182-183
    and risk assessment, 215-217
    role of, 56-58, 213-215
    self-care, 3
    Skills Development for the Therapist, exercise,
        168-170
    stress, 4
    The Therapist and Family Reunification, exercise,
        198
    The Therapist and Victim Empathy, exercise, 42
    Therapist Self-Assessment Regarding Work with
        Adolescents, exercise, 155
    Therapist Self-Assessment Regarding Work with
        Children, exercise, 154
    Therapists and Stressors, exercise, 91-92
    transference, 4
The Therapist and Family Reunification, exercise,
    198
The Therapist and Victim Empathy, exercise, 42

Therapist Self-Assessment Regarding Work with
    Adolescents, exercise, 155
Therapist Self-Assessment Regarding Work with
    Children, exercise, 154
Therapists and Stressors, exercise, 91-92
Thinking Distortions, exercise, 29-30
Thinking errors, 23
Thought stopping, 23
Thought switching, 23
Traders, sexual predator, 210
Transference, therapist, 5
Transvestic fetishism, 32
Travelers, sexual predators, 208
Treating Adolescents, exercise, 156
Treatment
    adolescents, sexually aggressive, 152-153
    antisocial personality disordered, 85
    children, sexually aggressive, 55-56, 151-152
    female sex offender, 79
    polygraph use in, 111-112
    progress, monitoring, 103
Triggers, Victim Choice, and Creation of environment
    (exercise), 93

UCSC Rape Prevention, 217
Undoing, defense mechanism, 159
Universality, change and, 180
Urophiliam, 32
U.S. Department of Justice, 217
Using the PPG, exercise, 110

Victim
    adult female, 217-220
    empathy for, 13, 33, 38, 41, 196
    legends and myths, 145-147
    letter from, 144-145
    safety, family reunification, 194-195
"Victim work," 143
Victim's Voice Letter, 144
    exercise, 148
Violence, family, 16
Voyeurism, 32

"What if" situations, 15

Yalom, Irvin S., 180-181

Zoophiliam, 32